�֍ V O L U M E 2 ✶

HOW DO WE KNOW THE BIBLE IS TRUE?

First printing: August 2012
Third printing: November 2014

Master Books®, P.O. Box 726, Green Forest, AR 72638

Master Books® is a division of the New Leaf Publishing Group, Inc.

ISBN: 978-0-89051-661-4
ISBN: 978-1-61458-261-8 (ebook)
Library of Congress Number: 2011932373

Cover by John Lucas

Unless otherwise noted, Scripture quotations are from the New King James Version of the Bible.

Please consider requesting that a copy of this volume be purchased by your local library system.

Printed in the United States of America

Please visit our website for other great titles:
www.masterbooks.net

For information regarding author interviews,
please contact the publicity department at (870) 438-5288

Master Books®
A Division of New Leaf Publishing Group
www.masterbooks.net

Acknowledgments

We would like to extend our sincere thanks to the many reviewers and editors involved in this book: Dr. David Crandall, Dr. Georgia Purdom, Dr. Tommy Mitchell, Tim Chaffey, Roger Patterson, Bodie Hodge, Ken Ham, Dr. Terry Mortenson, Steve Golden, Pastor Chuck Hickey, Greg Iocco, Mike Belknap, David Wright, Mike Matthews, Steve Fazekas, Dr. Don DeYoung, Dr. Kurt Wise, Frost Smith, Mark Looy, Jeremy Ham, Pastor David Chakranarayan and Troy Lacey.

Contents

Introduction: The World's Most Dangerous Book? — *Ken Ham* 7

1. Why Are Young People Walking Away from Our Churches?
   — *Ken Ham* 11

2. Harvard, Yale, and Princeton — Once Christian?
   — *Bodie Hodge* 17

3. Why Are Many Christian Colleges Shifting to a Secular Road?
   — *Dr. Greg Hall* 23

4. Who Created God? Where Did God Come From?
   — *Bodie Hodge* 33

5. Why Is the Bible Unique? — *Dr. Carl J. Broggi* 45

6. What Is Apologetics — and Why Do It?
   — *Ken Ham and Bodie Hodge* 61

7. Should We Trust the Findings of the Jesus Seminar?
   — *Tim Chaffey* 81

8. What about Theistic Evolution? — *Roger Patterson* 95

9. Being Consistent: Trusting the History in the Gospels
   and Genesis — *Roger Patterson* 107

10. Christian Unity . . . and the Age of the Earth — *Steve Ham* 117

11. Radiocarbon Dating? — *Dr. Andrew A. Snelling* 131

12. Radioactive Dating of Rocks? — *Dr. Andrew A. Snelling* 145

13. The Shroud of Turin — Was It in the Grave with Christ?
    — *Bodie Hodge* 161

14. Chronology Wars? — *Larry Pierce* 169

15. Has Noah's Ark Been Found? — *Bodie Hodge* 175

16. What about Theophanies (Appearances of God) in the Old
    Testament? — *Tim Chaffey* 189

17. What about Annihilationism and Hell? — *Bodie Hodge* 199

18. How Can I Use Hell in Evangelism? — *Ray Comfort* 209

19. The Importance of the Reformation — *Dr. Carl J. Broggi* 217

20. Were Adam and Eve Real People? — *Dr. Georgia Purdom* 229

21. The "Missing" Old Testament Books? — *Brian H. Edwards* 241

22. The "Missing" New Testament Books? — *Brian H. Edwards* 251

23. Has the Bible's Text Been Changed Over the Years?
    — *Dr. Ron Rhodes* 265

24. Nazca Lines — Defying Evolutionary Ideas? — *David Wright* 275

25. Did Atlantis Exist? What We Can Learn from Bible History
    — *Bodie Hodge* 281

26. The Authority Test — Christianity or Humanism?
    — *Bodie Hodge* 291

27. Was Jesus Wrong? Peter Enns Says Yes
    — *Tim Chaffey and Roger Patterson* 301

28. Were There Really Giants as Described in the
    Old Testament? — *Tim Chaffey* 311

29. Did the Ten Plagues of Egypt Really Happen? — *Steve Fazekas* 331

30. Spreading the Good News — *Roger Patterson* 339

31. Afterword: Where Do We Draw the Line? — *Bodie Hodge* 347

Introduction

The World's Most Dangerous Book?

Ken Ham

✿✿✿✿✿✿✿✿✿✿✿✿✿✿✿✿✿✿✿✿

B ecause this is an introductory chapter in an Answers in Genesis/
Master Books publication, some readers might answer by saying that
Darwin's *On the Origin of the Species* is the most dangerous book.

Certainly Darwin popularized a philosophy that has permeated the
world and has become the foundation for all sorts of evil thinking. For
example, Darwinian evolution fueled racist ideas — Hitler used evolution
as a so-called "scientific" justification for his racist attitudes. Scientists
ordered the killing of many Australian Aborigines to be collected as museum specimens — all in the name of evolution.

And it is true that when someone believes there is no God and is convinced that life can be explained by natural processes alone, as portrayed
in Darwin's book, then the worldview built on that belief of origins reflects such an atheistic philosophy. Morality, then, would be relative, for
such a person believes there is no absolute authority. Thus, "right" and
"wrong" would also be relative.

Such a philosophy has been practically applied in Marxism — resulting in the death of millions of people under Stalin, Hitler, and others. Yes,
Darwin penned a dangerous book and idea — but Darwin's book is **not**
the most dangerous today.

Because of the events of September 11, some people might claim that the Koran (Qur'an) is the most dangerous book. The terrorists who perpetrated these evil acts, and others in the terrorist network worldwide, claim they are only carrying out what they believe the Koran instructs them to do. After all, they say, the Koran states:

> . . . then fight and slay the Pagans wherever ye find them, and seize them, beleaguer them, and lie in wait for them in every stratagem; but if they repent, and establish regular prayers and practice regular charity, then open the way for them (9:5).

Also:

> "I will instill terror into the hearts of the Unbelievers: Smite ye above their necks and smite all their fingertips off them" (8:12).

Now, many Muslims would claim that the terrorists incorrectly understand the Koran — but it is true that in every Muslim-dominated country, Christians are not allowed full freedom of worship. Many claim that Islam is the fastest growing religion even though it is second to Christianity (though many affirm that in the US and many parts of the world the religion of secular humanism with its atheism is growing faster) — but the Muslim God is not the God of the Bible. Certainly, the Koran is a dangerous book, for millions have been led into a false religion — but it is **not** the world's most dangerous book today (http//fastestgrowingreligion. com/numbers.html).

The Answer

I do not want to be misunderstood, but I propose that the most dangerous book in the world is in fact...the Bible.

Consider what Peter states in 2 Peter 3:15–16. He says that Paul wrote his epistles with the wisdom that God gave him, including "some things hard to be understood, which they that are unlearned and unstable wrest [distort], as they do also the other scriptures, unto their own destruction" (KJV). As the Bible is the Word of God, it is a divine book, and it is the greatest book. And because of this, if we misread it, we can, as Peter states, twist it to our own destruction.

For instance, Peter was referring to misunderstandings some people had concerning the teachings of the Apostle Paul. In the Book of Romans, Paul says that some were slandering him concerning his teaching of justification by faith. Some falsely claimed that because we are justified by faith, Paul taught that we can sin as much as we like!

In Corinthians, Paul warns that some people claimed the resurrection that he spoke of as occurring in the future had already happened. And in Thessalonians, Paul tells us that some had claimed he had taught that the Day of the Lord had already come. Peter explains that these people were all "wresting," or distorting the Scriptures to their own destruction.

Because the Bible is the revelation from God explaining who we are, where we came from, our sinful state, our need of salvation, how to be saved, the future judgment, and so on, if people misread it, they distort the Scriptures to their own destruction.

Think about this — cults such as the Mormons and Jehovah's Witnesses quote the Bible, but they misread it, thus distorting it to their own destruction. Orthodox Jews quote the Old Testament — but again, they distort it to their own destruction as they reject Jesus as the Messiah (who is foretold and explained in the Old Testament).

Because the Bible explains the only way to be saved ("that if you confess with your mouth the Lord Jesus and believe in your heart that God has raised Him from the dead, you will be saved" Romans 10:9), it is the most dangerous book — if its message is not believed. After all, if its message of salvation is not obeyed, then this will lead to a person's destruction. The Bible warns that those who do not trust in Christ for salvation will be separated from God for eternity in hell.

Answers in Genesis is a ministry that is not just dealing with the creation/evolution issue, but it is challenging the world — and the Church — to believe God's Word from the beginning. Sadly, because there is so much compromise with billions of years and evolutionary ideas in the Church, generations have been taught to misread the Bible. The more this has happened, the more the Bible's teaching is distorted to their own destruction, as increasing numbers in the younger generations no longer have a respect for the Bible.

One of the major messages of Answers in Genesis is that we should not misread God's Word and make it conform to the world's (or our own) ideas. The Bible says:

Beware lest anyone cheat you through philosophy and empty deceit, according to the tradition of men, according to the basic principles of the world, and not according to Christ (Colossians 2:8).

We must come to the Scriptures with a spirit of humility and let God speak to us through His Word — and not "wrest" the Scriptures to our own destruction. God is the authority and is so in every area.

And fear not them which kill the body, but are not able to kill the soul: but rather fear him which is able to destroy both soul and body in hell (Matthew 10:28; KJV).

Chapter 1

Why Are Young People Walking Away from Our Churches?

Ken Ham

During the past 30 years of traveling the world and speaking in churches, I have been deeply burdened by distraught parents pleading for advice on how to reach their children who were brought up in the church but who no longer attend. "How can I reach them? How can we get them back to church?" I have been asked time and time again.

I have often thought how I would like to get into the heads of these young adults who have left the church to understand how they are thinking. What caused them to walk away from the church they were brought up in?

Thirty years of teaching thousands of children and adults in churches has given me a big-picture understanding of a number of issues — some of which greatly trouble me while some thrill me. For instance:

1. I have met so many young people who do not see the church as relevant and do not consider the Bible a real book of history that can be trusted.
2. I have found that most parents have delegated the training of their children to the Sunday school, youth group, or other Christian organization.

3. Whenever I ask a church audience if they have any questions, I find that they usually ask the same questions regardless of what country or church (conservative or liberal) I visit: How can we know the Bible is true and is God's Word? Where did God come from? Where did Cain get his wife? Can't Christians believe in millions of years, the big bang, and evolution as long as God was involved? Are the days of creation ordinary days or millions of years, and does it really matter? How could Noah fit all the animals on the ark? To name but a few.

As I saw such patterns across America, Australia, Europe, and the United Kingdom, I was sure there must be a connection. Could it be that the lack of teaching apologetics in our churches, youth groups, Sunday schools, and Bible studies is a major reason why young people leave the church? But how do we determine if this is so, and when in their lives is this becoming an issue?

As I talked with parents, an overwhelming number of them admitted they did not know how to answer their children's questions — whether about dinosaurs, the age of the earth, or the origin of the Bible. I also found that most parents believe their children's Christianity will not come under attack until college.

A supporter of Answers in Genesis wanted to help us obtain real data from a respected and trusted researcher, who could do a statistically valid study that had to be taken seriously.

So we contracted with Britt Beemer, from America's Research Group, to formulate questions and survey one thousand 20-somethings (ages 20–29) who had gone to church regularly as children but no longer attend. They had to have come from a *conservative* church background so the results would reflect what is happening to children from Bible-believing churches. And what did we find?

A Look at the Numbers

The Survey Results . . .

When

The study found we are losing our kids in elementary, middle school, and high school rather than college.

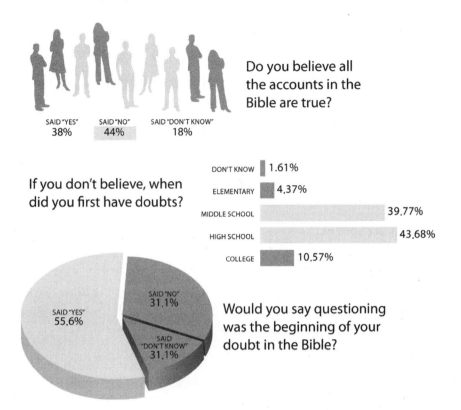

Do you believe all the accounts in the Bible are true?

SAID "YES"
38%

SAID "NO"
44%

SAID "DON'T KNOW"
18%

If you don't believe, when did you first have doubts?

DON'T KNOW	1.61%
ELEMENTARY	4.37%
MIDDLE SCHOOL	39.77%
HIGH SCHOOL	43.68%
COLLEGE	10.57%

SAID "NO"
31.1%

SAID "YES"
55.6%

SAID "DON'T KNOW"
31.1%

Would you say questioning was the beginning of your doubt in the Bible?

Why

Overall, the answer is the lack of teaching apologetics. The younger generations are not being raised to be able to answer the skeptical questions of our time, and so they begin doubting from a very early age whether they can trust the Bible.

Consider that most kids in Christian homes attend a state school (nearly 90 percent according the survey results), where they are being taught the religion of secular humanism (with evolution and millions of years and no God).[1] When Christianity was removed from the classroom, religion was not kicked out. Christianity was simply replaced with the godless religion of secular humanism (i.e., man's opinion rules as the ultimate authority rather than God).

---

1. Ken Ham and Britt Beemer, with Todd Hillard, *Already Gone: Why Your Kids Will Quit the Church and What You Can Do to Stop It* (Green Forest, AR: Master Books, 2009), p. 170.

Generations of children are being taught secular humanism in state schools, and then they go to church and question Christianity — but they do not receive answers based on the authority of God's Word. This is one of the main reasons kids are walking away from Christianity and gravitating to secular humanism.

What to Do About It

Sanctify the Lord God in your hearts, and always be ready to give a defense to everyone who asks you a reason for the hope that is in you, with meekness and fear (1 Peter 3:15).

Introduce apologetics (meaning "give a defense") curricula at all levels in church programs and at home. Parents need to take responsibility for their children's education and teach them from the moment they are born.

We need to answer the questions our kids have about the Bible (hence this and other book series such as the New Answers Books). Many times, even parents need to be trained to answer these questions so they can effectively train their children and grandchildren.

What Do the Twenty-Somethings Want from Church?

They want Bible teaching. It is not music that will bring them back to church but solid teaching that makes the Bible relevant. This was encouraging to find out. Many churches have become more like "social clubs," while Bible teaching and apologetics are almost extinct within many churches. Knowing that the 20-somethings want to hear what the Bible has to say should be an encouragement to most parents and church leaders.

Sometimes people have a tendency to think that kids *do not want* to know answers to questions about the days of creation, how we know the Bible is true, the 66 books of the Bible, Noah's ark, and so on, so they simply make them "side issues" of little importance. But they are not side issues; these are important and relevant issues to the youth of the next generation.

Are Sunday Schools Able to Handle the Situation?

Those who attend Sunday school are more likely to think God used evolution to create human beings, premarital sex is acceptable, and church is not relevant.[2]

---

2. Ham and Beemer, *Already Gone*, p. 39.

One of the shocks of the study was that, of these 20-somethings surveyed, those who went to Sunday school were more likely to be anti-church and defend gay marriage and abortion than those who didn't go to Sunday school. Again, the basic reason comes down to being taught the Bible as a book of fictional "stories" rather than real history that can be defended in this scientific age.

When many of these kids walked away from the church, they resented the church for not providing answers and viewed it as place of false doctrine. This is why many who have walked away from the church today are the most vocal in opposing the church, God, the Bible, and Christianity.

Analyzing the Survey Results

As I have been explaining the survey results during interviews, some radio hosts have asked me, "But why the disconnect — after all, surely the churches are teaching the gospel to these children."

My answer is something like this:

> Yes, that is true, but let's consider where we get the message of the gospel. How do we know Jesus rose from the dead? We were not there to see the Resurrection, and we do not have a movie of it, so how do we know it happened? We know because we trust the authority of the book from which we get the gospel — the Bible.
>
> We take the words of that book as God-breathed, letting them speak to us from God. But these young people have been brought up in a culture where Genesis, in particular, has been attacked. They have been taught the world was formed in millions of years through evolution. And sadly, most Christian leaders (Sunday school teachers and others) have told these kids that Genesis doesn't matter, that they can believe in secular history over millions of years, as long as they trust in Jesus. Ninety percent of these kids go to a public school where God, the Bible, and prayer have been thrown out. They are being educated in a secular philosophy — in naturalism and atheism.
>
> These children have been led to doubt that the Bible can be trusted in the beginning. They are not being taught how to take a stand for its authority from the very first verse. They are not taught the answers to the skeptical attacks on the Bible. So when

the message of Jesus is taught to them, they don't really believe it because they don't believe the book from which it comes. The next generation in the church needs to be taught not just what to believe as Christians, but also *why* we believe what we do, and how to answer skeptical questions. Let's begin equipping the next generation to stand solidly on the authority of God's Word![3]

---

3. For a complete treatment of the statistics from this study, see Ham and Beemer, *Already Gone.*

Chapter 2

Harvard, Yale, and Princeton — Once Christian?

Bodie Hodge

༺❀❀❀❀❀❀❀❀❀❀❀❀❀❀❀❀❀❀❀❀༻

M ost older colleges in the United States were Bible-proclaiming schools at one time. Harvard and Yale (originally Puritan) and Princeton (originally Presbyterian) once had rich Christian histories.

Harvard was named after a Christian minister, John Harvard, of Charleston. Yale was started by clergymen, and Princeton's first year of class was taught by Reverend Jonathan Dickinson. Princeton's crest even says *Dei sub numine viget*, which is Latin for "Under God she flourishes." In fact, a great many other colleges and universities have Christian roots founded as institutions to train pastors.

Even my alma mater, Southern Illinois University at Carbondale (SIUC), had Christian origins when it was founded in 1869. Our school motto was *Deo Volente*, which is Latin for "God willing." By the time I attended SIUC in the 1990s, there was almost no vestige of that Christian heritage. The university emphatically teaches the "facts" of millions of years and evolutionary ideas, and has blatantly rejected biblical authority (that the Bible is true — authoritative — and that we therefore need to adjust our beliefs and actions to its teaching).

So what happened to cause so many schools to abandon their Christian foundation?

The Beginning of Compromise

Undoubtedly, compromise with belief in an ancient earth and evolution contributed greatly to the downfall of these schools. For example, Yale had a long line of ministers as president, until Arthur Twining Hadley was installed in 1899. Though Hadley was a Christian, even though he bought into evolution, the trend was now set to have non-ministers as presidents. Hadley's adherence to evolution was obvious in his book *The Relations between Freedom and Responsibility in the Evolution of Democratic Government* where he states, "In some way or other man has acquired the possibility of forming groups which vary their customs without correspondingly varying their structure. It is this characteristic which distinguishes the evolution of mankind from the evolution of the lower animals. The main difference is not, as is so frequently said, that the human struggle for existence is a struggle between groups instead of individuals; for in more highly organized forms of animal life the subordination of the individual to the group is just as marked as in any section of the human race. The main difference is that the evolution of these human groups is a mental rather than a physical process."[1] By the end of the 1800s, the anti-biblical concept that earth's history had occurred over millions of years (geological evolution) overtook the school, where Darwinism (biological evolution) had a strong following.

Yale's next president was James Rowland Angell. Though raised in a Christian home, he believed the teachings of the religion of secular humanism (evolution and millions of years) over Christianity. He even wrote an article in 1909, "The Influence of Darwin on Psychology," that was pro-Darwinism. The school's changeover to naturalism had reached the top.

The ideas of millions of years and evolution came out of the belief that man's opinions are the ultimate standard *above* God and His Word. This type of thinking is known as humanism or secular humanism. These humanistic ideas began to permeate the culture, and as a result people began to treat God's Word as being subject to their own thinking. But we should

---

1. Arthur Twining Hadley, *The Relations between Freedom and Responsibility in the Evolution of Democratic Government* (New York: Yale University, 1903, p. 50).

carefully consider what John 12:48 says about those who reject God's Word — they will be held to account in the last day.

The Changing of the Worldviews

The Sacred and the Secular University is an insightful study by Roberts and Turner, two secular historians who show no evidence of overt Christian bias. They discuss the change in American universities from the Christian worldview to naturalistic philosophy (secular humanism).

They point out that universities across the board fell first in the area of science: "In the sciences, the critical departure from this hegemonic construct took place in the 1870s." They add that " 'methodological naturalism'[2] was the critical innovation."[3]

The religion of naturalism is in opposition to God's Word in Genesis, the foundational book of the Bible. Naturalism is the man-made idea that there is no supernatural and all things proceed the way they always have (2 Peter 3:4–5). In other words, naturalists would hold that there were no catastrophes in the past like Noah's Flood (Genesis 6–8), no supernatural creation during the creation week, and so on. As Psalm 11:3 states, "If the foundations are destroyed, what can the righteous do?" Cracks in the foundation led the universities to crumble in their Christian worldview and adopt secular humanism with its naturalistic aspects.

A Fractured Foundation

The cracks first appeared in the late 1700s and early 1800s, culminating with the influence of Charles Lyell's three volumes of *Principles of Geology* in the 1830s. Belief in old-earth geology (millions of years/geological evolution) seriously wounded widespread acceptance of the Flood and the biblical chronology, and Lyell just "finished off the victim and nailed the coffin shut," as history of geology expert Dr. Terry Mortenson says.[4]

---

2. Scientists that believe in methodological naturalism must do their work as if there is no God and that everything they study must be explained by three things: time, chance, and the laws of nature. Such a methodology for studying the physical world rules out the miraculous and providential works of God in His creation, even before investigation begins.
3. Jon H. Roberts and James Turner, *The Sacred and the Secular University* (Princeton, NJ: Princeton University Press, 2000), p. 11.
4. Terry Mortenson, *The Great Turning Point* (Green Forest, AR: Master Books, 2004).

This belief permeated universities by the mid-1800s, setting the stage for Darwin's evolutionary model in 1859 (*Origin of Species*), and his later work on human evolution, *The Descent of Man* (1871), both of which required long ages. After Christian universities adopted these compromises, the slide from biblical Christianity to naturalism and atheism soon followed.

Roberts and Turner explain why Christians compromised with naturalistic scientists:

> The determination of scientists to bring phenomena within the purview of naturalistic description evoked a mixed response from Christians outside the scientific community. . . . Many clergymen and theologians — most commonly those who embrace a "liberal" approach to Christian thought — sought to avoid that outcome by *joining* scientists in *embracing* an immanentist conception of God's relationship to the world[5] [emphasis added].

An immanent position holds that deity would be bound *within* the universe, which is what these naturalistic scientists were teaching. They gave up on God and the Bible, and told others not to even mention God or the Bible in their work.

Leaving the Bible Behind

Some liberal Christians gave up the Bible as their starting point and accepted naturalistic science in its place. How sad it must have been when Christians mixed these two religions — and how sad it still is when they mix the two today.

Once Christians began adopting a naturalistic view, including evolution or earth history over millions of years, it did not take long for the rest of their faith to come crumbling down.

Genesis is written as literal history, so it should be taken as such.[6] The demise of former Christian universities should be a lesson to individuals, churches, Christian colleges and universities, and seminaries to stand

---

5. Roberts and Turner, *The Sacred and the Secular University*, p. 31–32.
6. See Steven W. Boyd, "The Biblical Hebrew Creation Account: New Numbers Tell the Story," *ICR Impact Article* #377 (Nov. 2004).

firm on the Bible's clear teachings and beware of any doctrine that is not biblically sound.[7]

> For the time will come when they will not endure sound doctrine, but according to their own desires, because they have itching ears, they will heap up for themselves teachers; and they will turn their ears away from the truth, and be turned aside to fables (2 Timothy 4:3–4).

For more on how this problem is still infecting modern Christian colleges, please see Dr. Greg Hall's chapter in this volume as well as the book *Already Compromised* by Ken Ham and Dr. Greg Hall with Britt Beemer.

---

7. Ken Ham and Greg Hall, with Britt Beemer, *Already Compromised* (Green Forest, AR: Master Books, 2011).

Chapter 3

Why Are Many Christian Colleges Shifting to a Secular Road?

Dr. Greg Hall

༺༄༄༄༄༄༄༄༄༄༄༄༄༄༄༄༄༄༄༄

God's Word has been attacked since the earliest days of history (Genesis 3:1). The first sin that led to the fall of mankind through Adam and Eve was brought on by the enemy's casting doubt upon the veracity of the Word of God. Ever since, the truth claims of Scripture have been challenged and discredited by those who deny the Bible's inspiration, inerrancy, and authority.

That the Bible has been repudiated, discredited, or disgraced in a secularized culture is to be expected. To contend with those of the secular mindset about the truth and trustworthiness of Scripture is an effort in futility. However, to refute those Christian believers who side with those of the secular worldview when it comes to Scripture is a high calling indeed.

Disregard for the Word of God within secular institutions is the norm; however, it is unexpected by many, but a fact nevertheless, that Christian institutions also have a habit of falling into the same error. This is where Christian colleges fall short. In an effort to be considered acceptable among our secular counterparts, we too show a tendency to give up on the authority of Scripture.

Today, there is an extremely important work to standing up for the Word of God, teaching on its inspiration, inerrancy, and infallibility — especially among Christian colleges and universities. It may be because of higher criticism, liberal theology, or affinity for secular philosophies, but Christian colleges and universities have a history of departing from the orthodox Christian position of the inspiration, inerrancy, and infallibility of the Bible.

I have watched in amazement over the course of time as churches and Christian institutions of higher learning have marched away from important faith commitments, particularly as it relates to belief in the Bible. The contention seems the most intense over the issue of the inerrancy (utter truthfulness) of Scripture. Dr. R.C. Sproul writes:

> We believe that history has demonstrated again and again that all too often there is a close relationship between rejection of inerrancy and subsequent defections from matters of the Christian faith that are essential to salvation. When the church loses its confidence in the authority of sacred Scripture, it inevitably looks to human opinion as its guiding light. When that happens, the purity of the church is direly threatened.[1]

Some will find it hard to imagine that Christian institutions would employ those who discredit the Bible in any way. In his article "Total Capitulation: The Evangelical Surrender of Truth," Dr. Albert Mohler reacts to the position of evangelicals Karl W. Giberson and Randall J. Stephens in their book *The Anointed*. Consider these quotes from Dr. Mohler:

> Evangelicals, they [Giberson and Stephens] argue, "have been scarred by the elimination of prayer in schools; the removal of nativity scenes from public places; the increasing legitimacy of abortion and homosexuality. . . ."[2]

> Appearing on the October 20, 2011, edition of NPR's *Talk of the Nation* program, Giberson argued that homosexuality should

1. For more on this subject please see R.C. Sproul, *Can I Trust the Bible?* (Lake Mary, FL: Reformation Trust, 2009).
2. Albert Mohler, "Total Capitulation: The Evangelical Surrender of Truth," October 25, 2011, http://www.albertmohler.com/2011/10/25/total-capitulation-the-evangelical-surrender-of-truth/.

not be much of a concern at all. He revealed even more of his own approach to the Bible by asserting that "there's just a handful of proof text[s] scattered throughout the Bible on homosexuality," adding: "Jesus said absolutely nothing about it."[3]

Or consider this passage that Dr. Mohler quotes from *The Anointed*:

Christians have long been called "People of the Book." The label is especially appropriate for evangelicals. But the Book is thousands of years old, written in obscure languages, from a mysterious and incomprehensible time and place.[4]

That just about says it all. Dr. Mohler concludes, "They have, however, set the central issue before us. Evangelical Christians will either stand upon the authority and total truthfulness of the Bible or we will inevitably capitulate to the secular worldview."[5]

To further illustrate how some Christian educators deal with Scripture, consider these quotes from their own work:

The everyman reading of the creation story understands the Fall as an allegory representing every human's individual rejection of God. In this light, the Fall was not a historical event but an illustration of the common human condition that virtually everyone agrees is deeply flawed and sinful. The deeds of Adam and Eve simply represent the actions of all humans and remind us of this troubling part of our natures.[6]

Dr. Dan Harlow, professor of biblical and early Jewish studies in the Department of Religion at Calvin College, stated this in a recent paper:

Recent research in molecular biology, primatology, sociobiology, and phylogenetics indicates that the species Homo sapiens cannot be traced back to a single pair of individuals, and that the earliest human beings did not come on the scene in anything like paradisal physical or moral conditions. It is therefore difficult to

3. Ibid.
4. Ibid.
5. Ibid.
6. BioLogos, "Were Adam and Eve historical figures?" http://biologos.org/questions/evolution-and-the-fall.

read Genesis 1–3 as a factual account of human origins. In current Christian thinking about Adam and Eve, several scenarios are an offer. The most compelling one regards Adam and Eve as strictly literary figures — characters in a divinely inspired story about the imagined past that intends to teach theological, not historical, truths about God, creation, and humanity.

Taking a nonconcordist approach, this article examines Adam and Eve as symbolic-literary figures from the perspective of mainstream biblical scholarship, with attention both to the text of Genesis and ancient Near Eastern parallels. Along the way, it explains why most interpreters do not find the doctrines of the Fall and original sin in the text of Genesis 2–3, but only in later Christian readings of it. This article also examines briefly Paul's appeal to Adam as a type of Christ. Although a historical Adam and Eve have been very important in the Christian tradition, they are not central to biblical theology as such. The doctrines of the Fall and original sin may be reaffirmed without a historical Adam and Eve, but invite reformulation given the overwhelming evidence for an evolving creation.[7]

In our book, *Already Compromised*, Ken Ham and I researched how select individuals at Christian colleges and universities responded to important basic concepts of Christian faith. It was not surprising to me to see the variance of opinion among these leaders about the issues related to the Bible, especially that of inerrancy (utter truthfulness).

Now, if the Bible is compromised in whether or not it is completely true, what will the logical outcome be? If Scripture is not entirely true, then it is possible, even probable, that the creation account of Genesis 1 and 2 will be trumped by so-called scientific explanations of origins, which include evolution and the billions of years evolution requires. If Scripture is not inerrant, then perhaps there was a pre-Adamic race, as some teach, instead of the first man and woman, Adam and Eve. If Scripture is not inerrant, maybe the Fall of man in Genesis 3 is just an allegory or myth. If Scripture is not entirely true, maybe there was not a global

---

7. Daniel C. Harlow, "After Adam: Reading Genesis in an Age of Evolutionary Science," *Perspectives on Science and Christian Faith* 62, no. 3 (2010): p. 179.

Flood after all, and uniformitarianism really is the explanation for how our world came to be. Maybe there is no supernatural and the natural is all there is. Maybe the Bible is all allegory and myth — no virgin birth, no substitutionary death upon a Cross by Christ, and no Second Coming. If the Bible is not inerrant and given to us to be read in its plain, straightforward sense, then these false teachings could all be true.

But none of them are true. God's Word is true. Science does not trump Scripture. God speaks with clarity and power. The scripture is true — inspired, inerrant, infallible. We would do well to consider these words from Dr. John MacArthur:

> And Scripture always speaks with absolute authority. It is as authoritative when it instructs us as it is when it commands us. It is as true when it tells the future as it is when it records the past. Although it is not a textbook on science, wherever it intersects with scientific data, it speaks with the same authority as when it gives us moral precepts. Although many have tried to set science against Scripture, science never has disproved one jot or tittle of the Bible and it never will.
>
> It is therefore a serious mistake to imagine that modern scientists can speak more authoritatively than Scripture on the subject of origins. Scripture is God's own eyewitness account of what happened in the beginning. When it deals with the origin of the universe, all science can offer is conjecture. Science has proven nothing that negates the Genesis record. In fact, the Genesis record answers the mysteries of science.[8]

In the late 1700s and early 1800s, the idea of a long age (millions of years) for the earth was being popularized by atheists and other non-Christians.[9] They were attempting to use a so-called "scientific investigation of the world" to justify their rejection of God and His Word. At the

---

8. For more on this subject please see John MacArthur, *The Battle For The Beginning: The Bible on Creation and the Fall of Adam* (Nashville, TN: Thomas Nelson, 2001).

9. Some of these were Comte de Buffon, James Hutton, Abraham Werner, but it culminated with Charles Lyell in the 1830s. For more, see Bodie Hodge's chapter "How Old Is the Earth?" in Ken Ham, editor, *The New Answers Book 2* (Green Forest, AR; Master Books, 2008).

time, their primary tactic was to undermine the plain reading of the Bible concerning the Flood of Noah (and its consequence of rock layers and worldwide fossil deposits) and a young age for the earth. This was really an attempt to undermine the authority of the entire Bible.

At that time, there were church leaders who adopted the idea of millions of years into Scripture (e.g., Thomas Chalmers with gap theory, Hugh Miller with day-age ideas). This was no different than what happens today, and no different than what happened with the religious leaders in the Apostle Paul's day, and also no different from what was happening with the priests and false prophets in ancient Israel when they mixed things like Baal worship with their worship of God.

Fallible, sinful man, ever since Genesis 3, has had the propensity to believe the fallible words of humans rather than the infallible Word of God. That is our nature. At heart, because of sin, we are against God and what He teaches. People will go out of their way to trust in man rather than trust what God has clearly revealed.

In the early 1800s, there were church leaders in England who began to reinterpret the days of creation and the Flood account in Genesis to fit in the idea of millions of years. Some advocated the idea of a gap between Genesis 1:1 and 1:2, like Chalmers. Others, like Hugh Miller, said that Christians could interpret the creation days as long ages. Others realized that if one interpreted the fossil layers as representing millions of years, then how could one believe in the global Flood of Noah's day? Such a flood would destroy those layers and deposit more layers with fossils. Thus, it was postulated that Noah's Flood was only a local (regional) flood in the Mesopotamian Valley (modern-day Iraq).

As the 19th century progressed, Darwin popularized his ideas of biological evolution, which built on the ideas of geological evolution. There were church leaders who then reinterpreted Genesis to fit into evolution, even human evolution. When the idea of the big bang (astronomical evolution) was popularized in the early 20th century, in the same manner many church leaders adopted this into God's Word.

Over the past 200 years, many different positions regarding the creation account of Genesis have arisen in the church, such as the following:

- Day-age idea
- Gap theory

- Local flood
- Theistic evolution
- Progressive creation
- Framework hypothesis

There are other positions or variations on those listed above, but they all have one thing in common: they each attempt to fit man's ideas of millions of years into the Bible.

A number of Christian scientists actually opposed these compromise positions. Various books and articles were written to challenge the Church to stand on God's Word and not compromise with the fallible ideas of man that, intentionally or unintentionally, seriously undermined the authority of the Bible.

Biblical creation scientists and theologians have been able to conduct tremendous research and have provided many answers in geology, biology, astronomy, anthropology, archaeology, and theology, which have equipped Christians to stand uncompromisingly in Genesis. The several thousand articles on the Answers in Genesis website,[10] as well as the hundreds of books, DVDs, and other resources now available there, are a good example of providing well-researched answers.

Compromised ideas on the origin of life have made their way into our Christian schools. And when these ideas are fully adopted, they either replace the Bible as an authority or seek to relativize it or reconstruct it to fit human ideas, as some of their quotes reveal. Consider this quote from Dr. John MacArthur:

> The evolutionary lie is so pointedly antithetical to Christian truth that it would seem unthinkable for evangelical Christians to compromise with evolutionary science in any degree. But during the past century and a half of evolutionary propaganda, evolutionists have had remarkable success in getting evangelicals to meet them halfway. . . . So–called theistic evolutionists who try to marry humanistic theories of modern science with biblical theism may claim they are doing so because they love God, but the truth is that they love God a little and their academic reputations a lot. By undermining the historicity of Genesis they are undermining

---

10. www.answersingenesis.org.

faith itself. Give evolutionary doctrine the throne and make the Bible its servant, and you have laid the foundation for spiritual disaster.

Scripture, not science, is the ultimate test of all truth. And the further evangelicalism gets from that conviction, the less evangelical and more humanistic it becomes.[11]

There are probably numerous reasons why Christian educators deny or otherwise try to reconstruct Scripture (especially the early chapters of Genesis).

Some of them honestly do not believe in the authority of Scripture — they do not believe in its inspiration, inerrancy, or infallibility. Not everyone who teaches in a Christian institution is convinced of the truth claims of Christianity. Some consider themselves believers, but still cannot believe God's Word as inspired, inerrant, or infallible. These hold the view that the Bible is just another human text of antiquity and should be used as such. To them, Scripture is not the "vox Dei" — the veritable voice of God. When a teacher takes such a position, he will be more inclined to line up his beliefs with his discipline or guild when it comes to issues of Scripture, especially on matters of origin. There is a tremendous pressure in higher education and Christian higher education to conform to the guild and especially to make peace with "science." When this begins to happen, the science text will trump the sacred text — and that is a deadly error.

So when we give up on Scripture, marginalize it, or try to make it fit into the current understanding of science, what is the result in Christian schools?

When Ken Ham and I wrote *Already Compromised*, I was surprised both positively and negatively about the research we commissioned among Christian leaders. It was good news to find that there was a strong commitment to important New Testament themes, but there was also great confusion and disconnect with Old Testament themes, particularly related to Genesis 1–3 and the Bible's historical record of origins.

But the greatest surprise for me was the unsolicited response to the book from constituents of Christian higher education, particularly parents

---

11. MacArthur, *The Battle for the Beginning: The Bible on Creation and the Fall of Adam*, p. 25–26.

and students. I heard several times about students who went to Christian colleges and either had their faith broken down or in some cases abandoned it, at least for some time. One mother said, "It's about time somebody addressed what is going on in Christian colleges." One father told me he appreciated the book, but after having visited several Christian colleges said, "It's worse out here than you know." I've heard from numerous students who cannot understand why Christian institutions have such weak and at times strange ideas about Scripture. I heard from students who described lectures on scriptural concepts that would be considered heretical to the orthodox Christian faith.

These things ought not be so. I believe in Christian higher education because it provides a great hope for our culture. I believe in it enough to criticize it and to try to inspire it to present the Word of God in all its truth. It is time for the Church to hold us accountable for how and what we teach our youth.

The message to parents and students is clear and simple: Christian education is a great opportunity for education and spiritual development. But it may be that we are falling short in the most important issue of all: fidelity to Scripture and the God who gave it.

Learn to discriminate on this important matter. Ask the questions you know are important. God's Word is at stake in this, and so are the souls of our youth. You must realize too the academic dynamic of any institution, and that includes Christian schools. It is unrealistic to think a president or dean controls what professors think or teach. Rarely do the opinions of professors reach a public setting; it is usually in the intimacy of a class or during one-on-one moments with students that these opinions are brought up. An institution can have a faith statement, but it cannot guarantee conformity. At the end of the day, students will have to take responsibility for their own thinking and never allow anyone to do anything but "shape" their thinking. Students must be taught (at home and at church predominantly) to trust ultimately in an unchanging God and His Word.

Parents, you may be asking the question of which Christian college you should send your children to, given the fact some of these Christian institutions, in some ways, are secular. I advise you not to face the issue that way. You may be surprised even in the most solid Christian institution. There are no guarantees that wherever your children go they will be immersed in only clear Christian teaching.

The way to prepare for this is to make sure in your home that you are adequately preparing your children to base their lives completely upon the Word of God and to defend why they do so. Do not leave up to any school, Christian or otherwise, what is ultimately your primary responsibility.

Here is the first key: help your children understand Scripture from the first chapter and first verse of the Bible. If they do not understand the biblical creation account and learn to build on this foundation, everything that follows will lack for needing to have the creation truth as a firm foundation. Consider:

> In other words, objective truth is possible only if there is a Creator who has spoken to us — giving us divine revelation. As Schaeffer put it in the title of one of his books, *He Is There and He Is Not Silent.*[12]

> The only way of escape from postmodern skepticism is if God has revealed something of His own perspective to us — not about spiritual matters only, and not just a non-cognitive emotional experience, but revelation of objective truth about the cosmos we live in.[13]

---

12. Albert Alschuler, *Law without Values: The Life, Works, and Legacy of Justice Holmes* (Chicago, IL: University of Chicago Press, 2000), p. 59.
13. Nancy Pearcey, *Total Truth, Liberating Christianity from Its Cultural Captivity* (Wheaton, IL: Crossway Books, 2005), p. 246.

Chapter 4

Who Created God? Where Did God Come From?

Bodie Hodge

᯾᯾᯾᯾᯾᯾᯾᯾᯾᯾᯾᯾᯾᯾᯾᯾᯾᯾᯾᯾

Introduction

I had the opportunity to speak to some students, where many in the audience were rather "hostile" to the Bible and God. One student blurted out in a rather harsh tone, "Where did God come from? Who created God?"

This person was clearly not happy with the fact that I trusted the Bible and believed in God. Normally, those who ask these questions do so in an attempt to disprove the existence of God or at the very least to make themselves feel like they have an excuse not to "believe in God." I immediately responded to their question with a question and asked: "On what page of Shakespeare's book *Hamlet* could I find Shakespeare?"

I can recall the silence in the room — you could have heard a pin drop! So I asked again. The person responded by saying something like, "Shakespeare's not confined to his book. He created it and wasn't bound to it."

And this was indeed a brilliant answer. See, Shakespeare wrote the book and isn't *confined to* it — he is not *bound to* it, he is *beyond it*. It came about by his creativity. He is not *part of* the book. So with this, I responded, "In the same way, the God of the Bible is also not bound to His creation, He is beyond it, He created it, He is not limited to it. Let me explain.

When you ask the question who *created* God or where did God *come* from, you are using the action verbs 'created' and 'come.' This implies that time is in existence for God to "show up" on the scene at some point *after time* had begun (to be created or to come about). This is not the God of the Bible, who created time and is not bound to it. So in the same way that Shakespeare, being confined to his book, was essentially an illogical question, so is limiting God to being confined to His creation as *a creation* within time."

I remember seeing people sit up and take notice of this short answer. In fact, I doubt many of these kids ever heard anyone actually try to give a reasoned answer to that question. But let me re-explain this in more detail and add to it so you don't miss it.

The Answer

The key to the answer is the action verbs "come" and "created." Using these action verbs reveals an assumption on the part of the person asking the question. This question *presupposes* that time is infinite in the past, and that God is bound by time. However, time is finite; it has a beginning and even scientists recognize this, and those who have read the Bible have known this for quite some time.

God is beyond time; He did not come into existence at some point within time. Instead, He claims that, rather than having a beginning, He *is* the Beginning and the End (Revelation 22:13[1]). In light of this, the question is an illogical one. God didn't come from anywhere or anyone. God is the source of everything, and He created time. Time is not absolute; *God is absolute*. When someone asks "where God came from" or "who created Him," they are assuming *time is absolute* and God isn't — but this isn't the God of the Bible.

Now apply this to God. God created time. Yet people ask, "Who created God?" and "Where did God come from?" They are assuming that God is bound by time when asking a question like this. In other words, they believe that time was first and then God came onto the scene. From the Bible we learn that time had a beginning (Genesis 1) — that it was started by God, thus God is not bound by time.

---

1. Revelation 22:13: "I am the Alpha and the Omega, the Beginning and the End, the First and the Last."

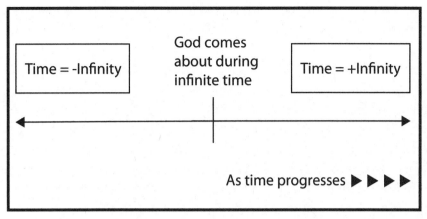

Figure 1. Fallacious view that time is infinite and God is bound by it

The misconception lies with the view of time. Either time is infinite and God is bound by it, or God created time and time is not infinite. This can be visualized by figure 1.

God, in Job 38 and Genesis 1, has laid claim that He created time (since time is part of the physical world, along with the three dimensions of height, width, and length), thus the time-line of history and the future should be viewed as figure 2.

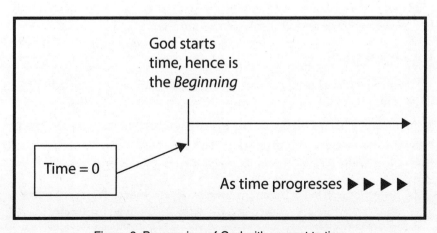

Figure 2. Proper view of God with respect to time

When people say that God is bound by time, they are saying that God is bound inside of what He created. This is a fallacy. Recall that God created everything physical — including time — because there was a beginning (Genesis 1:1). *God* had no beginning, and thus does not have a cause.

Now that this has been answered, let's move to some related discussion on the subject: Which God are we talking about? Now if there was a "god" who was created or showed up in the universe after its creation, that "god" really isn't the true God, is he? In fact, I would join in refuting all such false "gods," as there is only one God. This answer that we've been discussing is in reference to the God of the Bible, not to a false god, and hence, Christian theism. And now we turn to a discussion of God's existence.

Non-Christian Theism

God opens the Bible with the statement of His existence and there is so much we can learn from this. Being that He is the ultimate authority on every subject, including His existence, then there is no reason that He should not be taken at His Word. Consider Genesis 1:1: "In the beginning God created the heavens and the earth."

Elohim is the Hebrew word for God here. It is one of many names used of God throughout the Old Testament. As you may have noticed, names have significance in Hebrew. *Jehovah Jireh* means *The Lord provides*. *Elohim* is no different. It is often denoted as a majestic plural of the singular *El* (which is also a name for God). So why, of all the names, is this one used to open the Bible? Because it reveals a fascinating aspect of God, especially when used in conjunction with the rest of Scripture. This signifies the very power and kingship of the Lord God.

Unitarian God?

When *Elohim* is used of God, it retains *singular* verbs. This gives hints toward plurality and yet a single unity. Not that this means multiple *gods* . . . by no means. This coupled with the many passages that Jesus is God and the Holy Spirit is God are a confirmation of a triune God, not a Unitarian "god."[2] It means that the God of the Bible is clearly not Unitarian in essence.[3]

---

2. Bodie Hodge, "God Is Triune," Answers in Genesis website, February 20, 2008, http://www.answersingenesis.org/articles/2008/02/20/god-is-triune.
3. Jehovah's Witnesses have a Unitarian view of God even though they view Jesus as a separate "god," and so does Islam.

As the Lord reveals more and more through the Scriptures, we find that God is *triune* in nature. One God ("Hear, O Israel: The LORD our God, the LORD is one!" Deuteronomy 6:4; see also Romans 3:30[4]; 1 Corinthians 8:4[5]; Ephesians 4:6[6]; etc.), yet three persons — the Father, the Son, and the Holy Spirit. A table revealing passages that clearly show the triune nature of God are listed in *How Do We Know the Bible Is True?* Volume 1.[7]

When discussing the Trinity, people are often at a loss to understand how something can be one and yet three at the same time. The classical view of how to simplify this is by envisioning an equilateral triangle:

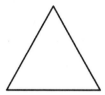

There is one triangle (think one God) with three identical points and angles (think Father, Son, and Holy Spirit), and yet each point is unique and if you follow the lines of the triangle from each point, they *are* the lines of the other two points. So, one point is ultimately *one* with the other points as well. They are identical in essence with the same line length and angles.

Others have postulated a way to understand it as envisioning the triple point of water, where at a particular pressure and temperature, water can be solid, liquid, and gas at the same time! Now these simple analogies will never fully be able to dive into the understanding of a triune God, but should be sufficient to show that such concepts are easily possible. Nor should such images or concepts be put in place of God — they are merely ways to help understand the character of God.

The use of *Elohim*, with singular verbs is a great confirmation of the character of God right from the start. And theologically, it makes sense. Consider John's statement that "God *is* love" in 1 John 4:8.

---

4. ". . . since there is one God who will justify the circumcised by faith and the uncircumcised through faith."
5. "Therefore concerning the eating of things offered to idols, we know that an idol is nothing in the world, and that there is no other God but one."
6. ". . . one God and Father of all, who is above all, and through all, and in you all."
7. Ken Ham and Bodie Hodge, editors, *How Do We Know the Bible Is True?* Volume 1 (Green Forest, AR: Master Books, 2011), p. 76–77.

Having plurality in the Godhead allows love to emanate from one person to another in perfect synchronicity as love is something that is shared, not withheld, regardless if creation exists or not. A Unitarian god would fall short in this area. For an absolute Unitarian god could *not* be love because love would not exist until something was created to love. A Unitarian god would be incomplete until creation occurred for love to become a reality. A triune God could love without the necessity of being bound to the creation, showing the great majestic power and kingship of God over His creation — which is what *Elohim* truly signifies anyway.

Now, not all instances of *Elohim* are in reference to God in the Old Testament. Although all 26 times it is used in Genesis 1, it is in reference to God. And most of the uses of *Elohim* in the Old Testament are in this form (well over 2,000) and refer to God.

This same word, *Elohim*, when used with *plural* verbs (and *plural* adjectives) is used when referring to cases where alleged "gods" or "pagan gods" are being spoken of in Scripture, such as The Ten Commandments where God says, "You shall have no other gods [*Elohim*] before Me" (Exodus 20:3). This is called a *numerical plural* meaning multiplicity, as opposed to the *numerically singular* majestic plural, which means God. So the context determines the meaning, which is common in Hebrew anyway, and these are easily discernible by the language.

But let's consider Genesis 1:1 and the rest of Scripture to alleged polytheistic "gods."

Polytheism?

Since Elohim is not used with plural verbs or adjectives, it does *not* mean that God should be plural as in "gods." This refutes any idea that the creation was created by multiple "gods." Polytheism, which has many gods, is thoroughly debunked by the Bible. Of course, there are a number of other passages that further interpret Genesis 1, even by Moses, who also penned Genesis:

> To you it was shown, that you might know that the LORD Himself is God; there is none other besides Him (Deuteronomy 4:35).

> Hear, O Israel: The LORD our God, the LORD is one! (Deuteronomy 6:4).

Now see that I, even I, am He, and there is no God besides Me; I kill and I make alive; I wound and I heal; nor is there any who can deliver from My hand (Deuteronomy 32:39).

Some polytheistic religions such as Mormonism have gods arriving *after* the fact (i.e., people *becoming gods* within the creation), but since they are not the Creator of all things including time and space, then are they really on par with the Creator-God of the Bible? Absolutely not.

Shinto, which has multiple gods, has them arriving on the scene after creation as well. It is a form of ancestor worship, where people become gods. But again, if they are not the Creator, then they are lesser (i.e., created), and cannot be equal to the God of all creation and hence are not "gods" at all. Any polytheistic religion (from these . . . to Greek mythology . . . to Hinduism) is refuted by the Bible, where God is one.

Many religions that have multiple "gods" have some link to a form of ancestor worship where great men of the past have been embellished and raised up to "god-like" status. Besides Shinto, which is obviously ancestor worship, Oden (Woden), for example, is found in the genealogies of Anglo-Saxon and Norse royal genealogies.[8] Hercules is a Greek embellishment of the account of Samson and so on.[9]

Atheistic Religions?

Obviously, atheism and variant atheistic religions are refuted by the mere mention of a God in the Bible. This explains why *humanists* (man is seen as the ultimate authority apart from any alleged god(s) — a form of atheism), *atheists/non-theists* (who say *emphatically* that there is **no** God), *agnostics* (who say they can't know if God exists), and *materialists* (another form of atheist who denies anything beyond a natural world) avoid the Bible if at all possible.

These atheistic variants can't get past Genesis 1:1 in the Bible without putting up their defenses. Hence, they often turn to attack the Bible, which is what we see in today's culture and the example we saw at the opening of this chapter. But God refutes any form of atheism with the first verse in the Bible.

---

8. Bill Cooper, *After the Flood* (West Sussex, England: New Wine Press, 1995), chapters 6 and 7.
9. Adam Clarke, Commentary notes Judges 16:31 drawing the clear parallels, http://www.studylight.org/com/acc/view.cgi?book=jud&chapter=016/

Humanism and Atheism: Refuting atheism is rather easy logically. To say there is no God would mean that one has looked in the entire universe at the same time, both in the natural world as well as the transcendent or spiritual world. This means they are claiming to be *omniscient,* as they are claiming to be all-knowing on the subject of God's existence. They would also be claiming to be *omnipresent* by claiming to be everywhere. So really, an atheist (or humanist) is claiming to be God and thereby refuting his or her own position. And God reveals that atheists really do know that God exists, but suppress that knowledge (Romans 1:18–20[10]).

Agnosticism: An agnostic claims there is no way of knowing if God exists or not. But frankly, how does an agnostic even know that? Without the truth of the Bible and the biblical God, how can anything be known? Knowledge is predicated on the fact that the biblical God exists (Colossians 2:3[11]).

Materialism: (see also the response on atheism above). In a materialistic view, any nonmaterial aspects are denied — that is, the spiritual realm, abstract realm, etc. But if this were the case, then other nonmaterial entities must also be denied. So in a materialistic worldview logic, truth, knowledge, and other abstract concepts must also be denied. If this is the case, nothing could make sense!

Existence of God

Take note of an important fact here. God does not take the time to build a logical or scientific case for His existence, but merely *presupposes* it. We live in a culture that tries to demand that things be proved, using science through empirical means (our senses) and/or by logical analysis. And yet God begins with a declaration of His Existence.

Many people instantly get "up in arms" because God didn't try to "prove" Himself first on man's fallible basis. So they assume that the existence of God cannot be proven but merely assumed on blind faith. But consider if God had set out to prove His existence to fallible sinful human

10. "For the wrath of God is revealed from heaven against all ungodliness and unrighteousness of men, who suppress the truth in unrighteousness, because what may be known of God is manifest in them, for God has shown it to them. For since the creation of the world His invisible attributes are clearly seen, being understood by the things that are made, even His eternal power and Godhead, so that they are without excuse."

11. ". . . in whom [Christ] are hidden all the treasures of wisdom and knowledge."

beings just to please us. In such an attempt, God would have to appeal to something greater than Himself in order to prove His existence.

For example, if God tried to use scientific means to prove His existence, then God would be lesser than science and forfeiting His claims to be the greatest thing in existence. If God tried to use a logical argument, then logic would be raised up to be greater than God, and again, God would be reduced to something lesser. But God, being all-knowing (Colossians 2:3[12]), knew better.

> For when God made a promise to Abraham, because He could swear by no one greater, He swore by Himself (Hebrews 6:13).

God is the ultimate authority on His existence, and therefore His statement is of the greatest authority and proof. In fact, such things as logic and uniformity in nature (basis for science) stem from or are founded on God and His power. Logic is the extension of the way God thinks. Laws of science are merely studying the way that God upholds the universe. These are tools that stem from God and His Word being that ultimate authority.

But consider the converse. What authority are these non-Christians really appealing to when they say that logical analysis or empirical senses are the ultimate authority? Themselves! They are claiming that they are the absolute authority, which is arbitrary, where God who is the ultimate authority on the subject of authority is not arbitrary! A question to ask to reveal this fallacy is, "What ultimate authority should God, who is the ultimate authority, have appealed to prove He is the ultimate authority?" He could *only* appeal to Himself if He is what He claims to be.

This hasn't stopped people, particularly Christians, from trying to use logical or scientific means to prove the existence of God. For example, some have tried using arguments such as:

1. First cause
2. Design in nature
3. Cosmological
4. Ontological
5. Mind/body separation
6. etc.

---

12. Ibid.

However, these arguments each have shortcomings. They assume a neutral position and then try to deduce that God exists by agreeing that logic is the ultimate authority over God instead of recognizing that logic and reason are the natural outworkings of a God and is predicated on the truth of the Bible. In a consistent manner, Christ affirms, though, that there is no such thing as neutrality, so falling into that trap means Christians are giving up the authority of the Word of God for an arbitrary humanistic view as their starting point.

> He who is not with Me is against Me, and he who does not gather with Me scatters (Luke 11:23).

If they start with an alleged neutral starting point, they have already lost the battle by giving up God's Word for human reason that is *apart from God*.

These arguments also have another problem that is predicated on this. They assume logic exists in a neutral worldview, then proceed to make arguments. But why would logic exist in a non-Christian worldview (or if Christians try to arrive at this conclusion without the Bible)? Logic, being a reflection of the way God thinks, means the arguer is already assuming the existence of God, while claiming not to, before they even begin to make the argument. So they are forced to start with the presupposition that God exists, just to try to argue against it. They have no basis outside of Scripture for logic to exist.

To avoid a vicious circle, we must start with the self-attesting God and His Word, which is not arbitrary, and then we will have a basis for logic, truth, knowledge, morality, science, and so on — these are Christian presuppositions. In other words, don't start from an arbitrary starting point (such as neutrality), but start with God and His Word and see where it goes. God explains the aspects of the world coherently. The non-Christians have difficulty with a starting point because they have no basis for such things — so they *must borrow* from Christian presuppositions.

Some have objected and said, "You can't start with God and His Word because that is what you are trying to prove!" However, a person *can* stand on a hill to defend a hill. In the same way a person has the right to get on the witness stand and defend himself. God has a right to defend Himself. And by starting with God's Word, that is how this is done.

Laws of logic, for example, require the biblical God. Yet to prove anything they are required, so the only way to begin is with God and His Word. So, if God did not exist, reasoning would be impossible.

Some may object and say they "don't believe in God and yet they can reason," but it is not a matter of whether they *believe* or not, but a matter of the truth of God and His Word — whether you believe it or not is irrelevant. So even the non-Christians are borrowing from a biblical worldview when they even try to make an argument, thus verifying the truth of God and His Word! Only the biblical God can account for the laws of logic (as well as morality and uniformity of nature). This doesn't mean that non-Christians don't believe in these things, but they have no *basis* for it apart from the biblical God.

In essence, this is a brief uttering of the transcendental argument for the existence of God as espoused by great philosophers such as Drs. Cornelius Van Til and Greg Bahnsen of the 20th century, by recognizing the way biblical authors and ultimately God Himself approached the subject — in a presuppositional fashion. All other arguments for the existence of God rest upon this one, which starts with God and His Word and show that only the biblical worldview makes sense of the world. Others will ultimately lead to absurdity. So by the impossibility of the contrary, God must exist. These other arguments for the existence of God are a confirmation of the transcendental argument for the existence of God.

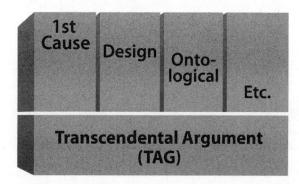

Sadly, when non-Christians try to attack the biblical God or His Word, they are ultimately attacking the very basis of their own borrowed presuppositions — oftentimes unknowingly. Christians need to help non-Christians realize they are standing on borrowed ground, before it is too late.

Conclusion

When it comes to the issue of who created God or where did He come from, these are illogical questions that assume that God is "bound to" or "was created" within His creation. This is not the God of the Bible who is beyond time and beyond His creation. He is not limited to it. He is the uncreated Creator of all existence, and existence is not possible without Him.

This God is the triune God of the Bible, not some other false god, such as unitarianism or polytheism would have us believe. And by the Word of God itself we can know that God exists and those who deny such things are really suppressing that knowledge, all the while borrowing from the truth of the Bible in an effort to deny and argue against God and His Word.

Chapter 5

Why Is the Bible Unique?

Dr. Carl J. Broggi

✿✿✿✿✿✿✿✿✿✿✿✿✿✿✿✿✿✿✿✿

Introduction

Before I became the pastor of a local church, I was involved in campus ministry for over a decade. I was consistently sharing the claims of Christianity with college students and almost daily I met students who would make such statements as:

> I don't believe sex outside of marriage is wrong. I don't believe there is a hell where people will spend an eternity in torment without God. I don't believe Jesus Christ is the only way to heaven. I think Jesus was a great man and a good religious teacher, but I don't believe that He is God in human flesh. I think if a person lives a decent life, in the end all will be well between him and God.

Whenever I would hear assertions like these, I would remind the person that he/she has some sort of basis for believing what he believes. He may have read it in a book, maybe his parents taught this viewpoint, maybe he heard some professor pontificate this perspective, or maybe he even came up with the idea on his own. But just believing something does not make it true. You can believe that two plus two equals five, and you can believe it passionately, sincerely, and with all your heart, but belief does not make it true. You can be sincere, but sincerely wrong.

A foundational question a wise person seeks to ask and answer for himself is this, "How do we know the Bible is the Word of God and is the Bible the only book that God ever inspired?"[1] If you can definitively, dogmatically, and accurately conclude that the Bible is God's Book, then you have a plumb line on which to evaluate everything you believe. You can take any idea about God, heaven, hell, Christ, and salvation and put it into the mirror of Scripture to see if your belief is accurate.

Many people think Christians are "stupid" or "ignorant" or both. Many think Christians have no basis whatsoever for why they believe what they believe. What they fail to understand is that Christians do not believe the Bible is the Word of God by mere blind faith. Faith as described in the Bible is not blind faith. Faith is rooted in evidence (Hebrews 11:1); faith is rooted in fact and truth (Titus 1:1). When you begin to examine the evidences demonstrating the unique inspiration of the Scriptures, you soon discover that believing the Bible it is not a leap in the dark but a step into light.

So what evidence do we have that the Bible is a unique book, God's Book, the very Word of God? There are many evidences that we might explore, but in this chapter we will examine just five. Each one supports the uniqueness of the Bible.

1. The Bible's Personal Claims

Even a casual reader of the Bible will soon discover he is reading a very unusual book. Though he may not accept its claims, if he carefully and reflectively reads, he will clearly see that the Bible makes some very unique claims about itself. In hundreds of passages, the Bible declares explicitly or implicitly that it is nothing less than the very Word of God. A computer concordance demonstrates that some *3,800 times* the Bible declares, "God said," or "Thus says the Lord."[2]

---

1. For a more complete treatment of the subject, please see: *How Do We Know the Bible Is True?* Volume 1, by Dr. Jason Lisle, Ken Ham, and Bodie Hodge, editors (Green Forest, AR: Master Books, 2011), chapter 1.
2. For example, Exodus 14:1; 20:1; Leviticus 4:1; Numbers 4:1; Deuteronomy 4:2; 32:48; Isaiah 1:10, 24; Jeremiah 1:11; Ezekiel 1:3.

Christians historically have claimed a "verbal plenary inspiration" of the Scriptures. The word "plenary" comes from the Latin and means *full* and the term "verbal" means *word*. The claims the biblical authors make are not just that the thoughts are inspired, but the very words are inspired . . . right down to the letters and verb tenses of the words.[3] If only the thoughts are inspired as some have said, then those "thoughts" would be open to wide and varied interpretation. But you cannot have thoughts without words anymore than you can have mathematics without numbers. If you change the numbers, you change the math, and if you change the words, you change the thoughts. Every word as God gave it is inspired.

So when conservative, Bible-believing Christians say the Bible is inspired, we do not mean *partial inspiration*, because it says, "all Scripture." If the Bible is only partially inspired then the reader becomes the judge of what is inspired and what is not. Nor do we mean progressive inspiration, as if some sections are more inspired and therefore truer than others.

All Scripture, Old and New Testament alike, is equally inspired. Leviticus 3:16 is no less inspired than John 3:16, and Genesis 1:1 is no less inspired than Revelation 22:21. Leviticus 3:16 may not be as "inspiring" to you as John 3:16, but it is just as much inspired by God and is just as much the Word of God. When Christians speak of *verbal plenary inspiration*, they are affirming that the Bible is not partially inspired, or progressively inspired, but fully inspired down to the words and letters.

The Apostle Paul recognized that his own writings were the Lord's commandments, and his writings were acknowledged as such by the Christians who read his letters.[4] He wrote in 2 Timothy 3:16–17, "All Scripture is given by inspiration of God, and is profitable for doctrine, for reproof, for correction, for instruction in righteousness: that the man of God may be perfect, thoroughly furnished unto all good works." The Bible claims to be "inspired by God."

The Greek New Testament literally reads, "All Scripture is God-breathed." The Scripture is the literal breath of God — just as when I

---

3. Jesus gave an argument for his deity based on the tense of a verb (John 8:58) and Paul defended Jesus' messiahship on the singular verses the plural form of a word (Galatians 3:16). Jesus taught that the Scriptures were inspired down to exact words and even to the smallest letter in Hebrew and the shortest stroke of a pen (Matthew 4:4; 5:18).

4. 1 Corinthians 14:37; 1 Thessalonians 2:13.

speak my voice is my breath coming up from my diaphragm out of my lungs over my larynx and then articulated by my tongue, lips, and teeth to reflect my very thoughts. Even so, the Bible is the Word of God as much as if God had a larynx, tongue, and lips to convey His very thoughts. Scripture claims to be the very breath and voice of God.

Just as Paul claimed to be writing the words of God, in similar fashion the Apostle Peter proclaimed that he, too, was writing God's Words and that those reading needed to heed it (2 Peter 1:16–21). Likewise, the Apostle John also recognized that his teaching was from God and that to reject his teaching was to reject God (1 John 4:6).

Of course, the skeptic is quick to say that this claim is purely a circular argument, and therefore not a valid argument. Obviously, anyone can write a book and some indeed have, claiming that the writings contained are the very words of God, when it is not so. However, when defending the uniqueness of the Bible, a very important place to start is the Bible's own claim to be inspired by God. If the Bible did not claim to be inspired, and we as Christians tried to prove it through some other means, then we would have a serious problem on our hands. But the Bible does claim to be the Word of God and that is an important piece of evidence that cannot easily be dismissed. Even in a court of law, the accused has the right to testify on his behalf and his testimony should be considered in the light of the evidence and in light of the credibility of the testimony given by the accused.

When we consider the human authors of Scripture who made the claim that they were writing the very Words of God, we need to ask, "Were these men trustworthy?" A simple examination of history documents that the human authors of Scripture defended the integrity of the Bible at great personal sacrifice, many with their own lives. For instance, Jeremiah received his message directly from the Lord, yet because of his defense of the Scripture some attempted to kill him and his own family rejected him (Jeremiah 11:1–3, 11:21, 12:6). When considering this, remember that the people of his day did not have an aversion to embracing a prophet from God, because counterfeit prophets were readily recognized (Jeremiah 23:21, 23:32, 28:1–17). So one is left only to ask, "Was Jeremiah a glutton for unnecessary punishment or did he have the truth?"

The testimony of reliable witnesses, like Jesus Christ (Matthew 4:4, 5:17–18, 22:23–32) and scores of others like Moses, Joshua, David, Daniel,

Nehemiah, and the Apostles, cannot just be brushed aside without first discrediting their integrity. While not everyone is ready to embrace Jesus Christ as God the Son, very few will write Him off as an evil man or as an unreliable person. Neither must we ignore men like the Apostles Peter and Paul. These men died martyrs' deaths believing that what they were writing and living for was the very Words of God.

Everything we know about the moral quality of the Apostles, most of whom died the death of martyrs, demonstrates that they were men of integrity. Take Peter, Paul, and John who gave us much of the New Testament. They were not dishonest men, but Apostles who in their writings condemned lying, stressed honesty, and encouraged Christian followers to be respectful, law-abiding, citizens.[5] These men had nothing to gain financially, yet they were willing to suffer for what they proclaimed because they believed the Bible to be the infallible Word of God.

Simon Greenleaf, one of the principal founders of the Harvard Law School, was once a skeptic himself until he examined the evidences for the reliability of the Resurrection from the biblical record. When he considered the Apostles who were willing to die for the truths of which they wrote in Scripture he said of them: "The annals of military warfare afford scarcely an example of like heroic constancy, patience, and unflinching courage. They had every possible motive to review carefully the grounds of their faith, and the evidences of the great facts and truths which they asserted."[6] The Apostles demonstrated the genuineness of their testimony, that the Bible is the Word of God, by their willingness to suffer persecution for the faith they recorded. One can only conclude they were either greatly deceived or what they said and embraced was true.

There is not any evidence to say that the authors of the Bible were untrustworthy men and that their claims, that they were writing the Words of God, are invalid. Even the careless reader of the Bible soon discovers that the human authors of Scripture believed that they were recording the God-breathed Word. When you read the Bible, the ever-present assumption of the writers is that they are recording the God-breathed

---

5. John 8:43-47; Revelation 21:7–8; Ephesians 4:25; Romans 13:1–7; 1 Peter 3:13–17.

6. Simon Greenleaf, *An Examination of the Testimony of the Four Evangelists by the Rules of Evidence Administered in he Courts of Justice* (Grand Rapids, MI: Baker Book House, 1965).

Word.[7] Their claim is either true or it is blatantly false. Certainly, if the only evidence we had for the Bible being inspired was its claim to be inspired, our argument would be very weak. If all we could say is, "I believe the Bible is the Word of God because it says it is inspired by God," then one could conclude that our defense is circular (having an arbitrary starting point). God, being the ultimate authority on all subjects (Hebrews 6:13), even on His own Word, is not an arbitrary starting point and doesn't violate an arbitrary vicious logical circle. However, if the Bible never claimed to be inspired, then Christians who defend it to be the Word of God would have a serious problem on their hands.

2. The Bible's Proven Accuracy

A second reason for believing the Bible to be a unique book is its proven accuracy. The Bible is unequaled in its historical accuracy, as one might expect if God inspired each of the writers. For instance, Dr. Luke, who was a medical doctor, who actually gave us more of the New Testament than any other single writer,[8] said this about the gospel that bears his name:

> Inasmuch as many have taken in hand to set in order a narrative of those things which have been fulfilled among us, just as those who from the beginning were eyewitnesses and ministers of the word delivered them to us, it seemed good to me also, having had perfect understanding of all things from the very first, to write to you an orderly account, most excellent Theophilus, that you may know the certainty of those things in which you were instructed (Luke 1:1–4).

Luke claimed to be an historian, and to this day he is considered a first-rate historian. Sir William Ramsay, a Nobel Prize recipient and professor of humanities at Aberdeen University in Scotland, was reputed to have been the foremost expert on geography and history of ancient Asia Minor during the 20th century. Considered to be one of the world's most eminent scholars, Ramsay was at one time highly critical of the Bible. But

---

7. For example, Psalm 19:7–11; 119.
8. Most Christians assume the Apostle Paul was used to give us most of the New Testament because he wrote 11 books. However, the Gospel of Luke and the Book of Acts combined is longer than all of Paul's letters put together.

eventually he was compelled to consider the writings of Dr. Luke, and after much research he concluded that Luke was one of the world's greatest historians. In fact, after carefully evaluating Luke's records, he wrote a book entitled *Luke, the Beloved Physician*! In one of Ramsay's classic works he wrote of Luke, "I take the view that Luke's history is unsurpassed in regards to its trustworthiness. You may press the words of Luke in a degree beyond any other historian, and they will stand the keenest scrutiny and the hardest treatment. Luke is a historian of the first rank. This author should be placed along with the very greatest of historians."[9]

One example of what Ramsay is speaking about is found in Luke 2 where we are told that the birth of Jesus took place when Quirinius was the governor of Syria (Luke 2:1–2). The opponents used to be quick to point out that Jesus was born before the death of Herod,[10] of whom history records died in 4 B.C., and that Quirinius was governor from A.D. 8–10. These critics concluded that there was an inaccuracy recorded by Luke and that he could not be trusted as a reliable historian. But the so-called "error" was cleared up when Sir William Ramsay and other archeologists discovered that Quirinius was governor twice; the first time when Jesus was born, and then a second time after Herod's death. Yet faultfinders, who are looking for errors in the Bible, have found it to be unreliable without having all the facts necessary to make a sound judgment.

Another example that was used for many years by those wanting to discredit the Bible concerns King Belshazzar. You will remember that he was the king who witnessed the mysterious handwriting on a wall when he was preparing a great banquet (Daniel 6). God informed him by the prophet Daniel that his kingdom would be divided and given to the Medes and the Persians. Critics scoffed at the written record, claiming the Book of Daniel was a fabrication because, according to ancient secular history, the last king of Babylon was not Belshazzar but a man named Nabonidus. For centuries, the historical record clearly showed that the last king of Babylon was Nabonidus until one day some archeologists unearthed a cylinder. On that cylinder was the name Belshazzar.[11]

9. William Ramsay, *Bearing of Recent Discoveries on the Trustworthiness of the New Testament* (Grand Rapids, MI: Baker, 1953), p. 222.
10. See Matthew 2:16–20.
11. In 1881 at Abu Habba, Hormuzd Rassam discovered the cylinders of Nabonidus which are now on display in the royal palace in Berlin.

With time, the archeologist's spade found more and more writings about Belshazzar, only to discover that the last king of Babylon was Nabonidus who co-reigned with Belshazzar. Nabonidus was the father of Belshazzar and they reigned together as co-regents. This explains why Belshazzar promised Daniel that if he could read the handwriting on the wall that he would make him "as third ruler in the kingdom" (Daniel 5:7). But suppose modern archeology had never found the cylinder about Belshazzar — would that make the Bible any less true? No, the Bible would still be true; we would just be limited in our information.

Another classic example that liberal critics use to discredit the reliability of the Bible is the repeated mention of the Hittite culture. Forty-eight times in the Scriptures, a people called the Hittites are mentioned, beginning in Genesis and ending in 2 Chronicles.[12] Up until 1875, in all the records of antiquity, there was not a single reference to these people. The skeptics attributed them to imagination and fiction.

This all changed when in 1876 George Smith began a study of monuments at a place called Djerabis in Asia Minor, uncovering the vast empire of the ancient Hittites. Historians now rate the Hittites on equal terms with both Egypt and Assyria, and at the University of Chicago there is an entire department dedicated to their study. The Hittites not only proved to be a real people, but their empire was shown to be one of the great ones of ancient times. Once again the critics of the Bible were proven to be wrong.

In the year 1806, the French Institute of Science listed no less than 80 historical/archeological/geological inaccuracies found in the Bible. By 1940, every single accusation on the list was proven to be wrong, such that today not a single item is held to be inaccurate. The Bible is an historically accurate record because it is inspired by the one true omniscient God who infallibly recorded the past.

3. The Bible's Supernatural Construction

A third reason for believing the Bible to be a unique book is its supernatural construction. Suppose you were to challenge ten different authors living today to write a book about the same general subject independently of one another. How similar do you think the book would turn out?

---

12. For example, we find them blocking Israel's path as they sought to enter the Promised Land (Numbers 13:29) and we learn of Uriah the Hittite, whom David sent to his untimely death (2 Samuel 11:21).

One of the amazing facts about the Bible is that although it was written by a wide diversity of authors (as many as 40), over a period of 1,600 years, from many different locations and under a wide variety of conditions, the Bible is uniquely one book, not merely a collection of 66 books.

The authors of the Bible lived in a variety of cultures, had different life experiences, and often were quite different in their personal make-up. They wrote their material from three continents (Africa, Asia, and Europe), in very diverse places[13] while employing three languages in their writings (Hebrew, Aramaic, and Greek).[14]

In addition, they represented a wide variety of backgrounds and professions.[15] And what is so amazing is that while most of the human authors never met each other and were unfamiliar with each others' writings, the Bible is still a unified whole without a single contradiction! There is a perfect unity that runs from Genesis to Revelation.

Compare that with other religious books. For instance, the Islamic Koran (Qur'an) was compiled by one individual, Zaid ibn Thabit, under the guidance of Mohammed's father-in-law, Abu-Bekr. Additionally, in A.D. 650, a group of Arab scholars produced a unified version based on Uthman's copy (third successor of Muhammad) and destroyed all variant copies to preserve the unity of the Koran.[16]

There is no other book ever produced in recorded human history like the Bible. It is apparent that no person or persons could have orchestrated the harmony found in Scripture. The Bible is beyond the ability of any man or group of men to create such a book. The only explanation is that the Bible is the Word of God. The only explanation is that behind the 40 human authors there was one Divine Author, God the Holy Spirit.

---

13. Moses in a desert, Solomon in a palace, Paul in a prison, John in exile, etc.

14. The Old Testament is almost entirely in Hebrew with a handful of chapters written in Aramaic. The New Testament is almost entirely in Greek with a few sentences written in Aramaic.

15. For instance, Moses was a political leader; Joshua a military leader; David a shepherd; Nehemiah a cupbearer; Solomon a king; Amos a herdsman; Daniel a prime minister; Matthew a tax collector; Luke a medical doctor; Paul a rabbi; and Peter a fisherman.

16. Samuel Green, "How and Why the Qur'an was Standardized," Answering-Islam website, accessed April 30, 2012, http://www.answering-islam.org/Green/uthman.htm.

4. The Bible's Prophetic Nature

Another amazing illustration of the divine origin of the Bible is its many fulfilled prophecies. The Bible is a unique book in that it has foretold the future, hundreds of years in advance, in a very specific and precise way. If someone told you that 300 years from today your great, great, great, great grandson is going to cross Park Avenue in New York City, where he will be stuck by a blue pick-up truck, driven by a woman with blonde hair, bearing the license tag W98-665, and it came true exactly as that person predicted, you would probably conclude he had a unique ability to foretell the future.

Well, no one has ever foretold the future hundreds of years in advance, in minute specificity, where the predictions came true. No one has ever made prophecies of this nature, except the writers of the Bible. For instance, in the Old Testament, hundreds of prophecies were made concerning the first coming of Christ. These were not predictions of a vague nature, but very specific predictions concerning His birth, life, death, Resurrection, and His return from heaven that is yet to take place. Only God, who knows all, can accurately and specifically foretell the future (Isaiah 46:10).

And that is precisely what He did through the various human authors of Scripture. Fulfilled prophecy is a powerful proof for the divine inspiration of Scripture. The following chart is just a brief sampling from over 300 prophecies that Jesus Christ fulfilled the first time He came into this world.

Of course, the critics say that the Lord Jesus, who knew the Old Testament, just arranged to have the prophecies fulfilled so that He could look like He was the Messiah. Think carefully about their criticism. Do you think Jesus Christ arranged to be born in Bethlehem? Do you think He arranged for the prophet Isaiah to describe His virgin birth in Isaiah 7:9 and to describe in Isaiah 53 His death by crucifixion centuries before it was a known form of execution? Yet that is precisely what these prophets wrote about 700 years before Christ left heaven and was born in Bethlehem.

Do you think Christ arranged nearly 1,000 years before His entrance into this world to have King David describe His death as if he were an eyewitness standing at the foot of the Cross? (Psalm 22). Do you think that Jesus arranged to be crucified between two thieves? Do you think He

Sampling of Fulfilled Prophecy in Relation to Christ			
1.	Isaiah 7:14	Virgin Born	Luke 1:26–35
2.	Micah 5:2	Born in Bethlehem	Matthew 2:1
3.	Isaiah 7:14	Called Immanuel	Matthew 1:23
4.	Isaiah 9:1–2	Ministry in Galilee	Matthew 4:12–16
5.	Zechariah 9:9	Triumphal entry	Matthew 21:1–11
6.	Psalm 41:9	Betrayed by a friend	Matthew 26:20–25
7.	Psalm 35:11	Falsely accused	Matthew 26:59–68
8.	Isaiah 53:7	Silent before accusers	Matthew 27:12–14
9.	Isaiah 53:9	Buried in tomb of rich	Matthew 27:57–61
10.	Isaiah 53:12	Crucified with robbers	Matthew 27:38
11.	Psalm 22:16	Hands and feet pierced	John 20:25
12.	Psalm 22:15	Thirsted on the Cross	John 19:28
13.	Psalm 22:18	Lots cast for clothes	John 19:23–24
14.	Psalm 34:20	Bones not broken	John 19:33
15.	Zechariah 13:7	Disciples flee	Matthew 26:31–35

arranged for Judas to betray him for 30 pieces of silver as Zechariah the prophet foretold?[17] Do you think He arranged for His own Resurrection from the dead? Do you think He arranged His appearance to over 500 individuals who were so convinced that they were willing to lay down their lives and die for Him? The truth is that He did arrange all this because He is God! In fact, Jesus Christ is the only one who ever arranged anything before He was ever born. He didn't arrange it after He was born, but even before He left heaven's splendor and came into this world through a miraculous virgin conception. This all happened as Matthew recorded in the gospel that bears his name: "All this was done that the Scriptures of the prophets might be fulfilled" (Matthew 26:56).

There is no other book on the face of the earth with fulfilled prophecy like the Bible. There are no verifiable fulfilled prophecies in the Muslim's *Koran*, in the Latter Day Saint's *Book of Mormon*, in the Hindu's *Upanishads,* or in any other religious or secular book. Only the Bible has fulfilled prophecy — and not just a few random things! Certainly there have been people who have appealed to secular works like Nostradamus. I have read his so-called "prophecies" and they are so vague and broad they

---

17. Zechariah was a prophet from 520 B.C. to 518 B.C. in Jerusalem.

could apply to hundreds of different scenarios. Rarely did he ever get specific, and when he did, he was always proven wrong, like his prediction that the world would end in 1999.[18] The Bible is a unique book because the Bible is a Divine-human book. Yes indeed, men wrote it, but men who were uniquely inspired by God.

5. The Bible's Preservation

The Bible is a very unique book in the manner by which it has been preserved. If the Bible is the Word of God, as it claims, then you would expect God to take care of and protect His Word as He said He would.[19] Yet sometimes one will hear critics say, "You Christians say the Bible is the Word of God, but it has been translated so many times through so many people through so many centuries that what we have today can no longer be trusted as the Word of God." If you have not heard statements like this, you will. So how should we respond?

While it is true that we no longer have the original manuscripts because the Bible is such an ancient book and paper will only last so long, we can still verify the authenticity of the Bible as we have it today by seeking out early copies or manuscripts.[20] Even beyond the ancient copies of Scripture, virtually all of the New Testament can be reproduced from early Christian writers who quote the Bible in their works. But sometimes people do not want to believe that the Bible is reliable because they do not like the implications it makes on their lives.

The argument that "today's Bible" is unreliable is quickly refuted when examining the manuscript evidence. By comparison to other documents of antiquity, the manuscript evidence for the Bible is unsurpassed. Take Julius Caesar's military battles known as "The Gallic Wars" fought from 58 to 51 B.C. Today there are just ten remaining copies of Caesar's work, with the earliest copy dating some 900 years after the original but no one questions its accuracy.[21]

---

18. Nostradamus or Michel de Nostredame (1503–1566) is best known for his book *Les Propheties* (The Prophecies), the first edition of which appeared in 1555.
19. If we believe that God is all-powerful, then we must believe that He has accurately preserved His will for man in the Scriptures as promised in numerous passages like Psalm 119:160; Isaiah 40:8; John 12:48; 2 John 2; and 1 Peter 1:22–25.
20. See chapter 23 in this book for more on textual criticism.
21. The Gallic Wars are described by Julius Caesar in his book *Commentarii de Bello*.

The first complete copy of Homer's *Odyssey* is 2,200 years after the original and no one questions its reliability. We have three copies of the works of Catullus with the earliest copy being about 1,600 years after he wrote, and yet the copies are esteemed to be reliable. When one considers the manuscript evidence for the Bible, it is unsurpassed by no other ancient work in history. There exists over 5,500 copies of the New Testament that contain all or part of the Greek New Testament with copies dating as early as A.D. 120–140.Early on in the life of the Church, the New Testament was translated into other languages of which we have over 18,000 copies further authenticating the reliable transmission of Scripture. Furthermore, there exist some 86,000 citations from early writers in their commentaries and letters (e.g., Clement quoting Hebrews in his letter to the Corinthian church in the first century, and he died before John the Apostle did). In addition, the accuracy of the copying process used for the Old Testament manuscripts has been further confirmed through the discovery of the Dead Sea Scrolls. The Dead Sea Scrolls were discovered in Qumran, Israel, in 1949 by a shepherd boy out in the wilderness caring for his sheep. Due to the dry arid climate of this section of Israel, these ancient scrolls were wondrously preserved. The vast majority of the Dead Sea Scrolls were simply copies of books of the Old Testament from 250–150 B.C., and a copy or portion of nearly every Old Testament book was found. This discovery only further confirmed what Jews and Christians already knew to be true. For instance, a complete copy of the Book of Isaiah was discovered providing a manuscript dating 100 years before Christ. When compared with copies dating 900 years after Christ, there was a difference of only 17 letters. The differences were minor, like the stylistic insertion of a conjunction, or differences in the spelling of certain words.[22] These minor differences between the Dead Sea Scrolls and those that the Masoretes provided did not in any way change the meaning of what was originally recorded. The argument that the Bible has changed through the centuries through the copying process does not stand up against the manuscript evidence. There is more support for the reliability of the biblical manuscripts than any other writings in the ancient world.

---

22. In Old English our word "Savior" is spelled "Saviour." The change in spelling that took place over three centuries has not changed or altered the meaning of the word. These are the types of changes reflected between the Dead Sea Scrolls and copies written hundreds of years later.

No Other Book Like the Bible

No other book has survived like the Bible. The Bible is not the book of the year . . . it is the Book of the Ages! The Bible is indestructible because, as it promises, "the word of our God stands forever" (Isaiah 40:8). The Bible has been laughed at, scorned, and laws have been made against it. It has been burned, it has been treated as contraband, and yet the Bible stands. God has preserved His Book, a Book that claims to be the very Word of God. Its accuracy demonstrates it is the Word of God. Its supernatural construction verifies it is the Word of God. Its prophetic nature and *fulfilled prophecy* should be enough to conclude that it is indeed the Word of God.

In light of the Bible's claims, accuracy, construction, and prophecies, one is left with two choices. Either God was involved in inspiring men to write it or He was not. If God was not involved in writing the Bible through various men, then you are left to conclude that either *good men* or *bad men* wrote it without God's help (but how would one define good and bad without the Bible anyway!). If the Bible is the product of *good men*, then they were really not "good" because they would be liars. Good men would deceive hundreds of times by saying, "Thus says the Lord," if God was not really inspiring them. And because of what these men wrote, millions of people have died for the claims of Jesus Christ. Such men would not be "good men" but evil men.

On the other hand, if the Bible is the product of *bad men*, it seems highly unlikely that they would write a book that forbids sin, commends good, and condemns their unbelieving lifestyles to an eternity in hell. The only viable alternative is that God wrote this book through the men He chose to write the inspired Word of God.

One anonymous poem summarizes it well:

> The Holy Bible must have been,
> Inspired of God and not of men.
> I could not if I would, believe
> That good men wrote it to deceive.
> And bad men could not if they would,
> And surely would not if they could,
> Proceed to write a book so good.

And certainly no crazy man
Could e're conceive its wondrous plan.
And pray, what other kinds of men
Than do these three groups comprehend?
Hence it must be that God inspired,
The Word which souls of prophets fired.

The only question that remains is, "Do you believe that the Bible is the Word of God and therefore the authority for your life?" The Bible is a unique book with a unique message. All of the other major religions in the world claim that a person can achieve heaven by how he lives. However, the Bible teaches that man cannot save himself, because the penalty for sin is death (Genesis 2:16–17; Ezekiel 18:20; Romans 6:23). So it is not surprising that the Bible teaches that if good works could save a person then there was no need for Christ to die (Galatians 2:21). This same book informs us that Christ did not have His life taken from Him, but that He gave His life for us (John 10:17–18). It claims that Christ became the substitute for the punishment ours sins deserve (Romans 5:8; 1 Peter 3:18). He then demonstrated His sinlessness, and therefore His ability as an innocent person to take our punishment, when He was resurrected from the dead (Romans 1:4). The message of the Bible is that we cannot earn salvation but that we must receive salvation by placing our faith in Jesus Christ (Ephesians 2:8–9). Jesus Christ did not claim to be a good way to God. He did not even claim to be the best way to God. In the only Book that God ever inspired, He claimed to be the *only* way to God (John 14:6; Acts 4:12). We must all decide what we will do with the message found in this unique book.

Chapter 6

What Is Apologetics — and Why Do It?

Ken Ham and Bodie Hodge

❦❦❦❦❦❦❦❦❦❦❦❦❦❦❦❦❦❦❦

The Bible is under attack in today's age. In fact, the Word of God has been under constant attack since the Garden of Eden, when the serpent, which was influenced by Satan, questioned Eve about God's command in Genesis 3 ("Has God indeed said . . ."). We call this the "Genesis 3 attack."

In our day, what is the main Genesis 3 attack? We believe it is the teaching of evolution and millions of years that attacks the historicity of Genesis 1–11, and thus undermines the authority of Scripture. The first step is to recognize these attacks and their consequences, and then understand how to deal with it.

First Chronicles 12:32 states:

> Of the sons of Issachar who had understanding of the times, to know what Israel ought to do. . . ."

Christians need to understand our times so that we can know what the church ought to do.

So what is going on today? There are numerous false claims about the Bible (especially in regard to the historicity of the first 11 chapters of the Bible), even by many professing Christians themselves. Subsequently, we are seeing kids walk away from the faith having no answers for the world.

Statistics reveal that two out of three young people are walking away from the Church, and research clearly shows this is related to doubt and unbelief because of compromising teaching in regard to the first book of the Bible. Sadly, much of the Church does not understand this problem and therefore is not doing what needs to be done to counteract this terrible situation of a generational loss of biblical authority.

So what do we do? Well, God's Word says:

> But sanctify the Lord God in your hearts, and always be ready to give a defense to everyone who asks you a reason for the hope that is in you, with meekness and fear (1 Peter 3:15).

It is time for the Church to respond to these attacks that are undermining Scripture and greatly contributing to the loss of the next generation from the Church, and to begin equipping generations to know how to answer the skeptical questions in our modern scientific age. The Church needs to "return fire" on these attacks that have had devastating consequences on the spiritual state of coming generations and the culture. The professional research we initiated shows clearly that the Church needs to be teaching apologetics at every age level (see *Already Compromised* [Master Books, Green Forest, AR, 2011]).

What Is Apologetics and What Is Its Purpose?

The phrase translated "to give a defense" or sometimes "give an answer" in 1 Peter 3:15 comes from the Greek word *apologia*, which literally means "reasoned defense." It does not mean to *apologize*, which is a common misconception among some who are not acquainted with this thrust of Christianity. It means to give a logical defense of the Christian faith.

Apologetics is a branch of Christianity that defends the authority of God's Word, the character of God, and Christianity as a whole, *and also* uses the Bible as an offensive "weapon" (e.g., like a sword) against all other worldviews and opposition. Not only do we need to teach general Bible apologetics in this age, but we also need to teach creation apologetics (dealing with the evolution/millions-of-years issues).

Apologetics is an exciting area of study to help strengthen your faith, defend Christianity, and close the mouth of the attacking unbeliever. But please don't misunderstand. Apologetics is *not* a tool to make people believe in Christ. The Bible makes it clear that "faith comes by hearing, and hearing by the word of God" (Romans 10:17). But apologetics can help answer people's skeptical questions and be used to point them to God's Word and the gospel. They can be shown clearly that the history in the Bible is true, that's why the gospel based in that history is true.

When under attack, there are two primary defenses available to you: defend (answer) and/or disarm (go on the offense). These are essentially the basics of Christian apologetics. Let's consider an analogy to help you understand. Let's say there is a crazed person who comes at you with a knife and tries to strike you down. You can defend yourself by blocking or moving out of the way every time the attacker strikes. Or you can disarm your opponent by taking the knife out of his hand.

Now to apply this to our situation concerning a defense of the Christian faith. You can defend by answering the questions, but then you can also disarm their arguments by attacking the very basis of their attacks, pointing out that they have a faulty starting point for their worldview. Of course, all this should be done with meekness and fear (gentleness and respect) as God's Word instructs us.

It's important to understand that in Christendom, there are some different types of apologetic approaches — though we would insist not all are correct and therefore it is important to ensure you are using the right one.

The main types (each with an ever-so-brief definition) are:

- Classical: essentially, this method assumes that rational thought is the absolute standard regarding philosophical debates. Evidence is used in conjunction with the argument — though it is important to understand all evidence is interpreted (i.e., rational thoughts first to point to the Bible's truthfulness).[1]
- Evidential: essentially assumes that rational thought is the absolute standard and that when people see evidence (as in miracles in the Bible, or historical evidence and scientific evidence), they will come to the right conclusion (i.e., evidence first to point to the Bible's truthfulness).[2] This method really assumes people are

---

1. Popular classical apologists are William Lane Craig, Thomas Aquinas, Norm Geisler, R.C. Sproul, and J.P. Moreland.
2. Popular evidential apologists are B.B. Warfield, William Paley, and John Warwick Montgomery.

"neutral" — which is against what the Bible clearly states about the nature of man (there is none righteous, and none seeks after God, etc.).

- Presuppositional:

  Van Tillian; God and His Word are the absolute standards of morality, logic, uniformity in nature, dignity, etc. The Bible is the only basis for a worldview that makes knowledge possible. All other worldviews must borrow from the Bible to make sense of the world (i.e., Bible first and final to look at all things.)[3]

Other popular semi-presuppositional methods:

- Clarkian: The best worldview is the most logical and Christianity is the most consistent in its logic. So Christianity appears to be the best.[4]
- Shaeferian: The best worldview will give the best answers to life. Christianity gives the best answers to life. So Christianity appears to be the best.[5]
- Carnellian: The best worldview is the most coherent. Christianity is the most coherent via the internal text. So Christianity appears to be the best.[6]

Others (cumulative case, reformed epistemology, fideism, etc.)[7]

The above was not meant to be an exhaustive list, but it helps give an idea of the different styles that are used to defend the Christian faith. Naturally, some work better than others.

The Answers in Genesis position has been in the vein of presuppositional apologetics. We use the Bible as our absolute authority in every area to build a worldview so we have the right basis to have the ability to then correctly understand the world (the evidence) around us. This is the overall style of apologetics used in our apologetics resources.

---

3. Named for Cornelius Van Til who articulated it in modern times, espoused by Van Til, Greg Bahnsen, Kenneth Gentry, Michael Butler, and Jason Lisle. Early presuppositional apologetics examples are claimed from the Bible itself, as well as numerous others such as Augustine (in some aspects) and John of Damascus.
4. Variant developed by Gordon Clark.
5. Variant developed by Francis Schaefer.
6. Variant developed by Edward J. Carnell.
7. We simply can't hit all the methods in this short introduction, so we are going to stick to the most popular views in the treatise.

Apologetics in the Bible

The Bible commands that we give a reasoned defense of the faith in 1 Peter 3:15. Peter also makes it clear this is to be done by first setting apart Christ as Lord in your heart and to do this with gentleness and respect.

Far too often Christians obtain a few answers and they think they are then ready to "force" those answers on to people so they can beat their opponent. Instead, this should be done with gentleness and respect. We need to show the same grace, mercy, and love that the Lord showed to us. This is why apologetics should always be used in conjunction with the Gospel (Matthew 28:18–20); in other words, don't do apologetics for the sake of doing apologetics to try to win an argument, but do it for the sake of the gospel of Jesus Christ.

But consider other pertinent passages also:

> We destroy arguments and every lofty opinion raised against the knowledge of God, and take every thought captive to obey Christ, being ready to punish every disobedience, when your obedience is complete (2 Corinthians 10:5–6; ESV).

> If anyone teaches otherwise and does not consent to wholesome words, even the words of our Lord Jesus Christ, and to the doctrine which accords with godliness, he is proud, knowing nothing, but is obsessed with disputes and arguments over words, from which come envy, strife, reviling, evil suspicions, useless wranglings of men of corrupt minds and destitute of the truth, who suppose that godliness is a means of gain. From such withdraw yourself (1 Timothy 6:3–5).

Furthermore, discernment must be used when discussing the things of God. Many apologists get caught up debating one person (who refuses to be corrected) over the course of years. The Bible speaks on this subject:

> But avoid foolish disputes, genealogies, contentions, and strivings about the law; for they are unprofitable and useless. Reject a divisive man after the first and second admonition, knowing that such a person is warped and sinning, being self-condemned (Titus 3:9–11).

Do not give what is holy to the dogs; nor cast your pearls before swine, lest they trample them under their feet, and turn and tear you in pieces (Matthew 7:6).

And whoever will not receive you, when you go out of that city, shake off the very dust from your feet as a testimony against them (Luke 9:5).

If people are not willing to learn and really shows no sign of being challenged and willing to consider they could be wrong, do not continue wasting time with them (on the account of their hard hearts). You may find much more fruitful evangelism with others who are willing to listen. Some may think that the Bible commands us to give an answer back to these those people who are arguing against the Christian faith repeatedly (for years even) because of 1 Peter 3:15. But take note of the careful wording: "always be prepared to make a defense" (ESV).

First Peter 3:15 doesn't say to always give an answer, but always "be prepared to give an answer." There are, in fact, times to refrain. For example, when people fail to listen (even professing Christians who refuse to listen) (2 Peter 2:3), when you can discern that they obviously do not want to be instructed (Proverbs 1:7), or when their purpose is to be divisive (Romans 16:17), then it is time to move on.

Practical Apologetics

There are several things the apologist should strive for when defending the faith. The first is to present the Christian worldview from the starting point of the Bible (Mark 16:15; Proverbs 26:4). This would include but not be limited to:

1. Creation week was a period of six ordinary 24-hour days. How can one stand on the authority of Scripture and then question the history in the Bible? If Genesis is not true, then why is the rest of the Bible true?

2. Man was made in the image of God. Man is not just the product of random chemical reactions over million of years. Therefore, man is not just an animal; human life has value (the most common worldview today is secular humanism with its foundation in man's beliefs of evolution, millions of years, and that you are just an animal with no value).

3. God created a perfect world where there was no death. Man's sin brought death and corrupted this perfect world. The Bible describes death as an "enemy." The Fall of mankind explains death and suffering in the world and the need for a Savior and the need for a new heavens and new earth.

4. The Flood that accounts for most of the rock layers that contain fossils; and also that God does judge sin, but also sends a means of salvation (i.e., the ark). The righteous judge is also a God who is merciful.

5. The Tower of Babel, which helps us understand why we speak different languages and why we all look a little different, even though we are one race, all sinners, and all in need of a Savior.

6. Moses and the Law, which gives more detail as to what sin is as it reigned from the time of Adam. Also relate how Christ fulfilled the law and offers grace.

7. Christ and His work on the Cross when God became a man to die and pay the penalty for our sin and offer the free gift of salvation to those who believe in Jesus Christ and His Resurrection.

8. New heavens and new earth to fulfill what God has promised. (Christians look forward to this, when there will be a time with no more death and suffering.)

Many times when we present a Christian worldview to the unbeliever, it involves clearing up misconceptions about Christian theism. A few examples are:

1. God is one God who is triune (three persons: Father, Son, and the Holy Spirit), not three separate "gods."

2. Christianity should be based on the Bible, not the words of fallible humans — even if they are Christians (who often fail to live up to the standards in the Bible).

3. God created the world perfect, not the way it is today. It has been subjected to death and decay due to man's sin (Genesis 1:31; Deuteronomy 32:4; Genesis 3; Romans 8). Death and suffering are a result of sin, and God stepped into history as Jesus Christ the God-man, to die in our place and save us from sin and death.

Second when defending the faith, in a sin-cursed and broken world, it is good to understand the way an unbeliever thinks. This is important to be able to refute their false worldviews because of their wrong starting point (starting with man's word instead of God's Word) (Ephesians 4:17–18; 1 Corinthians 1:21; 2:14; 3:19; Colossians 2:8; Romans 1:18–28; and so on). We need to know as much as possible about the other person's professed worldview so that we can kindly refute it when the time comes.

Third, the Christian apologist should do an internal critique of the unbeliever's worldview (Proverbs 26:5; 2 Timothy 2:25). Point out where they are being arbitrary, inconsistent, where their worldview's ultimate conclusion leads (e.g., reduced to absurdity), and even cases where they borrow from the Bible.[8]

Lastly, in our apologetics we must strive to continually point people to God's Word and present the gospel. Many times this can be done when presenting the Christian worldview. But make sure the gospel is "front and center" in apologetics, as the gospel of Jesus Christ is of utmost importance.

Presuppositional Apologetics (Van Til)[9]: What Is It?

Van Tillian presuppositional apologetics places God and His Word, the Bible, as the absolute authority in every area. God, who knows all things, has stated in the Bible that all other worldviews are wrong, so by extension all other worldviews have inconsistencies and must borrow from the Bible to make any sense of the world, whether they realize it or not.

Christian theism is not arbitrary, it is consistent, and has the preconditions of intelligibility (preconditions to make knowledge possible; e.g., we are made in the image of a logical and all-knowing God). Other worldviews are arbitrary, inconsistent, and lack the preconditions that make knowledge possible. So presuppositional apologists do an internal critique of the unbelievers' worldview to show where it is arbitrary, inconsistent, and where they lack the preconditions necessary for knowledge.

---

8. For more on these topics please consult Dr. Greg Bahnsen's book *Always Ready* (Nacogdoches, TX: Covenant Media Press, 1996), or Dr. Jason Lisle's book *The Ultimate Proof of Creation* (Green Forest, AR: Master Books, 2009).

9. In this short section, we will merely hit a brief highlight of Van Tillian presuppositionalism. For a more complete treatment, please see: *Van Til's Apologetic: Readings and Analysis,* Dr. Greg Bahnsen (Phillipsburg, NJ: Presbyterian and Reformed Publishing Company, 1998).

Presuppositional apologetics is a well-known method by which apologists "go on the offensive" to confront false worldviews (hopefully in a nice way, of course). In other words, an apologist makes adherents of other worldviews, like secular humanism, atheism, Hinduism, Islam, cults, and the like, try to defend their worldviews so they can show the problems within their professed view. And in all this, point out clearly where these other religions borrow from the Bible to make sense of the world.

For example, when the Creation Museum opened in May of 2007, the atheists protesting the opening hired a plane to fly above the museum with a banner quoting "Thou shalt not lie." The atheists have no reason not to lie in their own worldview, so they had to borrow from the Christian worldview to make this statement.[10] Interestingly, these atheists who say there is no right and wrong were arguing that the Creation Museum was teaching something wrong (Bible history). Right and wrong exist because we have an absolute authority, the God of the Bible, who defines what is right and wrong in the Bible. These atheists didn't have a foundation to determine right and wrong — only their subjective opinion!

Atheists who argue that we are just animals are almost always wearing clothes. Do animals wear clothes? No. So instead of making a consistent argument that we are only animals, atheists are instead confirming a literal Genesis 3 where we wear clothes due to sin and shame! God gave Adam and Eve clothes after sin. This works with many other things: Why do we have a seven-day week — the Bible. Why does logic and reason exist — the Bible. Why does knowledge exist — the Bible. Why is marriage defined as a man and a woman — the Bible.

This list can go on for hours! But in an unbeliever's worldview, they lack the very foundational basis for such things.

Here is a checklist to look for problems in the unbeliever's worldview[11]:

1. Is it arbitrary — mere opinions, relativism, mere conjectures (perhaps prejudicial) — biases that have no ultimate basis?
2. Is it inconsistent (fallacies, behavior doesn't match what one professes, their presuppositions do not mesh together)?

10. Atheism has no God who sets what is right and wrong, so there is no ultimate basis not to lie.
11. Due to the limited space in this chapter these will not be expanded upon. But to know more about this, please consult Dr. Greg Bahnsen's book *Always Ready* or Dr. Jason Lisle's book *The Ultimate Proof of Creation*.

3. Violations of preconditions for knowledge (any ultimate basis for logic, uniformity in the universe, morality, and so on)?
4. Will this view be reduced to absurdity (a form of inconsistency when taken to its ultimate conclusion)?

Some may argue that non-Christians don't believe the Bible to be true and yet they can do logic, insist on a view of morality, do excellent scientific research that builds outstanding technology, and so on. But they miss the point then. The issue isn't that they can do it, but they don't have *a basis* to do it. They must borrow from the Bible to actually make sense of it. In other words, the Bible has to be true, whether they acknowledge it or not, just to make sense of things.

Shortcomings of Other Presuppositional Views

There have been several "presuppositional" methods proposed over the years outside of the Van Tillian method.[12] Many of these people have contributed some excellent material to the debate and mesh well with

---

12. Some say that they like Van Tillian (or even Bahnsen's) presuppositional apologetic, but they don't want to promote it because Van Til had specific denominational views that they do not agree with. Please do not get us wrong; our intent here is not to make people follow all of Van Til's positions but to understand and make use of the philosophical method outlined in his works in regard to his apologetics method.

Van Tillian presuppositional apologetics in many areas. But there are some overarching flaws that reduce the potency of their overall thrust such as:

> Clarkian: Gordon Clark essentially says that the best world-view is the most logical, and Christianity is the most consistent in its logic. So Christianity appears to be the best.

> Schaefferian: Francis Schaeffer essentially says that the best worldview will give the best answers to life. Christianity gives the best answers to life. So Christianity appears to be the best.

> Carnellian: Edward J. Carnell essentially says that the best worldview is the most coherent. Christianity is the most coherent via the internal text. So, Christianity appears to be the best.

Of course, there are other variations (e.g., Nash), but we cannot be exhaustive in this short chapter.[13]

Clark's view (one of the more popular) is in essence similar to the evidential/classical methods. Even though he made some great presuppositional arguments in certain places, his overall viewpoint falls short of the typical presuppositional viewpoint. In other words, Clark really moved to a position that man's autonomous reasoning (man apart from God) should be used as the absolute starting point, over God's Word.

Carnell actually began with Van Tillian presuppositional apologetics and then moved to a form that was based on autonomous human reason looking at coherency. Schaeffer's ultimate apologetic does something similar as well, by ultimately appealing to man's authority over God's Word.

But even so, the problem with each of these is by what standard is "best" to be determined — autonomous human reason or God's Word? By moving away from God's Word as the absolute standard, these other methods really move away from true presuppositional apologetics. Such faulty "supposedly presuppositional" views still fall short. They actually fail because they still need to stand on the preconditions of

---

13. To understand these viewpoints and their overarching flaws please consult *Presuppositional Apologetics: Stated and Defended*, by Greg L. Bahnsen, Joel McDurmon, editor (Powder Springs, GA: American Vision Press; Nacogdoches, TX: Covenant Media Press, 2009).

intelligibility in regard to the Bible's absolute standard, just *to make* their case.[14]

Hence, each of these other methods are still inherently adopting a Van Tillian basis and and fail to properly connect it. Christian theism based on the Bible as the absolute truth, is the precondition that must be borrowed for knowledge to even be possible.

Each of these other views ultimately rely on fallible human logic as the absolute standard — instead of God, who is the ultimate standard.[15] Furthermore, each of their propositions are pseudo (false) presuppositional views as these views consequentially *can't* really allow one to know the Bible is true or be certain that God even exists — or be certain of one's own salvation. For these other views, in essence, their position is that this is the "best possible worldview right now," "likely the most coherent so far," and "gives the best possible answers right now," but could still be wrong.

Essentially, each of these other alleged presuppositional views are forced into a position that biblical matters are likely true or likely the best, but we can never *know* it 100 percent for sure. Interestingly, the Bible says we *can know* numerous things, for example:

> And we know that all things work together for good to those who love God, to those who are the called according to His purpose (Romans 8:28).

> But whoever keeps His word, truly the love of God is perfected in him. By this we know that we are in Him (1 John 2:5).

> These things I have written to you who believe in the name of the Son of God, that you may know that you have eternal life, and that you may continue to believe in the name of the Son of God (1 John 5:13).

---

14. Preconditions of intelligibility (knowledge) are the things that need to be in place for knowledge to exist. For example, the Bible gives a precondition for intelligibility where man is made in the image of an all-knowing logical God. Hence, we can relate to logical reasoning about knowledge and knowledge transfer. Also, God being all-knowing is the basis for knowledge to exist, and so on.

15. The problem here is that logic is elevated above God, whereas in a presuppositional debate, logic is a tool but subservient to God and His Word being the ultimate authority. Logic is possible because God and the Bible are true.

Neutrality vs. Common Ground

Have you ever had anyone ask you to "leave the Bible out of it" when you are discussing a subject? Perhaps they say something like, "Let's discuss this, but since I don't trust the Bible, you are going to have to use better sources, so we can meet on neutral ground."

This is a subtle tact to try to get you to throw out the Bible and have a "civilized" discussion about a topic, without all that supposed "religious stuff" — in other words, to be supposedly "neutral." But there is actually no neutral position. The Bible makes it clear than man's heart is evil and we are either for Christ or against (Genesis 8:21, Jeremiah 17:9).

What they are subtly trying to do is to get you to give up the Bible as your ultimate authority (your starting point) and trust theirs (man becomes the authority or starting point on the subject at hand, not God). In other words, they are trying to get you to act like a secularist, and if you do so, you have already lost the debate.

Consider this analogy: You see a person who is sniffing cocaine. As an apologist you want to inform this person of addictive problems associated with this illegal drug (e.g., 1 Corinthians 6:12). And they say, "Listen, we can talk about this, but first you need to sniff this cocaine with me." Would you do it? Of course not — you don't give up your morality based on the Bible's authority and accept theirs, so why give up the Bible's authority in any other area to trust theirs?[16]

Be on the lookout for those who propose that there is such a thing as neutrality in the debate. There is no such thing as neutrality:

> He who is not with Me is against Me, and he who does not gather with Me scatters abroad (Matthew 12:30).

> Because the mind set on the flesh is hostile toward God; for it does not subject itself to the law of God, for it is not even able to do so (Romans 8:7; NASB).

> Adulterers and adulteresses! Do you not know that friendship with the world is enmity with God? Whoever therefore wants to be a friend of the world makes himself an enemy of God (James 4:4).

---

16. No analogy is perfect, but hopefully this gets the point across.

Secular
Presuppositions

Biblical
Presuppositions

We don't want to get caught "giving up the Bible" to meet on supposed neutral ground, otherwise the non-Christians, especially the many secularists today, win! This is because they are getting you to leave the Bible out of the debate and thus debate on the terms of man's opinions being the ultimate authority (if the Bible is left out, then God is left out, which means man is the ultimate authority by default). In other words, they want you to give up your starting point of God's Word, and replace it with their starting point of man's word — so they win!

But there is common ground. The unbeliever will often repeat that it is wrong to lie, murder, and so on. But what are they doing? They are borrowing from the Bible. This is what we need to point out! We do have common ground, but that is because they are borrowing from the Bible. They actually have to use the Christian starting point of God's Word to discuss such things.

So apologists need to recognize this and "pull the rug

out from underneath" the unbeliever. Then when they realize they have no reliable foundation, we pray God will convict them to step aboard the biblical foundation — to change their starting point (which is a work of the Holy Spirit on their heart — a work of the Word of God that convicts and saves). Actually, in such discussions when they are obviously borrowing from the Christian starting point (the Bible), then when they attack the Bible they are essentially trying to blow themselves up too — whether they realize it or not. Hence, their position is self-refuting.

When we meet on common ground, we need to point out that the unbeliever is actually standing on borrowed ground — God's ground!

Correct Aspects of Classical and Evidential Apologetics

Many may have already realized the similarities in classical and evidential apologetics. And rightly so! Evidential apologetics is actually a modern outworking of classical apologetics. In fact, many clas-

sical apologists appeal to evidential thinking on certain arguments and vice versa. Often, we find classical and evidential apologists accepting positions that actually undermine biblical authority (like belief in an earth that is billions of years old), because they really have such a trust in autonomous human reasoning.

We would be the first to admit that classical and evidential methods would be great in a perfect world . . . but we are not in a perfect world. Let us explain. In a perfect world, everyone would use logic correctly! In a perfect world, everyone would view evidence the correct way. In a sin-cursed and broken world, logic and evidence are not used and viewed correctly because of false worldviews that have resulted due to sin, and thus the fallen state of man and how that affects our thinking.

Consider: We all have the same evidence (we all live in the same universe). We look at the same dinosaur bones, same DNA, same rock layers, same continents, and so on. And yet, the majority of the world's people are not coming to the conclusion that Jesus Christ is Lord. The evidence concerning Christ is not convincing them — even when we put it right in front of their faces! Evidence, by itself, doesn't convince people (Luke 16:31; John 6:65; 1 Corinthians 12:3; etc.); even Jesus when He offered His body as proof of the Resurrection did not remain silent but the evidence was presented in conjunction with the authoritative statements of Christ (Luke 24:36–41). Sadly, some still disbelieved (Luke 24:41).

Look now at the basis of the classical method. Everyone has the same logic and reasoning, but not everyone uses it correctly and hence the majority of the world's people are still not coming to Christ. In a broken world, these theoretical methods simply don't work the way they should due to human sin and the fact that man's heart is already biased against God — man is not neutral!

The point is, God Himself is the ultimate authority in every area. So God's Word has to be presupposed before we can even do a debate on logic/reasoning or evidence.

Follow us here, in the classical and evidential methods; it is assumed that logic is the absolute standard. But if logic is the absolute standard, then God would *not* be. Essentially, evidential and classical apologists are (inadvertently) appealing to another absolute standard (system of logic) to claim that God is the absolute standard. Classical and evidential defenders readily appeal to God as the absolute authority (and this is correct), but their method appeals to something else as the absolute authority. By default then, man's ideas (autonomous human reason) become the authority over God.

But don't throw the baby out with the bath water! There is a time when an evidential-style method is useful — in fact, very useful. This is when both involved in the debate share the *same* biblical worldview.

When both debaters have the same biblical worldview, then it is a matter of understanding the evidence, not a debate about worldview. When a debate arises over some scientific evidence or the like, and both are biblical creationists (for example), then the debate can proceed almost identical to an evidential method. The difference is that the Bible is the authority and evidence is a good *confirmation* of the Bible's truthfulness. There is more on evidence later in this treatise.

The same sort of situation occurs with the classical method. When both share a common biblical worldview, then the debate is no longer over worldview, but can be carried on from the perspective of a classical style apologetic by making the logical case. The difference is recognizing the place of God and His Word above all — even logic, which is more of a reflection of the way God thinks and upholds.

For example, classical arguments for the existence of God (first cause, design, and so on) are a good confirmation of the *transcendental* argument for the existence of God (TAG)[17] that is actually presupposed prior to the classical arguments.[18] TAG is actually the natural outworking of presuppositional apologetics.[19] But classical arguments, building on the Bible as the absolute authority, are a great *confirmation* of what we expect.

---

17. TAG basically states that any alternative to the biblical theism would make knowledge impossible. In essence, it is the only book that has the preconditions for knowledge/logic (i.e., intelligibility). All other worldviews must borrow from the Bible for the world to make sense. Science, morality, and logic all stem from the Bible being true. So, to reiterate, if the Bible were not true, then knowledge would be impossible. In other words, if the Bible were not true, nothing would make sense — good or bad . . . everything would be meaningless and pointless.

18. Ken Ham, editor, *New Answers Book 3* (Green Forest, AR: Master Books, 2010), p. 263–270.

19. For a good summary of people's attempts to refute TAG, please see "The Transcendental Argument for God's Existence" by Michael R. Butler, http://www. butler-harris.org/tag/.

One needs to recognize that the Bible gives the very basis by which we can do logic and understand knowledge — for we are made in the image of an all-knowing, logical God (Genesis 1:27; Colossians 2:3). Only God knows everything. Therefore, it is only on the basis of what the all knowing God reveals to us we can even begin to construct the right worldview. The Bible also explains why we mess it up — sin (Genesis 3; Romans 5). It is the Bible that enables us to understand that our memory and sense are reliable (e.g., Job 38–41) and the world will be upheld in a certain fashion (e.g., Genesis 8:22). So we have a basis to look at evidence and draw conclusions — but such things are predicated on the truthfulness of the Bible as the ultimate authority.

Uses of Evidence

We commonly encounter the false perception that evidence is not used among presuppositional apologists. This cannot be further from the truth. That is a philosophy nearing "fideism" (when one believes there is no reason to use evidence, arguments, or the Bible, but let God do all the work) . . . essentially faith alone (*fides* in Latin means faith).

The presuppositionalist uses evidence. It is often done in a slightly different way than evidential or classical apologetics. Some of the uses of evidence are:

- Confirming a biblical worldview
- Introduction to worldviews
- Showing inconsistencies and arbitrariness in false worldviews
- To show the unbeliever they must use the Bible to properly understand evidence

Let's look at an example for each of these.

Confirming a Biblical Worldview

Often, we come across evidence that is a great confirmation of the Bible's truthfulness. One excellent example of that is the Flood of Noah's day. When we see rock layers all over the

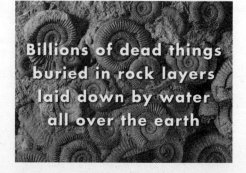
Billions of dead things buried in rock layers laid down by water all over the earth

world that have fossils in them, this is good confirmation of what we would expect to see as a result of a global flood. We can use this evidence when discussing a Christian worldview with an unbeliever to confirm that God's Word is the right starting point.

Introduction to Worldviews

When an unbeliever and biblical Christian engage in discussion, evidence is often used. And this can be good — an apologist can use evidence in regard to origins, for instance, to help the unbeliever realize it is really a worldview debate.

Then point out to the unbeliever that the debate is actually about starting points that build the two different worldviews. The real debate is actually at the starting point level.

Showing Inconsistencies and Arbitrariness in False Worldviews

This is a very effective use of evidence when evidence simply has no good explanation within the unbeliever's worldview. For example, the secular humanistic worldview (no God, evolution, and millions of years) teaches that dinosaurs evolved into birds over millions of years.

Recently, they found a group of feathers in rock layers supposed to be at the "dawn" of dinosaurs' existence![20] The secular response was to say that they look like feathers but they can't be true feathers because dinosaurs hadn't evolved into birds yet! Note the utter inconsistency!

---

20. Jeff Hecht, "Eighty Million Years Ahead of Its Time," *New Scientist* (March 24, 2012): p. 8.

To show the unbeliever they must use the Bible to properly understand evidence

Evidence can also be used to share with the unbeliever that the very *basis* to logically think about fossil feathers (using the example above) in rock layers below dinosaurs is predicated on the Bible's truthfulness about knowledge, logic, and correct reason. In other words, we can't even properly understand logic unless the Bible is true. By starting with the Bible, we cannot only make sense of the evidence, but have a basis to do so.

Conclusion

This short chapter on apologetics is merely scratching the surface of the topic. In fact, entire anthologies can be (and have been) written on the brief topics we discussed in this introductory chapter on apologetics. Our hope is that you learn the importance of apologetics in today's day and age and study the topic and how to answer and "give a defense."

But remember these key points: do this for sake of the gospel and the authority of the Bible. And do this with gentleness and respect. The unbeliever is not the enemy; it is the false philosophy that has taken them "captive" that is the enemy (2 Timothy 2:24–26; Colossians 2:8; 2 Corinthians 10:4–5). An unbeliever, whether he or she realizes it or not, is made in the image of God, your relative, and is in need of Jesus Christ to be saved.

Chapter 7

Should We Trust the Findings of the Jesus Seminar?

Tim Chaffey

꽃꽃꽃꽃꽃꽃꽃꽃꽃꽃꽃꽃꽃꽃꽃꽃꽃

Introduction

Imagine gathering over 70 conservative Christians, many of them scholars from various denominations, to meet twice a year for six years in Lynchburg, Virginia, to form the Easter Institute. Roughly 20 percent of this group would consist of respected scholars in their fields. The rest would be aspiring apologists, authors, theologians, and even a filmmaker who has directed some of the most staunchly theologically conservative films ever. Each of these folks would have to be faithfully walking with the Lord, and each would need to have demonstrated through his work that he has the utmost commitment to the authority, inspiration, infallibility, and inerrancy of the Bible.

Their job would be to examine every word attributed to Christ in Matthew, Mark, Luke, John, and the non-canonical Gospel of Thomas. Then they would make determinations as to whether Jesus actually spoke the words credited to Him in these works. After listening to a series of presentations and some friendly discussion pertaining to certain debated passages, each person would be given an opportunity to vote on the authenticity of the passage by using a colored bead. These Bible believers would use a red bead if they believed Jesus truly spoke the words in question, a pink bead if the words likely came from Jesus, a gray bead if they thought the words came from later sources and most likely were not spoken by Jesus but somewhat reflected His ideas, or a black bead if they were nearly certain Jesus did not speak the words.

What would the results of such an exercise be? Well, since the members of the hypothetical Easter Institute already have a firm commitment to the inerrancy of Scripture, then they would be nearly unanimous in affirming the words of Christ in Matthew, Mark, Luke, and John.[1] So the statements found in these books would receive a very high percentage of red beads. When examining the non-canonical Gospel of Thomas, they might offer a few red beads for statements that match what one of the four Gospels says, a pink bead for statements that are consistent with Christ's words in the canonical Gospels, a gray bead to those statements that are odd, and a black bead to every statement that promotes Gnosticism or contradicts the canonical Gospels.

Now imagine that when these meetings concluded, a handful of the top scholars from the Easter Institute published three books touting the fact that modern biblical scholars have confirmed that Jesus actually spoke the words attributed to Him in the Gospels and that all of His miracles really did happen. Furthermore, the mainstream media picks up this research and tirelessly promotes it without questioning the motives of the Easter Institute. The History Channel, Discovery Channel, A&E, National Geographic Channel, and other stations invite some of these scholars to make documentaries to promote their claims to the world, all the while treating them as the leading experts in their respective fields and acting as if anyone who disagreed with them was not a real scholar.

It sounds preposterous, doesn't it? This could never happen, right? Although you may agree with the findings of the hypothetical Easter Institute, I hope you are able to see some problems with such a scenario. Pooling together like-minded individuals who hold to the same presuppositions on biblical inerrancy and inspiration to *vote* on the authenticity of Christ's words is nothing but circular reasoning. They begin with the assumption that Jesus actually spoke the words in question, and they conclude that He

---

1. Some conservative scholars have legitimate concerns about the authenticity of certain passages, such as Mark 16:9–20 and John 7:53–8:11, so the words of Jesus in these passages would likely receive pink beads instead of red beads from these scholars.

really did speak those words. Even if their conclusions are right, this is not a scholarly exercise by any stretch of the imagination.

Enter the Jesus Seminar

As bizarre as the hypothetical scenario above sounds, something very similar has occurred, though with very unorthodox results, and the findings of the group are treated by the mainstream media as representing the pinnacle of New Testament scholarship.

In 1985, the "Jesus Seminar" met for the first time under a sponsoring organization known as the Westar Institute. They were led by the late New Testament and Greek scholar Robert W. Funk in Santa Rosa, California. The group was made up of atheists, liberal Protestants, Catholics, Jews, and even a filmmaker with no formal theological training and several raunchy films in his portfolio. Approximately half of the members had graduated from or taught at the noted liberal divinity schools of Harvard, Claremont, or Vanderbilt.[2]

With the possible exception of a couple of evangelical-leaning scholars in the group, the Jesus Seminar consisted of people who flatly rejected the inspiration and inerrancy of Scripture. They also rejected the supernatural, so they "demythologized" the Gospel accounts (i.e., they automatically rejected any passage in which Jesus performed miracles or taught His own deity). So when it came to voting on the sayings of Jesus, the group rejected the vast majority of Christ's words in the Gospels as being inauthentic.

The results of their efforts were published in three works: *The Five Gospels* (1993), *The Acts of Jesus* (1998), and *The Gospel of Jesus* (1999). The mainstream media treats the claims of the Jesus Seminar as "Gospel

---

2. In 1994, Craig Blomberg stated, "The final 'Fellows' of the JS [Jesus Seminar], as they are called, fall roughly into three categories. Fourteen of them are among the leading names in the field. . . . Roughly another 20 are names recognizable to New Testament scholars who keep abreast of their field, even if they are not as widely published. . . . The remaining 40 — more than half of the JS — are relative unknowns; most have published at best two or three journal articles, while several are recent PhDs whose dissertations were on some theme of the Gospels. A computer-search of the ATLA and OCLC databases of published books and articles turned up no entries relevant to New Testament studies whatsoever for a full 18 of the Fellows." Craig L. Blomberg, "Who Does the Jesus Seminar Really Speak For?" ChristianAnswers.net, http://christiananswers.net/q-eden/edn-t017.html.

truth," as was evidenced by the uncritical acceptance and popularization of their findings by the late Peter Jennings in the 2000 ABC documentary entitled "The Search for Jesus," which featured Jesus Seminar principals Funk, Marcus Borg, and John Dominic Crossan. Borg and Crossan are regulars on Christian-themed documentaries airing on the History Channel, Discovery Channel, A&E, and the National Geographic Channel. These men have advanced the following false notions of Jesus:

- He was the illegitimate child of Mary and a Roman soldier.

- The virgin birth was borrowed from the Roman myth of Apollo the sun god having sex with a woman. (But how would this inspire an account of a *virgin* birth?)

- Jesus was not born in Bethlehem.

- No Roman census took place during the time of Caesar Augustus.

- Judas was invented by early Christians as a sort of anti-Semitic slur.

- Jesus was not buried in Joseph's tomb but in a shallow grave, and his body was eaten by dogs and crows.

Apparently, this is what passes for scholarship for many critics of the Bible. Once again, this is nothing but circular reasoning. Grab a group of like-minded people and have them vote on the words of Christ when you already know they reject the possibility of many of the Lord's claims, and one can claim to be "on the cutting-edge of biblical scholarship."

Historical Methodology

When it comes to history, scholars generally follow certain criteria in determining the reliability of a given account. Since no human is completely objective and only records certain data, the historian (in theory) does not blindly accept every ancient account.[3] Events in the past several decades may have video and audio recordings to support the historicity of the event, as well as newspaper and magazine reports. Obviously, events that allegedly occurred in the distant past cannot be held to the same

---

3. Since the Holy Spirit is objective, and He inspired the writing of the Bible, we can accept the accuracy and historicity of Scripture.

standard, so historians follow different guidelines in trying to figure out what actually took place. While there are numerous approaches that can be taken, such as internal criticism, source criticism, and so on, there are several points that historians generally agree upon. Here are five of those principles, as outlined by respected historian and leading expert on the Resurrection of Jesus, Dr. Gary Habermas:

1. Testimony attested to by multiple independent witnesses is usually considered stronger than the testimony of one witness.

2. Affirmation by a neutral or hostile source is usually considered stronger than affirmation from a friendly source, since bias in favor of the person or position is absent.

3. People usually don't make up details regarding a story that would tend to weaken their position.

4. Eyewitness testimony is usually considered stronger than testimony heard from a second or thirdhand source.

5. An early testimony from very close to the event in question is usually considered more reliable than one received years after the event.[4]

Had the Jesus Seminar fellows followed these five principles, the canonical Gospels would have fared much better during their voting. However, these critics "stacked the deck" against the words of Christ in several ways.

Seven Pillars of Scholarly Foolishness

The seminar's initial publication, *The Five Gospels*, immediately introduces the reader to the so-called "Seven Pillars of Scholarly Wisdom," which served as the guiding principles of seminar members. These pillars set up a false dilemma in that they claim one must either accept the Jesus of faith, theology, and creeds, or the Jesus of "historical reason and research."[5] In other words, those who agree with the critical scholars are

---

4. Gary R. Habermas and Michael R. Licona, *The Case for the Resurrection of Jesus* (Grand Rapids, MI: Kregel Publications, 2004), p. 40.

5. Robert Funk, *The Five Gospels: What Did Jesus Really Say?* (San Francisco, CA: Harper SanFrancisco, 1993), p. 2.

reasonable and have history and science on their side, while those who believe in Jesus as described in the Bible simply have a blind faith in theology and creeds. Here are the "Seven Pillars of Scholarly Wisdom":

1. One must make a distinction between the historical Jesus and the Jesus of faith.

2. The Gospels of Matthew, Mark, and Luke are much closer to the historical Jesus than the Gospel of John, which portrays a spiritualized Jesus.

3. Mark was written before the other Gospels.

4. Luke and Matthew relied upon a hypothetical document called Q, allegedly an early collection of the sayings of Jesus.

5. Scholars have already determined that Jesus never spoke about a final judgment. Instead, He was a reformer and cynic sage.

6. First-century Israel was an oral culture, as opposed to a print culture like our own. As such, Jesus must have spoken in short phrases so that people would be able to easily remember His teachings.

7. The Gospels are guilty of error until proven innocent, and the burden of proof is on those who believe them to be accurate historical documents.[6]

The Historical Jesus and the Jesus of Faith

These "pillars" ensured the rejection of the biblical portrayal of Jesus in favor of a demythologized Jesus before they ever looked at the evidence. These assumptions are unscientific in nature because they automatically rule out certain legitimate explanations. They are also illogical on several counts. For example, the first point declares that a distinction must be made between the Jesus of faith and the historical Jesus. This is a bifurcation (either/or) fallacy, because it presents only two competing options, when there is obviously a third alternative. This third option is portrayed in the pages of Scripture and was fervently held by Christ's earliest

---

6. Ibid., p. 2–5.

followers even to the point of being executed in gruesome fashion. That is, the Jesus of history and the Jesus of faith are one and the same.

In 1 Corinthians 15, Paul made abundantly clear the link between the historicity of Christ's Resurrection and our faith in Him. He opened the chapter by showing that the gospel message is founded upon the Crucifixion and Resurrection of Jesus Christ, which occurred in fulfillment of prophecies in the Old Testament Scriptures (1 Corinthians 15:3–4). He proceeded to cite eyewitnesses of the resurrected Lord, including over 500 people who saw Him at one time, many of whom were still alive when Paul wrote the letter (meaning that an inquiring skeptical person could find some of these witnesses and ask them about what they saw). Then Paul stressed the importance of the historicity of the Resurrection of Jesus. If Jesus did not rise bodily from the grave, then "our preaching is empty and your faith is also empty" (1 Corinthians 15:14), we are "false witnesses of God" (v. 15), "your faith is futile; you are still in your sins" (v. 17), the dead are gone forever (v. 18), and we are to be pitied above all men (v. 19). Luke added that Jesus "presented Himself alive after His suffering by many infallible proofs" (Acts 1:3). Furthermore, Jesus predicted His own bodily Resurrection (Matthew 20:18–19; John 2:19). If Jesus was mistaken, then He would have been a sinner and could not die for our sins since He would have had to die for His own sin. We can state without reservation that without the physical Resurrection of Jesus Christ, Christianity would not exist.

By starting with the first pillar, the Jesus Seminar guaranteed that the essential elements of the person and work of Christ would be thrown out. Space does not allow for a full refutation of each point, but let's examine a couple more of these pillars.

Matthew, Luke, and Q

Because of what is commonly called the "Synoptic Problem," scholars have attempted to figure out the order in which the Gospels were written, thinking it would solve some of the differences in the order of events described in Matthew, Mark, and Luke and explain why the writers used different wording for the same passages and very similar or even identical wording in other passages. Throughout most of church history, it was assumed that the Gospels were written in the order they appear in the Bible:

Matthew, Mark, Luke, and John. In the 19th century, source critics proposed that Mark was written first and that Luke and Matthew borrowed from Mark, or from Mark and the hypothetical Q (from the German word *Quelle*, meaning "source").

Although no shred of Q has ever been found, and it was never mentioned in the extant writings of anyone in church history until the hypothesis was developed, its historicity is accepted as fact by many critical scholars and even by some conservative scholars. Critical scholars have even published copies of this theoretical work based on common statements found in Matthew and Luke. Such a document would help explain some of the difficulties, but it is not the only plausible solution, and it creates some more problems.[7]

By proposing that Mark and Q were the real sources for Matthew and Luke, the critics have essentially reduced the number of firsthand sources. If accurate, then Matthew would no longer be an account by one of Christ's disciples who was an eyewitness to many of the events described. In fact, critics have assigned to each of the Gospels a much later date of

---

7. The three major interdependence theories are known as "The Augustinian Proposal," "The 'Two-Gospel' hypothesis," and "The 'Two-Source' Hypothesis." It is beyond the scope of this article to explain the strengths and weaknesses of each view, but excellent summaries are available. For a favorable treatment of interdependence, see D.A. Carson, Douglas J. Moo, and Leon Morris, *An Introduction to the New Testament* (Grand Rapids, MI: Zondervan, 1992), p. 26–38. For a strong case against the interdependence views, see Robert L. Thomas, "Evangelical Responses to the Jesus Seminar," *Master's Seminary Journal* 7 (Spring 1996): p. 76–106. Thomas explains that even though many respected evangelical scholars hold to one of the various interdependence theories, these ideas inevitably undermine the historicity of the Gospel accounts because they are based upon a flawed methodology. He argues that "the assumption of literary dependence forces scholars to diminish the historical precision of a gospel account. This is no different in kind from the decision of the Jesus Seminar. Granted, these evangelicals do not carry their dehistoricizing to the same degree as those who radically reduce the biographical data in the gospels, but it is nevertheless the same type of dehistoricizing" (p. 94–95). For a more in-depth study, see also the enlightening work of Eta Linnemann, an evangelical German New Testament scholar, who as a former theological liberal once taught these critical views of the Gospels, but after coming to a genuine saving knowledge of Christ has since amassed strong textual evidence that the Gospels are independent eyewitness accounts of the life and ministry of Jesus. See her *Historical Criticism of the Bible: Methodology or Ideology? Reflections of a Bultmannian Turned Evangelical* (Grand Rapids, MI: Baker Books, 1990) and her *Is There a Synoptic Problem? Rethinking the Literary Dependence of the First Three Gospels* (Grand Rapids, MI: Baker Books, 1992).

authorship than what has been traditionally accepted throughout church history. If the Gospels were not written in the first century A.D., then they were not written by eyewitnesses, and legendary details about Jesus could indeed have been invented. Nevertheless, there are very solid reasons for accepting that the entire New Testament corpus was completed by the close of the first century.

Results of the Voting

Another way in which the Jesus Seminar fellows stacked the deck against the words of Christ lies in their anti-supernatural bias. These scholars began with the assumptions that prophecies and miracles are impossible and that God does not exist, or if He does, then we could not know anything about Him. Consequently, any passage that touched on the supernatural was automatically dismissed. This explains their use of the first pillar.[8]

When one looks at the results of their voting (see chart that follows), the biases of the Jesus Seminar fellows are readily apparent. Keep in mind, the Gospel of Thomas is not included in Scripture. Not only is it pseudepigraphal (false writings), but it was written in the 2nd century A.D., well after all of the Apostles had died, and it was never accepted by the Church as authoritative or authentic.

These results are quite telling and clearly reveal the biases of the Jesus Seminar. For example, look at the results of the votes on the Gospel of John. They voted that there is only one saying of Jesus that might be authentic (John 4:44, in which Jesus said that a prophet has no honor in his own country). This verse has parallels in other accounts, so the Jesus Seminar voters apparently did not believe that John contained any original material from the lips of Jesus.

Notice that the one non-canonical book (Gospel of Thomas) received the highest percentage of statements that Jesus may have actually said

---

8. Ironically, many Jesus Seminar members, as is true of liberal theologians in general, consider themselves to be Christians. Yet without the physical Resurrection of Jesus Christ, there is no basis for Christianity. There may be some "good" intentions behind liberal theology in the sense that many liberals try to figure out how to make the Bible believable to unbelievers with a secular mindset. However, it is not our task to remove objectionable parts of God's Word to appease those who reject God. Paul instructed Timothy to proclaim God's Word both when it is popular and when it is not popular (2 Timothy 4:2). He did not tell him to change it when it was not popular.

Results of the Jesus Seminar Voting on the Sayings of Christ				
Beads/Percent Book/Sayings	Red (truly spoken)	Pink (likely spoken)	Gray (other source)	Black (not spoken)
Matthew (420 sayings)	11 (2.6%)	61 (14.5%)	114 (27.1%)	235 (56.0%)
Mark (177 sayings)	1 (0.6%)	18 (10.2%)	66 (37.3%)	92 (52.0%)
Luke (392 sayings)	14 (3.6%)	65 (16.6%)	128 (32.7%)	185 (47.2%)
John (140 sayings)	0 (0.0%)	1 (0.7%)	5 (3.6%)	134 (95.7%)
Thomas (202 sayings)	3 (1.5%)	40 (19.8%)	67 (33.2%)	92 (45.5%)

From Norman L. Geisler, *Baker Encyclopedia of Christian Apologetics* (Grand Rapids, MI: Baker Books, 1999), p. 387.

(red and pink beads combined) at 21.3 percent and the lowest amount of statements they believe He definitely did not say (black beads) at 45.5 percent.

Why would the Jesus Seminar treat the Gospel of John with such a high degree of skepticism? Some may claim that the low score is due to the fact that it was the final canonical Gospel to be written, so according to historical methodology, it would not be viewed as reliable as those written closer to the events described in it. However, this reasoning fails since the number of red and pink beads assigned to the Gospel of Thomas were 30 times more (by percentage) than John, and it was written long after the fourth gospel.

Funk claimed that one of the reasons for treating John's Gospel in such a manner was because "Jesus speaks regularly in adages or aphorisms, or in parables, or in witticisms created as a rebuff or retort in the context of dialogue or debate. It is clear he did not speak in long monologues of the type found in the Gospel of John."[9]

---

9. John Dart, "Seminar Rules Out 80% of Words Attributed to Jesus: Provocative Meeting of Biblical Scholars Ends Six Years of Voting on Authenticity in the Gospels," *L.A. Times*, March 4, 1991, http://articles.latimes.com/1991-03-04/news/mn-77_1_jesus-seminar.

This particular statement by the seminar's founder highlights some of the biggest problems with the group. It is quite arrogant to assume that critics living nearly two millennia after the reported events are in a better position than the eyewitnesses to determine what really happened.[10] The rationale behind this thinking backfires at every point. This unwarranted skepticism against history so prevalent in our post-modern world would have us believe that one cannot know history with any certainty because all historians are merely products of their own time who cannot escape the biases and ignorance of their time. Furthermore, all historians have an agenda to push, so the Gospel writers cannot be trusted, because they had an ulterior motive — to promote Christianity. Since these men were ignorant of modern science, the things attributed as miraculous would be explained differently in today's enlightened world. However, if all history is suspect, then the members of the Jesus Seminar must also be products of their own time, complete with their own biases, agendas, and areas of ignorance. So as soon as the Jesus Seminar votes and publishes their work, then these documents become part of that suspect history, and consequently, cannot be trusted. Also, the fellows of the Jesus Seminar clearly had an ulterior motive — to undermine the historicity of the words of Christ in the New Testament.[11] Some may argue that these were unbiased scholars who only reached their conclusions during the sessions of the Seminar, but this is easily refuted. If these scholars truly were unbiased, then why weren't any strongly conservative scholars invited to participate? Only certain individuals were invited to ensure the results of the voting. Using the presuppositions of the Jesus Seminar members, one should absolutely reject the findings of this biased gathering.

---

10. This belief may also be a form of the logical fallacy known as chronological snobbery, which occurs when one assumes that a more recent idea is necessarily better than older ones, or vice versa. In this case, the critic assumes that modern historical approaches are more enlightened than the beliefs of the first-century Jews who witnessed the events and recorded them.

11. One should not uncritically accept all that is written as history, so investigation of the authenticity and reliability of historical writings is important. But the *a priori* rejection of the supernatural elements merely begs the question. That is, Jesus Seminar members voted against any statements that smacked of the supernatural because Jesus would never have said such things. How would they know this to be the case? Well, because they believe supernatural events just cannot happen, so Jesus would never teach these things.

A Spiritualized Jesus Who Spoke in Short Sayings

Furthermore, how would seminar participants know that Jesus "did not speak in long monologues of the type found in the Gospel of John"? The Lord's longest message appears in Matthew 5–7 and is popularly called the Sermon on the Mount, and His second longest, the Olivet Discourse, is found in Matthew 24–25. Even though there exist multiple attestations of these messages (abbreviated forms of both are recorded in Luke), the Jesus Seminar rejected the vast majority of these passages, too. Why? Because of their *a priori* (presupposed) belief that Jesus did not speak in long monologues.

It is true that the Gospel of John does not show Jesus teaching in parables, and it seldom cites the aphorisms accepted by the Jesus Seminar, but there is a clear reason for this, explaining why the seminar treated John with such contempt. The Apostle John included a purpose statement near the end of the book: "And truly Jesus did many other signs in the presence of His disciples, which are not written in this book; but these are written that you may believe that Jesus is the Christ, the Son of God, and that believing you may have life in His name" (John 20:30–31). By the time John wrote his Gospel, the other three Gospels were already written, and they were very similar in terms of content. John may or may not have been aware of that content, but he decided to focus on sharing only those things that would display Jesus as the Christ, the Son of God. Naturally, since the Jesus Seminar participants reject this notion, they reject the teachings of Christ in the Gospel of John.

Conclusion

The Jesus Seminar was a gathering of mostly liberal theologians who voted according to their own anti-supernatural biases in an effort to undermine the historicity, and thus the authority, of the Gospel accounts. Their "research" was based on an arrogant and flawed methodology that ignored the words of the eyewitnesses and the beliefs of Christ's earliest followers. Yet members of this group are continually held up as experts representing leading scholarship by media members who are willing to perpetuate the bogus claims of the Jesus Seminar. Christians need to be aware of the false claims of this group and how their ideas have permeated our culture.

Ultimately, this gathering was just another salvo in a long line of attacks on God's Word stemming from the serpent's question: "Has God indeed said?" (Genesis 3:1). Yes, God indeed said that Jesus was born of a virgin, lived a sinless life, performed miracles, died on the Cross for our sins, bodily rose again on the third day, appeared numerous times to His followers for 40 days, and then ascended bodily to heaven from where He will one day return bodily as the King of kings and Lord of lords and Judge of all the earth. Christians can have absolute confidence in the work of Christ and the Word of God. And non-believers need to repent of their sins and trust in Jesus Christ as Savior and Lord to escape the coming judgment and spend eternity with our loving and gracious Creator (Acts 17:30–31).

Chapter 8

What about Theistic Evolution?

Roger Patterson

꽃꽃꽃꽃꽃꽃꽃꽃꽃꽃꽃꽃꽃꽃꽃꽃꽃꽃

There has been an explosion in the intensity of the conversation regarding the creation/evolution debate in the last few years — but not where one might expect. It would make sense that the intensity of this discussion would continue to elevate between the world and the Church, but that is not where the fire is raging. The flames are being stoked by those within evangelical circles. Not only are there many who are demanding that Christians must embrace evolution in its various forms, some are also demanding that Adam and Eve were either evolved from ape-like creatures or that they did not even exist. These are the issues involved in the discussions surrounding theistic evolution.

In talking about this topic, there are two important points for readers to remember. First, make sure that the meaning of the term *theistic evolution* is clear. Unfortunately, there is a great deal of intentionally ambiguous language used by different groups within the discussion. There are those (who may believe in God) who fully believe in the idea that humans evolved from apes and that the universe began 14 billion years ago with a big bang, yet who will look people in the eye and say, "I am not a theistic evolutionist."

Second, readers engaging in discussions with those who hold evolutionary ideas should examine carefully what these people mean by the terms they use (e.g., theistic evolution, Intelligent Design, and so on). This examination should be done in a loving manner without making assumptions based on past experiences (cf., 2 Timothy 2:24–26).

Defining the Terms

The word *evolution* can certainly have different meanings in different contexts. It is important to define the terms, but many Christians who believe in evolutionary ideas use other terms that must be carefully uncovered with probing questions. To really understand this concept, it is helpful to think of a continuum. On one end is something close to a deistic view of God's role in nature and on the other end is a God constantly tinkering with His creation over billions of years to bring about His plans. A very basic way of understanding evolution is simply as change over long periods of time (i.e., hundreds of thousands to millions of years). But there is often a one-dimensional approach to thinking about evolution — the biological dimension. I would like to extend the discussion beyond that first dimension, however, to include the three basic forms of evolution: cosmological, geological, and biological (see chart that follows).[1]

Those whose views would fit within this continuum would generally agree on the following: 1) the universe is approximately 14 billion years old; 2) the big bang explains the origin of the universe; 3) the earth formed gradually beginning about 4.5 billion years ago; 4) life evolved on the earth as chemicals interacted to form the first "living" organism; and 5) organisms increased in complexity over time with all life on earth sharing a common ancestor. There are certainly those who would say that God guided each of these processes to different degrees, but they believe in a universe and planet that is billions of years old and in life progressing through gradual change to the complexity and variety seen today.

With this understanding, and knowing that many would reject the specific label, a theistic evolutionist is one who believes that God providentially acted at some point(s) in history to bring about the world as

---

1. Cosmological evolution generally involves the supposed big bang as the original beginning of the universe and the gradual formation of stars and planetary systems over billions of years. Geological evolution refers to the formation of the features present on the earth over billions of years. Biological evolution refers to the origin of life and its development from a single-celled organism into all forms alive and extinct.

Theistic Evolution Continuum		
Cosmological Big Bang 13.7 Billion Years Stellar Evolution	God caused the big bang and allowed natural processes to form the universe without guidance.	God constantly guides the processes forming the universe.
Geological Nebular Hypothesis 4.5 Billion Years Extent and Nature of the Flood	God allowed the earth to form gradually by unguided natural processes.	God constantly guides the processes forming the planet.
Biological Origin of Life New Species Humans	God allowed life to form gradually through unguided natural processes.	God specially creates some forms of life or certain features at various stages.

seen today. The degree of involvement is the only disagreement. Some may suggest that cosmological and geological evolution have occurred in "natural" ways while God was more intimately involved in the biological evolution, but all ascribe to some form of evolution.

The Name Game: What's in a Name?

Theistic evolution, old-earth creation, evolutionary creation, BioLogos, progressive creation, and intelligent design are all labels of groups interested in promoting evolution in one form or another. To be clear — it is difficult to put any single person's views into a box with a tidy little label. Even if they label themselves, there are shades of nuance coloring their understanding of specific topics related to the origins issue.

As biblical creationists discuss these ideas with others, they should demonstrate their love for others by asking sincere questions in order to understand their particular views. Ask people who subscribe to these ideas to explain how they support their ideas with Scripture. Biblical creationists should be willing to do the same for their own views. As soon as a biblical creationist hears that someone believes in evolution, he should not automatically assume that this person thinks Jesus was not born of a virgin or that Adam and Eve are allegorical.

Theistic Evolution/Evolutionary Creation

Many people would refer to themselves as "theistic evolutionists." They believe, openly, that God used evolution to create the universe — from the big bang right up to humans and the Grand Canyon. Books have been published with titles like *Thank God for Evolution, Finding Darwin's God, I Love Jesus and I Accept Evolution, Evolutionary Creation*, and others. In recent years, evolutionary views have been firmly embraced by many prominent and popular evangelicals, including Bruce Waltke, Tim Keller, Francis Collins, Peter Enns, Joel Hunter, Os Guinness, and many more.

Of late, the most aggressive promotion of an evolutionary understanding of the universe has come from the BioLogos Foundation. This work was initiated by Francis Collins, a prominent geneticist and professing Christian. Dennis Venema, one of the regular contributors to the articles on the BioLogos site, provides a helpful explanation of the distinctions between the various views of origins:

> Despite their (large) differences, [Young-Earth Creationism, Old-Earth Creationism, and Intelligent Design] deny some aspect of modern science. The only Christian perspective on origins that fully accepts mainstream science is the Evolutionary Creation / Theistic Evolution view. This view holds that science is not an enemy to be fought, but rather a means of understanding some of the mechanisms God has used to bring about biodiversity on earth. This view accepts that humans share ancestry with all other forms of life, and that our species arose as a population, not through a single primal pair. There are different views within the EC community on whether there was a historical couple named Adam and Eve – some hold that there was, and that they were selected by God from a larger population as representatives. Other folks in the EC community feel that Adam and Eve are typological figures, such as a representation of the failure of Israel to keep the covenant. The science (human population genetics) is clear that our species arose as a population, and that is what I have focused on (since that is my area of expertise). I try to leave the theology to others, but often folks want to talk theology on these points, not science.[2]

---

2. Dennis Venema, "Ask an Evolutionary Creationist: A Q&A with Dennis Venema," http://biologos.org/blog/ask-an-evolutionary-creationist-a-qa-with-dennis-venema.

Those involved with the BioLogos Foundation seek to promote discussion about the relationship between science and the Christian faith. However, they dismiss the Bible as the authoritative source for understanding the natural world. They claim, "We have found that the methods of the natural sciences provide the most reliable guide to understanding the material world, and the current evidence from science indicates that the diversity of life is best explained as a result of an evolutionary process. Thus we affirm that evolution is a means by which God providentially achieves His purposes."[3]

One might be tempted to say that these scholars do not consider the Bible an authority at all, but the same BioLogos document explains, "Foundational to the BioLogos vision is the belief that the Bible is the inspired and authoritative Word of God. The Bible is a living document through which God, by his Spirit, continues to speak to the church today."[4] With that claim, it would only be fair to ask what they mean by "authoritative." And asking those questions is an important part of discussing these ideas with those who hold to an evolutionary understanding of the universe.

Included among the contentious ideas within the evolutionary creation community are the identity, or even the historicity, of Adam and Eve and the nature of the Fall. Some insist that Adam and Eve must be actual people who were the actual ancestors of all humans. Others say that they were two members of the evolved human population that were selected by God to represent humanity. Others, still, see no need from the text for a real Adam and assign him some allegorical or symbolic position.[5] With the question of Adam's historicity comes the question of whether the Fall was an actual event or some form of allegory to explain the human condition. These differences provide another reason to lovingly ask questions as biblical creationists dialog with Christians who embrace theistic evolution.

Intelligent Design without a Designer

It may come as a surprise to some, but many who are part of what has been called the Intelligent Design (ID) movement would fit into the category of theistic evolution. Many involved in the ID movement believe in

---

3. BioLogos, "About the BioLogos Foundation," http://biologos.org/about.
4. Ibid.
5. See chapter 20 for a more detailed discussion of the historicity of Adam.

the big bang, an old earth, and the general concepts of evolutionary progression over time. They reject Darwinian (or neo-Darwinian) evolution because it has no goal or purpose and is random, but they embrace some form of guided evolution. When certain aspects of a biological system are determined to be "irreducibly complex," they suggest God may have guided the evolutionary process at this point to allow the process to continue to produce new kinds of organisms.

Among old-earth proponents within the ID movement, there would be some disagreement about how mankind came about. Some would suggest that this progression led to an advanced hominid that God used to begin the human race as He injected a spirit into the creature. Others say that God did, indeed, specially create Adam from dust and that Eve truly is the mother of all the living. Some of the popular figures in the ID movement have clearly laid out their views while others seem to shroud their ideas in vague phraseology that appeals to a wide audience.

In an interview with *World* magazine, Michael Behe stated, "When we study humans with a common genetic disease (such as sickle cell), we can often trace it back to a single mutation in a human forbear. With a few more assumptions, the same reasoning can be applied between species. We humans share with other primate species what look for all the world like common genetic accidents. If we inherited those from a common ancestor, it would neatly explain why we all have them now. I find that persuasive."[6] While Behe rejects the randomness of neo-Darwinism, he is an evolutionist, nonetheless. In a 2010 conference lecture, Behe responded to a question with, "I believe in, yes, I believe in non-Darwinian evolution, in the sense that I think evolution took place. And I believe that because I think it's at least a reasonable explanation for the similarities between creatures."[7]

Likewise, William Dembski has recently affirmed that evolution is compatible with the Bible's explanation of origins, including the possibility of mankind coming from an evolved hominid species (into which God inserted a spirit to make it truly human). In his book *The End of Christianity*, he has proposed an explanation for the existence of death

---

6. Marvin Olasky, "Darwin Slayer," *World* (July 21, 2007): p. 16.
7. Michael Behe, "Q&A: Intelligent Design/Theistic Evolution" (lecture, Fixed Point Foundation, In the Beginning Conference, Birmingham, Alabama, June 18, 2011).

and suffering before Adam sinned so that the natural evil of evolutionary processes can still be accounted for.[8] In other writings, Dembski has stated that he personally believes that Adam and Eve were specially created by God and that he rejects Darwinian evolution while embracing the idea of an earth that is billions of years old.[9] There are also many other leaders in the ID movement who endorse the big bang, geological evolution, and some form of biological evolution. The complexity of these intertwining issues should underscore the need for carefully and prayerfully considering how to discuss these ideas in a charitable manner with other Christians.

Another important thing to consider in thinking about the Intelligent Design movement is the identity of the designer. As a movement, there is no claim as to who that designer might be. Among the prominent leaders of the movement are Roman Catholics, Evangelicals, Protestants, Unification Church members, and others. Although individuals within the movement point to whom they believe the creator might be, ID is not intended to point to any specific designer. As such, the ID movement is embraced by those of the broad Christian tradition as well as Muslims, and its arguments could potentially be used by any religion that holds to some notion of a "higher power."

While the ID movement has produced scientific arguments that support what is already known from Scripture, the "big tent" nature of the program makes it problematic from a theological perspective. While there is little disagreement about the nature of cosmological and geological evolution, just how much change can be allowed for through biological evolution is not agreed upon. But, more significantly, people may put

---

8. William Dembski, *The End of Christianity* (Nashville, TN: B&H Pub. Group, 2009). Though Dembski states that he is not making any assumptions about the age of the earth or the extent of evolution or design (p. 10), he repeatedly denies a young earth in favor of what "science" has shown (p. 53ff) and affirms evolution, even of hominids that God made into humans, to be a possibility that should be considered as consistent with the Bible.

9. For example, in an interview with The Best Schools website, Dr. Dembski presents his acceptance of an old universe while rejecting purely Darwinian explanations for the development of life on earth (http://www.thebestschools.org/blog/2012/01/14/william-dembski-interview). Dr. Dembski also made his views on the historicity of Adam and Eve clear in a statement published in a white paper in response to reviews of his book (http://www.baptisttheology.org/documents/AReplytoTomNettlesReviewofDembskisTheEndofChristianity.pdf).

their trust in Allah, Jesus, or Reverend Moon and still stay dry under the tent flying the ID flag.[10]

Progressive Creation

The third basic view, one many would not typically consider part of the theistic evolution camp, is known as progressive creation — a form of day-age creation where the days of Genesis 1 represent vast periods of overlapping time. The most notable proponent of this idea is Hugh Ross of the organization Reasons to Believe. In general, progressive creationists accept that the big bang is the explanation for the origin of the universe, that the earth gradually formed from debris as it orbited the sun, and that the earth is 4.5 billion years old. However, they reject that biological evolution accounts for the history of life on earth. For this reason, progressive creation is not typically included within the range of theistic evolution. Those who hold to progressive creation also would not affirm point 5 in my description above. Progressive creation is included here, however, because of the elements of cosmological and geological evolution it embraces.

While this view is often referred to as old-earth creationism or day-age creationism, it still relies on the models of the big bang/nebular hypothesis and radiometric dating to determine the age of the earth. Rather than gradual biological change over the billions of years, God is supposed to have created organisms in progressive stages while allowing earlier forms to die out. Thus, the fossil record shows fully formed organisms appearing because God created them at various points and then wiped them out in major extinction events. As for mankind, Adam and Eve are thought to be real humans that God created about 100,000 years ago; the parents of all people. However, there were hominid species alive before God created humans.

View of Genesis

Many articles, and even entire books, have been written on the various views of Genesis 1–11.[11] However, in order to hold to an evolutionary

---

10. For more on the problematic nature of the ID movement, see Georgia Purdom, "Is the Intelligent Design Movement Christian?" in Ken Ham, editor, *The New Answers Book 2* (Green Forest, AR: Master Books, 2008).
11. For articles relating to these various views, see the "Get Answers: Creation Compromises" page at http://www.answersingenesis.org/get-answers#/topic/creation-compromises.

view of the universe, including our planet and its living things, a straight-forward reading of Genesis 1–11 must be abandoned. Instead, the days of Genesis 1 become long ages that, in some views, actually overlap so that day 3 really starts after day 4. Some set aside the day-age ideas and insert a gap between Genesis 1:1 and 1:2 and then find ways to make the rest of Genesis 1 read as six normal days. Others suggest that the whole section is some type of legend, myth, or allegory that contains truth about the origin of mankind or Israel, but should not be understood as presenting actual facts about the timing or conditions of that history.

To be certain, there is no straightforward way to read Genesis 1–2 and arrive at a history of the universe that approaches the evolutionary view held by so many Christians today. In fact, there are many blatant contradictions in the order of events described in Genesis and the evolutionary accounting of the events that formed the universe as known today. To reconcile these differences, it seems that much dismissal or twisting of the text must be performed to accommodate the various evolutionary processes.[12]

The table below presents a few of the differences with biblical text that must be reconciled if an evolutionary view is embraced. Many people have not considered these contradictions, and this is a great point of discussion as biblical creationists dialog with believers who hold evolutionary views.

Evolutionary History	Genesis Account
The sun forms before the earth	The earth is present before the sun
Land mammals appear before whales	Whales are created before land animals
The earth begins as a molten mass of rock without any water	The earth begins with water
Reptiles evolve before birds	Birds are formed before reptiles
Thorns and thistles evolve before man	Thorns and thistles are a result of man's sin

What Authority?

A very important question must be asked when thinking about the relationship between evolutionary views of the world and the biblical text.

12. Terry Mortenson, "Evolution vs. Creation: The Order of Events Matters!" Answers in Genesis, http://www.answersingenesis.org/articles/2006/04/04/order-of-events-matters.

To be fair, everyone mentioned in this chapter would affirm that the Bible is authoritative. But, just as biblical creationists must ask questions about exactly what *evolution* means, they must also ask what *authoritative* means. The following quotes are presented so that readers might evaluate what is meant by *authoritative* in each case. Is the Bible the authority in each of these cases, or is an interpretation of "mainstream science" the authority?

> The young-earth solution to reconciling the order of creation with natural history makes good exegetical and theological sense. Indeed, the overwhelming consensus of theologians up through the Reformation held to this view. I myself would adopt it in a heartbeat except that nature seems to present such a strong evidence against it. I'm hardly alone in my reluctance to accept young-earth creationism.[13]

Dr. Dembski is using the word *nature* in this case to refer to the naturalistic interpretation of the data (presumably including radiometric dating) that concludes the earth is billions of years old. Later in the same book he claims that people "study science to understand [the Book of Nature], theology to understand [the Book of Scripture]." Dembski goes on to explain how Scripture can change one's understanding of science and science can change Scripture, claiming that "if we are to reject an old earth (which the Book of Nature teaches), then we must have solid scientific evidence for doing so."[14]

As seen in his statement above, Dr. Venema believes that "science (human population genetics) is clear that our species arose as a population" and not as two individuals. Rather than two, there were around 10,000 according to recent population models produced by "mainstream science." It is not reasonable from the modern scientific understanding to think of an actual couple as the foundation of humanity.

All of those who write and work on behalf of the BioLogos Foundation would (presumably) adhere to the statement from their position page:

> We have found that the methods of the natural sciences provide the most reliable guide to understanding the material world,

13. Dembski, *The End of Christianity*, p. 55.
14. Ibid., p. 71–77.

and the current evidence from science indicates that the diversity of life is best explained as a result of an evolutionary process. Thus we affirm that evolution is a means by which God providentially achieves His purposes.[15]

From the view of a theistic evolutionist, of whatever variety or degree, man's ability to understand what the layers of rock, DNA sequences, and patterns of gas clouds in the universe certainly trumps the ideas contained in a straightforward reading of Genesis 1–11. The six days are surely something other than days; Adam and Eve are not necessarily real people; and the Fall is some form of allegory because people can trust that population genetics gives a true picture of human origins. But it is important that Christians believe Jesus was raised from the dead and that He died for their sins. Even though the Bible cannot be trusted when it comes to astronomy, anthropology, geology, and biology, it can surely be trusted when it tells about humanity's need for a Savior.

Or can it?

If the Bible is set aside as the authority over every area of believers' lives, including how they think about the history of the world, then man and his thinking about the world has become the measure of all things. If God did not really communicate how He created; if Adam and Eve were just representative hominids; if death and thorns and thistles were always present before sin . . . then why should believers place the Bible in a position of moral authority over their lives or trust it to tell what is going to happen in the future? Those are the kinds of serious questions that must be answered if "mainstream science" is allowed to become the authority in these areas. There is an important connection between the manner in which God created, how man fell into sin, the nature of the Flood, and the gospel of Jesus Christ — what did God really say?

Biblical creationists need to be loving yet firmly fixed upon Scripture as they engage others within the Church over this topic. They must recognize that great, godly men and women can make mistakes — including themselves. Consider Peter's denial that Christ would go to the Cross (Matthew 16:23) or his hypocrisy in front of the Jews (Galatians 2:11–13). It was through the proclamation of truth and the work of the Holy Spirit that Peter was able to repent of these actions and ideas. It is that same

---

15. BioLogos, "About the BioLogos Foundation," http://biologos.org/about.

truth and Spirit that believers must seek to find unity with other believers. It is that same truth and Spirit that will help each believer to become more like Christ. And that must be the ultimate goal as believers engage one another over the relationship between an evolutionary view of the world and a biblical view of the world.

Chapter 9

Being Consistent: Trusting the History in the Gospels and Genesis

Roger Patterson

༄༅༄༅༄༅༄༅༄༅༄༅༄༅༄༅༄༅༄

One of the common claims against the teaching of a biblical worldview and therefore of a young earth is that it would require science and reason to be set aside in our modern, scientific age. If we insist that the Bible accurately describes the history of the universe, the earth, and life on our planet, then we run the risk of alienating those who "know" better.

The rational person is supposed to look at the "mountains of scientific evidence" and conclude that the earth is billions of years old and that all life on earth, including humans, has a common ancestor. Furthermore, secularists will say that anyone who claims the Bible is the literal truth about the natural world must be "anti-science" and think the earth is flat.

These claims are certainly on the rise within the writings of evangelical Christians in the West. Those on the left are looking for creative ways of understanding Scripture so that there is no conflict with the "truths" of evolutionary beliefs.

On the right (theologically speaking), believers are looking for ways to describe the scientific data that confirm the truths of Scripture. The goals are contrary to one another and the stakes in this search for the true nature of the universe are very high. While those on both sides of the spectrum believe God is involved in His creation, foundationally this all comes down to an issue of authority. Can we trust our reasoning, under-standing the effects of sin on our human nature, to tell us how we came to be, or should we look to the words God has revealed to us to understand our origins — or is there some combination of the two that we can trust?

Consistency

Being consistent is a hallmark of rationality. Those who believe in a young earth and the biblical descriptions of the creation and history of the universe are commonly called "irrational" — though in somewhat backhanded ways. While some will claim that I am unreasonable to be-lieve that God created the earth about 6,000 years ago and yet ride in a car or type on a laptop, I reject such assertions.[1] I do so on the grounds that the *science* that has led to the development of computer technology is in a different category than the conclusions arrived at regarding the age of the earth and the origin of life in its various forms.

Operational science allows us to understand how things work in the present, but applying that knowledge to understanding events from the past introduces another level of uncertainty. For example, I trust that a mass spectrometer can give us accurate information about the isotopes that make up a specific mineral sample from a rock layer in the present. It is another thing to suggest that that ratio of atoms can then be turned into a date for the birth of that rock. To make the leap, I must assume that the ideas of uniformitarianism are the absolute truth.[2]

I do not reject uniformitarian thinking on the age of our planet out of hand; I do so because the Bible presents a different understanding of the history of the earth. I also accept the historicity of the Flood described in Genesis and its global nature because of what the text says, not solely be-cause there is immense evidence (most rock layers that contain fossils are from the Flood) that it really happened. Despite common scientific objec-

---

1. The biblical age of the earth is determined by adding up the genealogies from Adam (who was created on the sixth day of creation) to Christ. This is about 4,000 years based on most chronologies done with the Hebrew text. Christ lived about 2,000 years ago, so this gives us about 6,000 years as the biblical age of the earth.
2. Uniformitarianism is based on the idea that processes and rates have been constant in the past. In other words, no significant catastrophic or rapid changes happened in the past, like Noah's Flood, creation as God said, and so on. When people assume uniformitarianism, they are assuming the Bible is false to argue against the Bible being true. This is a fallacy of affirming the consequent.

tions to a global flood, I hold to that belief because I trust the Bible over the reasoning of man. This is not a rejection of reason, but a rejection of reasoning that does not take into account what the Bible says about mankind and the universe God has placed us in. I reject "autonomous human reasoning" — reasoning apart from God's revelation to mankind.

Most Christians would say that they believe that the Bible is authoritative. Most creeds and confessions of the Church through the centuries would affirm this idea. However, many Christians have adopted the view that the Bible is only authoritative on matters of *faith* and not on how the natural world operates.[3] Many would parrot Galileo's sentiment that the Bible tells us how to go to heaven, not how the heavens go. While the Bible is not a textbook on celestial mechanics, any scientific models or hypotheses that directly contradict the teaching of Scripture would be incorrect if I am going to be consistent in using the Bible as *the* authority. If I do not look to the Bible as the absolute authority, I have set myself above the Scriptures and cast judgment on their truthfulness based on my understanding of the world.[4]

Let's think through some of the issues together. You might think that there is no consequence to believing that the earth is millions of years old or that Adam and Eve were not real people. If that is the case, then is the Flood simply a story about how people need to trust God? Was Jonah really in a fish for three days? Did Jesus turn water into wine and rise from the dead?

I trust that there are many Christians who simply have not thought through some of the ideas that they hold — specifically, how those ideas

---

3. Of course, this philosophy of limiting the Scriptures to matters of faith and nothing else is inconsistent with many passages, such as 2 Corinthians 10:5; 2 Timothy 3:16–17; Colossians 2:3; and Psalm 119:160.

4. This is not to minimize the difficulties in translating the Hebrew and Greek texts into a form we can understand today. We must take into account the author's intent, the various forms of literature, cultural considerations, and so on. But to say that we can only understand Genesis 1 if we hold to a certain view of ancient Near East temple imagery is to assign the proper interpretation to an elite group of individuals who have studied such topics. For a thorough and scholarly discussion on these topics, see Terry Mortenson and Thane Ury, editors *Coming to Grips with Genesis* (Green Forest, AR: Master Books, 2008). Additionally, people who elevate their own thoughts and ideas to sit in judgment of Scripture are called humanists. Humanism is the religion that elevates man to the position of being greater than God. Humanistic thinking permeates today's society.

relate to one another. This was true of me in the past, and I am sure there are many more things God will teach me as I study the world around me in light of the truths contained in His Word.

The Age of the Earth

Some mainstream scientists have calculated the age of the earth at approximately 4.5 billion years. There seem to be very few evangelicals who doubt that this is an accurate number. A recent poll of Protestant pastors in the United States showed that 34 percent "strongly disagree" that the earth is 6,000 years old, while only 30 percent "strongly agree" with this biblically based date. The rest are not sure or take some tentative position.[5] To be consistent, anyone who doubts that the earth is 6,000 years old based on their understanding of the scientific evidence must also reject that the days of creation in Genesis 1 are literal days. Rejecting literal days of creation naturally leads to the acceptance of the supposed big bang as the evolutionary method God used to create the universe. Although we can simply add up the ages of the patriarchs mentioned in the Genesis 5 and 11 genealogies to arrive at a date after creation for Abraham, who lived about 4,000 years ago, many reject this as a reasonable way of determining the timing of creation.[6]

The Origin of Man

The same poll yielded other statistics: 74 percent of these pastors "strongly agree" that Adam and Eve were real people, and 64 percent "strongly disagree" that God used evolution to create people.[7] That means that a large group believes that the earth is billions of years old but that evolution did not lead to people. Why do they doubt the scientists who tell them humans evolved yet trust these same scientists when they say the earth is 4.5 billion years old? It is not consistent. In response, many

---

5. David Roach, "Poll: Pastors Oppose Evolution, Split on Earth's Age," LifeWay, http://www.lifeway.com/Article/Research-Poll-Pastors-oppose-evolution-split-on-earths age.

6. For a detailed explanation of the nature of the genealogies used to determine the date of creation, see Larry Pierce and Ken Ham, "Are There Gaps in the Genesis Genealogies?" in Ken Ham, editor, *The New Answers Book 2* (Green Forest, AR: Masterbooks, 2008), available online at http://www.answersingenesis.org/articles/nab2/gaps-in-genesis-genealogies.

7. Roach, "Poll: Pastors Oppose Evolution, Split on Earth's Age."

would allow for the evolution of animals and plants over billions of years, yet insist that God specially created people.[8] Why the inconsistency?

The modern consensus of population geneticists is that humans began from a group of individuals, probably several thousand, not the pair described in God's Word. Uniformitarian assumptions seem to be acceptable to determine the earth's age, yet those same basic assumptions are rejected when it comes to human origins.

If we look at the text of Genesis 1 and 2, there is not much difference in the description of the creation of the plants, animals, and man — all of them were created out of the earth; of course, God breathed life into man and made him in His image. While many insist that Adam and Eve were real people, they do so against the scientific consensus — a consensus that comes from the same people they trust to tell them the age of the earth. For example, Karl Giberson has attempted to be consistent in his thinking, saying:

> For more than two centuries, careful scientific research, much of it done by Christians, has demonstrated clearly that the earth is billions years old, not mere thousands, as many creationists argue. We now know that the human race began millions of years ago in Africa — not thousands of years ago in the Middle East, as the story in Genesis suggests.[9]

So if the Bible cannot be trusted to give an accurate account of human history, why should it be trusted to tell us about our condition as humans? Should we not also look to the same types of humanistic evolutionary thinking to tell us who we are as a species? If we were to be consistent, that would be our approach.

Even though the "story in Genesis suggests" that Adam was a real man, there must be another explanation that "careful scientific research" can reveal. If there was never a man named Adam, or if he was just one of a group of advanced hominids, then who was Eve? Was she the mother of all living (Genesis 3:20)? Did she really give birth to Seth who eventually led to Abraham who led to David who led to Jesus (Luke 3:23–38)? At

---

8. See chapter 8 for a detailed discussion on the various views of theistic evolution.
9. Karl Giberson, "My Take: Jesus Would Believe in Evolution and So Should You," CNN Belief Blog, http://religion.blogs.cnn.com/2011/04/10/my-take-jesus-would-believe-in-evolution-and-so-should-you.

what point in Genesis do we find the first truly historical event? It is hard to imagine that there are answers to these questions that are consistent with Dr. Giberson's scientific understanding and the text of the Bible.

To take this to the heart of the gospel, if there was no man Adam then the Apostle Paul makes a very significant error, under the inspiration of the Holy Spirit, when he teaches the Romans and the Corinthians that it is Jesus Christ, the last Adam, who has come to reverse the effects of the sin brought into the world by the first Adam (Romans 5; 1 Corinthians 15). It has become popular to question the existence of Adam and Eve among those who embrace the "careful scientific research" in order to be consistent in their thinking.[10] They are to be commended for taking their logic to its natural conclusions, but they do so at the risk of undermining the very nature of Christianity.

Hopefully you are beginning to see the doctrinal implications of being consistent and starting with the Bible as the foundation rather than man's fallible reasoning.

A Global Flood

Reading the account of Noah and the Flood from Genesis, it seems like a clear account of what happened. It has the marks of a historical account, including the exact timing — to the day — of the various parts of the experience, and many evangelicals believe it actually happened. The text talks of every air-breathing creature on the land dying, of the mountains under the whole heaven being covered by water, and of Noah building a truly massive vessel to save the people and animals. A recent survey of evangelical Christian colleges revealed that while 91 percent of their leaders believed the Flood happened, only 58 percent believed it was worldwide, with 35 percent believing it was a local event and 7 percent saying it never really happened.[11]

For those who believe the Flood account is telling of a local event, they must explain how the apparently universal language in the text describes only a localized region. They must explain why God called Noah to build such a massive ship to save people and animals who could have

---

10. One of the proponents of such a position is Peter Enns, who has written on the topic at the BioLogos website and in a book titled *The Evolution of Adam*.

11. Ken Ham and Greg Hall, *Already Compromised* (Green Forest, AR: Master Books, 2011), p. 19–24.

simply moved from the flooded area to the mountains. It just does not seem to be reasonable — yet they appeal to the mainstream scientific consensus to explain the "unreasonable" conclusion that the Flood was global. Apart from the prevailing scientific consensus that there was no globe-covering flood, is there really any reason to doubt that God flooded the entire earth?

For those that believe the Flood was non-literal, they have to accept that Jesus and Peter were using a myth to teach about the nature of the Second Coming and the creation (Luke 17:26–27; 1 Peter 3:20; 2 Peter 2:5). In a long-age scenario, this raises questions about the inspiration and inerrancy of Scripture (1 Timothy 3:16–17) and the deity of Christ (Hebrews 6:18).

Virgin Birth

Careful scientific research has shown that virgins do not give birth. While there are many species of animals that can reproduce from solitary females, called parthenogenesis, it has never been observed to occur naturally in mammals or people. Yet Christians who believe that the scientific evidence should be the standard for understanding natural phenomena, like the birth process in humans, insist that Jesus was born from Mary, who was a virgin. On what grounds do they make such an assertion? It can only be based on what the Bible says about the topic in Luke 1. But why trust the Bible in this historical detail and not on the miraculous "birth" of Adam or Eve?

Resurrection

Careful scientific research has also shown that dead men or women do not rise from the dead. Yet we find many examples of this happening in the accounts of Scripture. Surely God is free to accomplish miracles within the world He created, so this should not be a problem for those who believe what God has revealed in the Scriptures.

But neither should creating the universe in six days or causing the entire globe to be flooded. There seems to be an inconsistency. Having read many explanations from theistic evolutionists (those who believe in God, but replace much of Genesis 1–11 with evolutionary ideas) about the acceptable nature of the Resurrection of Christ, I am still left confused. They assure us that we can trust science to tell us about how the big bang formed the universe, how evolution has led to all of the life on the earth, and how humans began as a population (not a couple), but they fail to trust their colleagues on the Resurrection and the virgin birth. But on what basis? All of these events happened in the past. We cannot conduct observable, repeatable tests on any of them. All of them are recorded in the Bible as historical narrative. Why should we trust the Bible on the Resurrection, but not on the Flood or creation?

A Moving Sushi Bar

Though I have never eaten at one, there are sushi restaurants where the food moves past you on a conveyor belt. You snatch up the California rolls and let the slabs of raw tuna pass on by. The next guy loves the tuna and thanks you for letting it pass. While we have preferences about the food we eat, I would suggest that we cannot take such liberties with the truths God has revealed in the Bible.

Like choosing our food from a conveyor belt, it is inconsistent to accept those parts of the Bible that are presented as historical narratives as true in some places and untrue in others. However, this is what must be done in order to embrace the evolutionary views of the big bang, the gradual formation of our planet, the development of life on earth, and the arrival of humans on this planet. If you hold to one, several, or all of these explanations and call yourself a Christian, I ask you to carefully consider the question of the authority of Scripture in every area of your life: are you elevating your *own* thoughts to be greater than God's (humanism) on any of these points?

On what authority do those who say we can *set aside Genesis as real history* and yet believe in a literal Resurrection and the virgin birth make this claim? If Paul was wrong about the connection between Adam and Christ, then why should we trust what Paul said about the sins of murder, lying, and homosexuality and our need for forgiveness through Christ alone?

As you ponder these questions, I leave you to prayerfully consider these words of Jesus Christ:

> I do not receive honor from men. But I know you, that you do
> not have the love of God in you. I have come in My Father's name,
> and you do not receive Me; if another comes in his own name,

him you will receive. How can you believe, who receive honor from one another, and do not seek the honor that comes from the only God? Do not think that I shall accuse you to the Father; there is one who accuses you — Moses, in whom you trust. For if you believed Moses, you would believe Me; for he wrote about Me. But if you do not believe his writings, how will you believe My words? (John 5:41–47).

Chapter 10

Christian Unity . . . and the Age of the Earth

Steve Ham

❀❀❀❀❀❀❀❀❀❀❀❀❀❀❀❀❀❀❀❀

"I do not ask for these only, but also for those who will believe in me through their word, that they may all be one, just as you, Father, are in me, and I in you, that they also may be in us, so that the world may believe that you have sent me. The glory that you have given me I have given to them, that they may be one even as we are one" (Jesus, John 17:20–22).

If anyone has spent a large amount of time in a local church, he or she will soon come to the realization that the church is filled with redeemed sinners. These redeemed sinners are looking forward to the time when Christ returns and when on that day they will finally be made into His perfect image (1 John 3:2).

Until that day, believers groan with the rest of creation. This groaning visibly shows itself no better than when Christians witness disputes in the Church. Some disputes have been totally necessary. Throughout the history of the Church believers have witnessed councils, creeds, and confessions arising from the need to deal with the heretical views of those who would undermine clear biblical truth.

These evangelical confessional statements have helped to protect the Church and biblical doctrines in a world fraught with human error. In this way, I thank God for good men who were willing to stand on the authority of God's Word and against the false teaching of their times. Sadly, at other times, many have witnessed a church entertain disputes about such things as the color of the carpet, the use of pews or chairs, the starting time of worship services, or the style of the music.

Pastors are acutely aware of issues concerning unity in their churches. It would be rare to find a pastor who does not care about the church he leads acting like a functioning body with all the parts working in unison for the glory of Christ. Moreover, unity is a subject that should touch every Christian heart because the Scriptures directly and indirectly talk on the subject frequently.

The Scriptures tell believers that Christ has commanded them to love one another (John 13:34). In his closing statements to the Philippians, Paul exhorts two people to get along for the sake of Christ (Philippians 4:2). All through the Epistles are numerous appeals for unity. Unity in the Church is one of the gospel imperatives (i.e., things believers are commanded to do) seen as a sign of a truly redeemed community of believers (James 5:9).

Unity and Truth

If Christian unity is centered in the all-powerful gospel of Jesus Christ, surely every church member has a foundation for unity despite other disagreements. Christian unity is based on a salvation common to all believers. "Beloved, although I was very eager to write to you about our common salvation, I found it necessary to write appealing to you to contend for the faith that was once for all delivered to the saints" (Jude 3).

The faith Jude is talking about is something that has been delivered, or handed down. The faith believers are united in is a propositional objective body of truth that is already established and handed to us. Unity is not something Christians can build on their own but something they come into by faith in Christ and His propositional objective truth found in Scripture.

When it comes to unity, truth has a high degree of importance. If not for truth, there is no need to define anything, including the saving message of the gospel. The Apostle Paul believed so strongly in the foundational element of truth in unity that he reminded the Ephesians that there was only one truth from one God that the Christian can be united in. "There is one body and one Spirit — just as you were called to the one hope that belongs to your call — one Lord, one faith, one baptism, one God and Father of all, who is over all and through all and in all" (Ephesians 4:4–6; ESV).

Even so, Christians can and should make some distinctions. The Bible does call for grace in certain disagreements where there is liberty for Christian discernment. In these cases, where a doctrine does not undermine the Christian faith, the Christian is encouraged not to be a stumbling block for the sake of the gospel. Even in these issues, God's Word gives guidance (Romans 14:1–19).

Christian unity must also hold firm in the doctrines that are essential for salvation and doctrines that foundationally support the gospel. For example, the doctrine of the authority of the Bible is not a saving issue, but people only understand the gospel message from the Bible. In this way, a question of scriptural authority is only a step away from gospel integrity; therefore, biblical authority should actually be important for Christian unity (Psalm 11:3).

It is on this topic that Dr. Al Mohler writes of the necessity for theological triage. Just as a doctor in an emergency ward assesses the priority of patients according to the seriousness of the problem, Christians should also be engaged with theological triage in relation to the seriousness of a doctrine in its connection to an authentic gospel. Dr. Mohler ranks these in terms of first-order and secondary-order doctrines and states, "The truthfulness and authority of the Holy Scriptures must also rank as a first-order doctrine, for without affirming the Bible as the very Word of God, we are left without any adequate authority for distinguishing truth from error."[1]

What about the Book of Genesis?

How Christians interpret Genesis 1–11 (which incorporates belief about the age of the earth) impacts this subject at the core of understanding and maintaining the coherency of the gospel. Because of the foundational importance of the Book of Genesis, every doctrine concerning the

---

1. A. Naselli and C. Hansen, editors, *Four Views on the Spectrum of Evangelicalism* (Grand Rapids, MI: Zondervan, 2011), p. 79.

gospel is understood in light of the historical foundation in Genesis. This makes Genesis of first-order importance.

A misunderstanding of the history in the first 11 chapters of Genesis will inevitably undermine or cause someone to question the validity of the gospel message because so much of that history answers the necessity for a gospel in the first place. A reading of the first three chapters of Genesis answers all of the correlated gospel questions below:

- How do we know man is a sinner?

- How do we know we are all sinners?

- How do we know that death is the penalty for sin?

- How do we know that God would provide a Savior?

- How do we know Jesus needed to die and rise again physically?

- How do we know this world is not what it originally was?

Believers know these things because Genesis describes a "very good" original creation, a warning to obey God, the disobedience of the first man and woman, rebellious humanity's position under the wrath of the Creator, and a promise that the seed of the woman will crush the seed of the serpent. If the Bible cannot be trusted from the very foundational history in the first chapters of Genesis that is so closely correlated to the gospel message itself (e.g., Romans 5; 1 Corinthians 15), one has to ask if the gospel itself is reliable. After all, both accounts are part of the same history in the same book — the Bible.

The issue of Genesis and the age of the earth is also an issue that hits at the core of biblical authority. The Bible clearly reveals in Genesis that (among other things) death, disease, bloodshed, a carnivorous diet, and thorns and thistles are a consequence of God's curse because of Adam's sin (see Genesis 1:29–30 and 3:14–19).

With an allowance for millions of years prior to the creation of Adam and Eve on the sixth day comes an allowance for the above consequences to be present before sin causing them. If God's very good creation already contained the consequences of sin before Adam's Fall, this would call into question a very good creation, the character of the God who declared, and the need for any restoration by Christ at all. So the age of the earth is itself a gospel-related, biblical authority issue for the Christian.

Unity in Christ

Very few Christians would disagree that primarily their unity is in Christ. If believers are going to find unity in Christ, they must define who Christ is only as He has revealed Himself to them. The Bible says that Jesus is both God of creation and God of redemption (John 1; Colossians 1:15–20; Hebrews 1:3–13).

Scripture reveals Jesus as the self-existent, eternal Son of God, Creator of everything, and the One who has revealed Himself to us in person and through His Word from Genesis 1:1 to the last verse of Revelation. It is impossible to be unified in the God of the gospel without being unified in the God of creation and the God of the whole Bible because He is the same God, Jesus Christ.

Jesus Himself teaches that He is the way, the truth, and the life (John 14:6). Evangelical Christians know this and rejoice in it. It would not be difficult to get a room full of evangelical Christian leaders agreeing to and preaching the centrality of Jesus Christ in the message of Scripture. When it comes to accepting and preaching Jesus as the revealer of truth and the Creator, and getting specific about what that means, then unity starts to fray.

If Jesus is the pre-eminent, supreme revealer of truth, then the search for truth must start with His pre-eminence over man's philosophies. Our unity must be based first on the person of Jesus Christ and on His Scriptures. It is Christ and His truth that helps us to understand the truth about our world, and not man's interpretations of this world supposedly telling us what Jesus means in His Word. To start our search for truth with man's ideas is essentially to shift the supreme authority from Jesus to man. And this is something that those committed to unity in Jesus Christ should not tolerate.

This begs a very important question: Is the Church today trying to find unity in Christ as the center of truth, without recognizing Him as the revealer of truth in the entirety of the biblical record — from Genesis 1:1 to Revelation 22:21?

Unity and Consensus of Opinion

Christ Himself taught that truth is important. Today, however, one of the most common definitions of "Christian unity" revolves around a consensus of fallible man's opinion rather than the truth of God's infallible Word. Depending on which circles a Christian is in, he will find varying levels of pressure to accept the consensus of opinion as truth. Particularly in today's academic circles, immense pressure is placed upon students and professors to accept this consensus-centered view.

Every word of man must be viewed and scrutinized in the light of the revealed Word of God. While great respect should be given to teachers, believers must be careful that they are not placed in a situation similar to the time before the Reformation where it was insisted that only "clergy" could understand the Bible. Believers must not allow the ideas of professors to become the final word. Nowhere does Scripture teach that unity comes through consensus of opinion, even from the highest levels of academia. The truth of God trumps consensus every time.

It is in the biblical Book of John where the first key points of insight in answering these crucial issues are found. In John 17, Christ prays for the unity of the church:

> I will remain in the world no longer, but they are still in the world, and I am coming to you. Holy Father, protect them by the power of your name — the name you gave me — so that they may be one as we are one. While I was with them, I protected them and kept them safe by that name you gave me. None has been lost except the one doomed to destruction so that Scripture would be fulfilled.
>
> I am coming to you now, but I say these things while I am still in the world, so that they may have the full measure of my joy within them. I have given them your word and the world has hated them, for they are not of the world any more than I am of the world. My prayer is not that you take them out of the world but that you protect them from the evil one. They are not of the world, even as I am not of it. Sanctify them by the truth; your word is truth. As you sent me into the world, I have sent them into the world. For them I sanctify myself, that they too may be truly sanctified (John 17:11–19; NIV).

In verse 11, Jesus prays that unity may be kept among the Apostles, as it is in the Trinity. The unity that Jesus was looking for did not come from consensus. Jesus is talking about a unity that is already perfectly present in Christ; it is the *supremacy* of Christ.

In verses 17–19, He prays that believers may be *kept* in the *truth* — *His* truth. Unity for the believer is already available in Christ rather than something to be obtained by consensus of opinion. This unity is to be *kept*, not established. It is unity that is separate from this world and maintained in the truth of Christ and His Word.

Is the division over the interpretation of Genesis a result of an earnest desire to be unified around the Word of God, or a desire to be unified around the words of sinful fallible human beings (regardless of whether they are highly qualified scientists or theologians)? In days gone by, English pastor Richard Baxter said:

> Indeed, no truth is inconsistent with any other truth: but yet when two dark or doubtful points are compared together, it is hard to know which of them to reject. But here it is easy; nothing that contradicteth the true nature of God or man or any principle, must be held.[2]

Logic tells us that something cannot be both true and false at the same time and in the same sense, and truth is always consistent with itself. For the sake of unity, this logic particularly applies to the nature of God and man. God is holy, pure, and perfect. Man however has a heart that is "deceitful above all things, and desperately wicked" (Jeremiah 17:9).

The only truth consistent with the nature of both God and man is the literal interpretation of the historical narrative in Genesis. This is clear from several considerations. Genesis tells of a very good creation, unblemished by death, disease, suffering, extinction, and other natural evils (earthquakes, hurricanes, and so on). This correlates consistently with the constant biblical references to the holiness of God.[3] Scripture says that man is a creation of God. It explains that God's creations were good.

2. Martin Lloyd-Jones discussing John Owen and his teaching on schisms, *Diversity in Unity* (London: A.G. Hasler and Co.); The Puritan and Reformed Studies Conference December 1963, p. 63.

3. God's holiness is seen in Scripture in His perfect purity and inability to tolerate blemish. Sin in the Garden of Eden brought out the holiness of God through judgment and salvation. For example, read Scriptures such as Psalm 104, where the Psalmist gives a poetic discourse that involves the pre-Curse creation week (verses 1–5,19–20), the post-Curse Flood (verses 6–9), and the current time in which he lived. The cursed world people live in today does not bring God's holiness into question but shows His holiness in respect to His judgment shown in the consequences for sin.

Therefore, evil and death cannot be a part of man's beginning (or of any part of the creation for that matter), as such an addition to man's beginning would contradict the truth of who God is.

Death, thorns, a carnivorous diet, a cursed ground, groaning physical creation, and eternal judgment are the consequences of sin and will be removed from the creation when Christ comes again to complete His redemptive work (e.g., Romans 8:19–25; Revelation 22:3). Such things were not in existence before the Fall. It is only this understanding that is consistent with the truth that Jesus came to physically die and then to rise again to conquer the consequences of man's sin. Later, Scripture also says that man is essentially evil, destined to die, and will face judgment for sin. This correlates then to the truth that is seen in man and there is no contradiction in logic. The infallible inerrant Word of God is the only consistent starting point for understanding this world in the truth of Christ. By not upholding the historical accuracy of God's Word in Genesis, people inevitably walk away from truth and walk away from the unity of that truth, which is Christ's objective propositional body of truth delivered to us.

Keeping Unity Regarding the Issue of the Age of the Earth

Truth is critically important for biblical unity; this is echoed and emphasized throughout Scripture. Consider Ephesians 4:11–13:

> And He Himself gave some to be apostles, some prophets, some evangelists, and some pastors and teachers, for the equipping of the saints for the work of ministry, for the edifying of the body of Christ, till we all come to the unity of the faith and of the knowledge of the Son of God, to a perfect man, to the measure of the stature of the fullness of Christ.

It is the job of the leaders in the Church to utilize the unity Christians already have in the foundation of truth in Scripture and lead them toward the fullness of Christ. This foundation is essential for Christian growth and church leadership. Often, churches do not see that kind of unity today. In fact, more often churches see division. But is it division for the sake of unity on God's Word? Or is it division for the sake of unity on man's word? Therein lies the issue.

Sadly, the division seen in regard to Genesis really comes down to a unity many Christian academics have regarding man's word, where they go against the doctrines taught in Scripture (Romans 16:17). This is also a problem with the Church — and has been the problem with man since Genesis 3, when man was tempted to question God's Word and then decide truth for himself.

Ephesians 4:14 offers a very strong warning. Christians are to grow in the knowledge of Christ and His fullness "that we should no longer be children, tossed to and fro and carried about with every wind of doctrine, by the trickery of men, in the cunning craftiness of deceitful plotting."

Unity is not only in Christ and His truth, but it is maintained by committing to *that* truth and not being persuaded otherwise by men. In Colossians 2:8, a similar warning is given by Paul to a newly established church, as he desires to keep a strong unity within it:

> Beware lest anyone cheat you through philosophy and empty deceit, according to the tradition of men, according to the basic principles of the world, and not according to Christ.

Neither millions of years nor evolution can be found anywhere in the text of Scripture. Nor can such teachings fit consistently with the whole counsel of God's Word. Yet those who have not allowed the intrusion of man's ideas of millions of years into the first chapter of Genesis are often accused of causing division. These old-earth beliefs are philosophies and "empty deceit" according to the "traditions of men."[4] The Church is warned to be on the lookout for this and to shut the door to the compromise of human philosophies. Paul wrote to encourage the Colossian church to keep the truth and maintain the unity.

Dealing with the Academic Consensus

People today have been persuaded into thinking that if they do not adhere to the consensus of the scientific and/or theological establishment, they have "checked their brains at the door." The many PhD scientists and experts who do start with the truth of Scripture and use all of

---

4. See Terry Mortenson, *Millions of Years: Where Did the Idea Come From?* DVD of lecture (Hebron, KY: Answers in Genesis, 2005), and Terry Mortenson, *The Great Turning Point: The Church's Catastrophic Mistake on Geology — Before Darwin* (Green Forest, AR: Master Books, 2004).

the principles of logic in operational science to confirm biblical history certainly would disagree with that notion.

In Christian academic settings today, there is a great appeal to experts as the authorities. Christians are told they need to follow Professor "X," or Dr. "Y" on this point or that, seeking a unity around the words of an academic, instead of one based on the clear teaching of the Word of God. No matter the stature of a leader, the number of the consensus, or the multitude of letters in a title, our unity is not in man or his philosophies but in Christ and His truth. This is why Paul warned the Corinthians not to follow men even though he was one of them being mentioned with Cephas and Apollos (1 Corinthians 3:21–23).

Unfortunately, one of the intimidating problems faced by congregations today is that standing on the Word of God on the issue of the age of the earth is often associated with claims of denying others the freedom of academic pursuit. Combined with this, there are many academics, even in Christian colleges, who infer that there is actually no way for the common man to understand Genesis unless the reader first acquaints himself with the philosophical approach of the particular academic who has specialized in a particular area.

There are many books that can be purchased in Christian bookstores showcasing the latest academic research in such areas as ancient Near Eastern mythology and various historical, philosophical, and even theological pursuits from respected teachers and experts, including those with PhDs, endorsing conformity to their view first in order to understand Genesis.[5] Many of them are actually interpreting Genesis in a completely different ways from one another, resulting in great confusion in the Church.

The answer to this problem is found in a doctrine of Scripture that is too often and too easily overlooked — the doctrine of perspicuity. The word *perspicuity* means clarity, and the doctrine says that while there are some difficult passages that challenge the best of scholars, Scripture is generally clear and understandable to a non-scholar and even a child.

---

5. Just to name a few examples among many: John Walton, *The Lost World of Genesis One* (Downers Grove, IL: IVP Academic, 2009); Karl Giberson and Francis Collins, *The Language of Science and Faith* (Downers Grove, IL: InterVarsity Press, 2011); William Dembski, *The End of Christianity* (Nashville, TN: Broadman and Holman, 2009).

This doctrine is implied by the biblical commands for fathers to teach their children the Scriptures (Deuteronomy 6:1–9; Ephesians 6:4) and by the way that Jesus and the Apostles handle the Old Testament and New Testament for the common people. Eleven times in the Gospels it is recorded that Jesus said, "Have you not read?" and 30 times that He said, "It is written" and then quoted Scripture as if the meaning was obvious.

Perspicuity is one of the doctrines under attack in our time. This attack has a direct link to the potential for people to divide away from the truth that is in Christ. It is a devastating phenomenon that many published scholars have walked away from foundational truths of clear Scripture in an academic pursuit of human wisdom independent of Scripture.

The biggest concern comes when many respect the words of such men over the clarity of Scripture. This is something that the Apostle Paul warned of when he wrote to the church in Corinth. "But I fear, lest somehow, as the serpent deceived Eve by his craftiness, so your minds may be corrupted from the simplicity that is in Christ" (2 Corinthians 11:3).

The same attack upon the perspicuity of Scripture was one of the issues that Martin Luther was fighting in the Reformation. The result of a constant rhetoric and practice communicating that the Bible was out of reach for the common man caused a fateful disdain of Scripture itself. "Yet with such a phantasmagoria [bizarre illusion] Satan has frightened men away from reading the Sacred Writ, and has made Holy Scripture contemptible."[6]

Scripture says the following about its perspicuity:

1. All Christians without distinction are to search the Scriptures (Acts 17:11; 2 Timothy 3:15).
2. Perspicuity does not mean Christians do not need pastors and teachers to teach the depth of Scripture within its existing clarity (Ephesians 4:11–13).
3. Scripture itself affirms it has clarity (2 Peter 1:19).
4. The many commands in Scripture show that it is expected to be understood and obeyed by all believers.
5. Perspicuity does not mean that everything is equally clear or simple to understand.

---

6. Philip Watson and Helmut Lehmann, editors, *Luther's Works*, vol. 33, Career of the Reformer III (Philadelphia, PA: Fortress Press, 1972), p. 25.

A good example of this last point is the doctrine of the Trinity. It is clear from Scripture that God is one God and yet that the Father is God, the Son is God, and the Holy Spirit is God. While the doctrine of the Trinity is not as equally simple or clear as other doctrines, it is clearly taught in the Bible.

The historical narrative in Genesis is a clear historical narrative. It is a narrative that surpasses the folly of human wisdom. And starting with the literal truth of this narrative, one can confirm this history using the same observational science in this world that is available to all men. The mark of a good academic is one who starts with the assumption of the authority and perspicuity of God's Word and takes His clear truth to understand this world from the perspective of the only One who is able to claim omniscience. To deny this clarity and embrace and promote instead the fallible and arrogant ideas of sinful man is to be divisive in respect to Christ and His truth.

In today's Church, the accommodation of millions of years and evolution has undeniably increased the problem of division within the Church. It is time for Christians to again review the prayer of Christ in John 17 and commit to return to the keeping of the unity that is only in Christ and His Word. It is time to take heed of the warning in Colossians 2:8 and beware of the philosophies of men that keep believers from the truth that is *in Christ* and *from Christ.*

This phenomenon of people following the teachings of so-called great men rather than Christ is not new. In studying the Puritan pastors of the 1600s, Dr. Martyn Lloyd-Jones, the great 20th-century pastor in London, commented on the voluminous writings on Christian unity by John Owen. In relation to schisms in the Church, Lloyd Jones offers the following in reference to Owen:

> The trouble, as he points out repeatedly, over the whole question of schism is that people will defend the position that they are in. They shut their minds; they are not ready to listen, to be instructed, and to change.[7]

What Lloyd-Jones understood was that Owen in his day found that rather than being conformed to the truth that is in Christ and His Word,

---

7. Lloyd-Jones, *Diversity in Unity*, p. 63.

men were more likely to hold strongly to their own beliefs. This is called pride.

The great divide in the Church today has its roots in this pride. Few people are able to admit error even when it comes to biblical truth. Yet all want to rejoice and find unity in Christ. The Church is in need of those who will unite uncompromisingly on God's Word, because of the division caused by those who have allowed themselves to be persuaded by man's fallible word to reinterpret Scripture.

The Call for Unity

Our closing prayer echoes that of Christ. Yes, we pray and strive not for division, but for unity, that we might all be one, in truth, as Jesus prayed we would be. If someone wants to divide because they are not willing to conform to the truth that Jesus has given us in Genesis, then they will sadly divide (Romans 16:17).

While Christians should never stop treating a professing believer as anything other than a brother, they should also consistently hold to, preach, and exhort others in the truth of Christ that makes this world look only foolish. They should truly unite in Jesus who is the Jesus of the Gospel, the Jesus of creation, and the Jesus of the revealed Word of God from the first to the last verse.

Chapter 11

Radiocarbon Dating?

Dr. Andrew A. Snelling

Cℳ⅍⅍⅍⅍⅍⅍⅍⅍⅍⅍⅍⅍⅍⅍⅍⅍⅍⅍

The most well-known of all the radiometric dating methods is radiocarbon dating. Although many people think radiocarbon is used to date rocks, it is limited to dating things that contain carbon and were once alive (fossils).

How Radiocarbon Forms

Radiocarbon (carbon-14 or ^{14}C) forms continually today in the earth's upper atmosphere. And as far as we know, it has been forming in the earth's upper atmosphere at least since the Fall, after the atmosphere was made back on day 2 of creation week (part of the expanse, or firmament, described in Genesis 1:6–8).

So how does radiocarbon form? Cosmic rays from outer space are continually bombarding the upper atmosphere of the earth, producing fast-moving neutrons (sub-atomic particles carrying no electric charge) (figure 1).[1] These fast-moving neutrons collide with nitrogen-14 atoms, the most abundant element in the upper atmosphere, converting them into radiocarbon (carbon-14) atoms.

---

1. Sheridan Bowman, *Interpreting the Past: Radiocarbon Dating* (London: British Museum Publications, 1990).

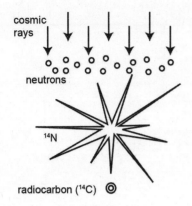

radiocarbon (^{14}C) ◎

Figure 1. The formation of radiocarbon (^{14}C or carbon-14) in the earth's upper atmosphere due to the influx of cosmic rays from outer space.

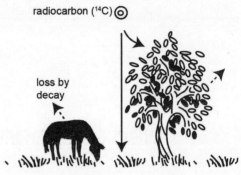

Figure 2. Radiocarbon (^{14}C or carbon-14) atoms combine with oxygen atoms in the atmosphere to form carbon dioxide (CO_2) that circulates into the biosphere. Radiocarbon is thus incorporated into plants by photosynthesis and into the animals that eat the plants. Continued photosynthesis and feeding replaces the ^{14}C atoms lost from the plants and animals by decay back to ^{14}N (nitrogen-14).

Since the atmosphere is composed of about 78 percent nitrogen,[2] a lot of radiocarbon atoms are produced — in total about 16.5 lbs. (7.5 kg) per year. These rapidly combine with oxygen atoms (the second most abundant element in the atmosphere, at 21 percent) to form carbon dioxide (CO_2).

This carbon dioxide, now radioactive with carbon-14, is otherwise chemically indistinguishable from the normal carbon dioxide in the atmosphere, which is slightly lighter because it contains normal carbon-12. Radioactive and non-radioactive carbon dioxide mix throughout the atmosphere, and dissolve in the oceans. Through photosynthesis carbon dioxide enters plants and algae, bringing radiocarbon into the food chain. Radiocarbon then enters animals as they consume the plants (figure 2). So even we humans are radioactive because of trace amounts of radiocarbon in our bodies.

Determining the Rate of Radiocarbon Decay

After radiocarbon forms, the nuclei of the carbon-14 atoms are unstable, so over time they progressively decay back to nuclei of stable

2. Steven S. Zumdahl, *Chemical Principles*, second edition (Lexington, MA: D.C. Heath and Company, 1995), p.171.

nitrogen-14.[3] A neutron breaks down to a proton and an electron, and the electron is ejected. This process is called beta decay. The ejected electrons are called beta particles and make up what is called beta radiation.

Not all radiocarbon atoms decay at the same time. Different carbon-14 atoms revert to nitrogen-14 at different times, which explains why radioactive decay is considered a random process. To measure the rate of decay, a suitable detector records the number of beta particles ejected from a measured quantity of carbon over a period of time, say a month (for illustration purposes). Since each beta particle represents one decayed carbon-14 atom, we know how many carbon-14 atoms decayed during that month.

Chemists have already determined how many atoms are in a given mass of each element, such as carbon.[4] So if we weigh a lump of carbon, we can calculate how many carbon atoms are in it. If we know what fraction of the carbon atoms are radioactive, we can also calculate how many radiocarbon atoms are in the lump. Knowing the number of atoms that decayed in our sample over a month, we can calculate the radiocarbon decay rate.

The standard way of expressing the decay rate is called the half-life.[5] It's defined as the time it takes half a given quantity of a radioactive element to decay. So if we started with 2 million atoms of carbon-14 in our measured quantity of carbon, then the half-life of radiocarbon will be the time it takes for half, or 1 million, of these atoms to decay. The radiocarbon half-life or decay rate has been determined at 5,730 years.

Using Radiocarbon for Dating

Next comes the question of how scientists use this knowledge to date things. If carbon-14 has formed at a constant rate for a very long time and continually mixed into the biosphere, then the level of carbon-14 in the atmosphere should remain constant. If the level is constant, living plants and animals should also maintain a constant carbon-14 level in them. The reason is that, as long as the organism is alive, it replaces any carbon molecules that have decayed into nitrogen.

---

3. Alan P. Dickin, *Radiogenic Isotope Geology*, second edition (Cambridge, UK: Cambridge University Press, 2005), p. 383–398.
4. Zumdahl, *Chemical Principles*, p. 55. For radiocarbon this number is ~6.022 X 10^{23} atoms per 14 grams of carbon-14.
5. Gunter Faure and Teresa M. Mensing, *Isotopes: Principles and Applications*, third edition (Hoboken, NJ: John Wiley & Sons, 2005), p. 614–625.

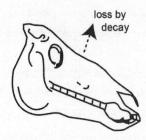

loss by decay

Figure 3. After the death of an animal it no longer eats and adds ^{14}C to its body, so the ^{14}C in it is steadily lost by decay back to ^{14}N.

After plants and animals perish, however, they no longer replace molecules damaged by radioactive decay. Instead, the radiocarbon atoms in their bodies slowly decay away, so the ratio of carbon-14 atoms to regular carbon atoms will steadily decrease over time (figure 3).

Let's suppose we find a mammoth's skull, and we want to date it to determine how long ago it lived. We can measure in the laboratory how many carbon-14 atoms are still in the skull. If we assume that the mammoth originally had the same number of carbon-14 atoms in its bones as living animals do today (estimated at one carbon-14 atom for every trillion carbon-12 atoms), then, because we also know the radiocarbon decay rate, we can calculate how long ago the mammoth died. It's really quite that simple.

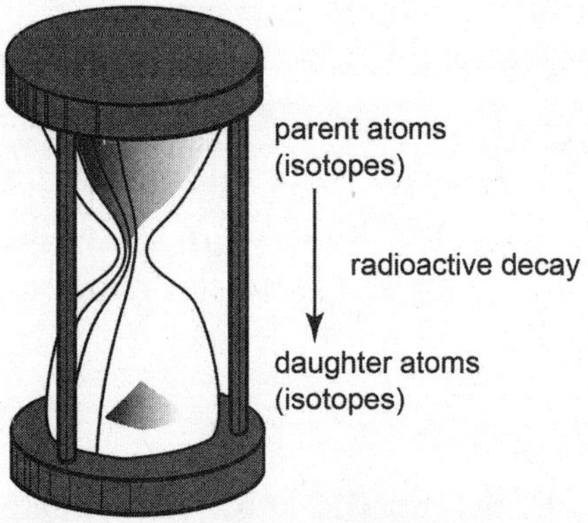

parent atoms (isotopes)

radioactive decay

daughter atoms (isotopes)

Figure 4. A simple hourglass clock. The sand grains in the top bowl fall to the bottom bowl to measure the passage of time. If all the sand grains are in the top bowl, then it takes exactly an hour for them all to fall. So if half the sand grains are in the top bowl and half in the bottom bowl, then 30 minutes has elapsed since the sand grains began falling. We can calibrate an hourglass clock by timing the falling sand grains against a mechanical or electronic clock. But there is no way of independently calibrating the radioactive clocks in rocks because no observers were present when the rocks formed and the clocks started.

This dating method is also similar to the principle behind an hourglass (figure 4). The sand grains that originally filled the top bowl represent the carbon-14 atoms in the living mammoth just before it died. It's assumed to be the same number of carbon-14 atoms as in elephants living today. With time, those sand grains fell to the bottom bowl, so the new number represents the carbon-14 atoms left in the mammoth skull when we found it. The difference in the number of sand grains represents the number of carbon-14 atoms that have decayed back to nitrogen-14 since the mammoth died. Because we have measured the rate at which the sand grains fall (the radiocarbon decay rate), we can then calculate how long it took those carbon-14 atoms to decay, which is how long ago the mammoth died.

That's how the radiocarbon method works. And because the half-life of carbon-14 is just 5,730 years, radiocarbon dating of materials containing carbon yields dates of only thousands of years, not the dates over millions of years that conflict with the framework of earth history provided by the Bible, God's eyewitness account of history.

So one would think that since the radiocarbon dating method works on organic (once living) materials, then radiocarbon could be used to date fossils. After all, we should be able to estimate how long ago a creature lived based on how much radiocarbon is left in its body.

Why Isn't Radiocarbon Used to Date Fossils?

The answer is a matter of basic physics. Radiocarbon (carbon-14) is a very unstable element that quickly changes into nitrogen. Half the original quantity of carbon-14 will decay back to the stable element nitrogen-14 after only 5,730 years. (This 5,730 year period is called the half-life of radiocarbon, figure 5).[6] At this decay rate, hardly any carbon-14 atoms will remain after only 57,300 years (or ten half-lives).

So if fossils are really millions of years old, as evolutionary scientists claim, no carbon-14 atoms would be left in them. Indeed, if all the atoms making up the entire earth were radiocarbon, then after only 1 million years absolutely *no* carbon-14 atoms should be left!

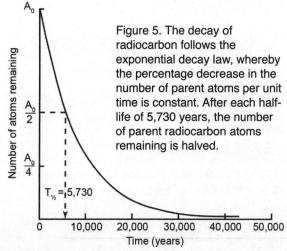

Figure 5. The decay of radiocarbon follows the exponential decay law, whereby the percentage decrease in the number of parent atoms per unit time is constant. After each half-life of 5,730 years, the number of parent radiocarbon atoms remaining is halved.

The Power of Radiocarbon Detection Technology

Most laboratories measure radiocarbon with a very sophisticated instrument called an accelerator mass spectrometer, or AMS. It is

---

6. Bowman, Sheridan, *Interpreting the Past: Radiocarbon Dating*, University of Californis Press, 1990), pg. 614-625.

able to literally count carbon-14 atoms one at a time.[7] This machine can theoretically detect one radioactive carbon-14 atom in 100 quadrillion regular carbon-12 atoms! However, there's a catch! AMS instruments need to be checked occasionally, to make sure they aren't also "reading" any laboratory contamination, called background. So rock samples that should read zero are occasionally placed into these instruments to test their accuracy. What better samples to use than fossils, coals and limestones, which are supposed to be millions of years old and should have no radiocarbon?

Radiocarbon Found!

Imagine the surprise when *every* piece of "ancient" carbon tested has contained measurable quantities of radiocarbon![8] Fossils, coal, oil, natural gas, limestone, marble, and graphite from every Flood-related rock layer — and even some pre-Flood deposits — have all contained measurable quantities of radiocarbon (figure 6). All these results have been reported in the conventional scientific literature.

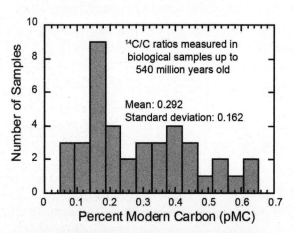

Figure 6. Distribution of ^{14}C values in samples of organic carbon from biologically derived materials such as fossils, limestones, coals, oils, natural gas, and graphite, as reported in the scientific literature. All these samples are supposed to be millions of years old and should contain no detectable radiocarbon, according to the standard geological time scale.

This finding is consistent with the belief that rocks are only thousands of years old, but the specialists who obtained these results have definitely *not* accepted this conclusion. It does not fit their presuppositions. To keep from concluding that the rocks are only thousands of years old, they claim that the radiocarbon must be due to contamination, either from the field or from

7. Dickin, *Radiogenic Isotope Geology*, p. 383–398.
8. Robert L. Whitelaw, "Time, Life, and History in the Light of 15,000 Radiocarbon Dates," *Creation Research Society Quarterly* 7 no.1 (1970): p. 56–71; Paul Giem, "Carbon-14 Content of Fossil Carbon," *Origins* 51 (2001): p. 6–30.

the laboratory, or from both. However, when technicians meticulously clean the rocks with hot strong acids and other harsh pre-treatments to remove any possible contamination, these "ancient" organic (once-living) materials still contain measurable radiocarbon.

Since a blank sample holder in the AMS instrument predictably yields zero radiocarbon, these scientists should naturally conclude that the radiocarbon is "intrinsic" to the rocks. In other words, real radiocarbon is an integral part of the "ancient" organic materials. But these scientists' presuppositions prevent them from reaching this conclusion.

Radiocarbon in Fossils Confirmed

For some years creation scientists have been doing their own investigations of radiocarbon in fossils. Pieces of fossilized wood in Oligocene, Eocene, Cretaceous, Jurassic, Triassic, and Permian rock layers supposedly 32 to 250 million years old all contain measurable radiocarbon, equivalent to "ages" of 20,700 to 44,700 years.[9] (Creation geologists believe that with careful recalibration, even these extremely "young" ages would be less than 10,000 years.)

Similarly, carefully sampled pieces of coal from ten U.S. coal beds, ranging from Eocene to Pennsylvanian and supposedly 40 to 320 million years old, all contained similar radiocarbon levels equivalent to "ages" of 48,000 to 50,000 years.[10] Even fossilized ammonite shells found alongside

9. Dr. Andrew A. Snelling, "Radioactive 'Dating' in Conflict! Fossil Wood in 'Ancient' Lava Flow Yields Radiocarbon," *Creation* 20 no.1 (1997): p. 24–27; Dr. Andrew A. Snelling, "Stumping Old-age Dogma: Radiocarbon in 'Ancient' Fossil Tree Stump Casts Doubt on Traditional Rock/Fossil Dating," *Creation* 20 no.4 (1998): p. 48–51; Dr. Andrew A. Snelling, "Dating Dilemma: Fossil Wood in 'Ancient' Sandstone," *Creation* 21 no.3 (1999): p. 39–41; Dr. Andrew A. Snelling, "Geological Conflict: Young Radiocarbon Date for 'Ancient' Fossil Wood Challenges Fossil Dating," *Creation* 22 no.2 (2000): p. 44–47; Dr. Andrew A. Snelling, "Conflicting 'Ages' of Tertiary Basalt and Contained Fossilised Wood, Crinum, Central Queensland, Australia," *CEN Technical Journal* 14 no.2 (2000): p. 99–122; Dr. Andrew A. Snelling, "Radiocarbon in 'Ancient' Fossil Wood," *Impact* #415, Acts & Facts, Institute for Creation Research (January 2008): p. 10–13; Dr. Andrew A. Snelling, "Radiocarbon Ages for Fossil Ammonites and Wood in Cretaceous Strata Near Redding, California," *Answers Research Journal* 1 (2008): p. 123–144.

10. John R. Baumgardner, Dr. Andrew A. Snelling, D. Russell Humphreys, and Steven A. Austin, *Proceedings of the Fifth International Conference on Creationism*, "Measurable ^{14}C in Fossilized Organic Materials: Confirming the Young Earth Creation-Flood Model," Robert L. Ivey Jr., editor (Pittsburgh, PA: Creation Science Fellowship, 2003), p. 127–147.

fossilized wood in a Cretaceous layer, supposedly 112 to 120 million years old, contained measurable radiocarbon equivalent to "ages" of 36,400 to 48,710 years.[11]

Radiocarbon is Even in Diamonds

Just as intriguing is the discovery of measurable radiocarbon in diamonds. Creationist and evolutionary geologists agree that diamonds are formed more than 100 miles (160 km) down, deep within the earth's upper mantle, and do not consist of organic carbon from living things. Explosive volcanoes brought them to the earth's surface very rapidly in "pipes." As the hardest known natural substance, these diamonds are extremely resistant to chemical corrosion and external contamination. Also, the tight bonding in their crystals would have prevented any carbon-14 in the atmosphere from replacing any regular carbon atoms in the diamonds.

Yet diamonds have been tested and shown to contain radiocarbon equivalent to an "age" of 55,000 years.[12] These results have been confirmed by other investigators.[13] And calculations have shown that any radiation from trace uranium in the earth near the diamonds would have been *totally* incapable of producing from any nitrogen in the diamonds these measured levels of in situ carbon-14.[14] So even though these diamonds are conventionally regarded by evolutionary geologists as up to billions of years old, this radiocarbon has to be intrinsic to them. This carbon-14 would have been implanted in them when they were formed deep inside the earth, and it could not have come from the

11. Dr. Andrew A. Snelling, "Radiocarbon Ages for Fossil Ammonites and Wood in Cretaceous Strata near Redding, California," *Answers Research Journal* 1 (2008): p. 123–144.

12. John R. Baumgardner, *Radioisotopes and the Age of the Earth: Results of a Young-Earth Creationist Research Initiative*, "¹⁴C Evidence for a Recent Global Flood and a Young Earth," Larry Vardiman, Dr. Andrew A. Snelling, and Eugene F. Chaffin, editors, (El Cajon, CA: Institute for Creation Research, and Chino Valley, AZ: Creation Research Society, 2005), p. 587–630; Don B. DeYoung, *Thousands . . . Not Billions: Challenging an Icon of Evolution, Questioning the Age of the Earth* (Green Forest, AR: Master Books, 2005), p. 45–62.

13. R. Ervin Taylor and John Southon, "Use of Natural Diamonds to Monitor ¹⁴C AMS Instrument Backgrounds," *Nuclear Instruments and Methods in Physics Research* B 259 (2007): p. 282–287.

14. Baumgardner, "¹⁴C Evidence for a Recent Global Flood and a Young Earth," p. 614–616.

earth's atmosphere. This is not a problem for creationist scientists, but it is a serious problem for evolutionists.

The Radiocarbon "Puzzle"

Evolutionary radiocarbon scientists have still not conceded that fossils, coals, and diamonds are only thousands of years old. Their uniformitarian (slow-and-gradual) interpretation requires that the earth's rocks be millions or billions of years old. They still maintain that the carbon-14 is "machine background" contaminating *all* these tested samples. Among their proposed explanations is that the AMS instruments do not properly reset themselves between sample analyses. But if this were true, why does the instrument find zero atoms when no sample is in it?

It should be noted that radiocarbon "ages" of up to 50,000 years don't match the biblical time frame either. The Flood cataclysm was only about 4,350 years ago. However, these young radiocarbon "ages" are far more in accord with the Bible's account than the uniformitarian time scale. The discovery that diamonds have 55,000-year radiocarbon "ages" may help us unravel this mystery.

However, it would be extremely helpful if it was possible to systematically recalibrate radiocarbon "ages." Once radiocarbon is interpreted properly, it should help creationists date archeological remains from post-Flood human history, showing how they fit within the Bible's chronology.

Assumptions Change Estimates of Age

To solve this puzzle it is necessary to review the assumptions on which radiocarbon dating is based. These include:[15]

1. The production rate of carbon-14 has always been the same in the past as now.
2. The atmosphere has had the same carbon-14 concentration in the past as now.
3. The biosphere (the places on earth where organisms live) has always had the same overall carbon-14 concentration as the atmosphere, due to the rapid transfer of carbon-14 atoms from the atmosphere to the biosphere.

---

15. Sheridan Bowman, *Interpreting the Past: Radiocarbon Dating* (London: British Museum Publications, 1990), p. 14.

None of these assumptions is strictly correct, beyond a rough first approximation. Indeed, scientists have now determined that the concentration of carbon-14 in the atmosphere varies considerably according to latitude. They have also determined several geophysical causes for past and present fluctuations in carbon-14 production in the atmosphere.[16]

Specifically, we know that carbon-14 has varied in the past due to a stronger magnetic field on the earth and changing cycles in sunspot activity. So when objects of known historical dates are dated using radiocarbon dating, we find that carbon-14 dates are accurate back to only about 400 B.C.

The conventional scientific community is ignoring at least two factors crucial to re-calibrating radiocarbon (so that it accounts for major changes in the biosphere and atmosphere that likely resulted from the Flood): (1) the earth's magnetic field has been progressively stronger going back into the past, and (2) the Flood destroyed and buried a huge amount of carbon from the pre-Flood biosphere.

The Effect of a Past Stronger Magnetic Field

The evidence for the earth having a progressively stronger magnetic field going back into the past is based on reliable historical measurements[17] and "fossil" magnetism trapped in ancient pottery.[18] [19]

---

16. Ibid., p. 16–30; Gunter Faure and Teresa M. Mensing, *Isotopes: Principles and Applications*, third edition (Hoboken, NJ: John Wiley & Sons, 2005), p. 614–625; Alan P. Dickin, *Radiogenic Isotope Geology*, second edition (Cambridge, UK: Cambridge University Press, 2005), p. 383–398.

17. Thomas G. Barnes, "Decay of the Earth's Magnetic Field and the Geochronological Implications," *Creation Research Society Quarterly* 8 no.1 (1971): p. 24–29; Thomas G. Barnes, "Electromagnetics of the Earth's Field and Evaluation of Electric Conductivity, Current and Joule Peaking in the Earth's Core," *Creation Research Society Quarterly* 9 no. 4 (1973): p. 222–230; D. Russell Humphreys, "The Creation of the Earth's Magnetic Field," *Creation Research Society Quarterly* 20 no. 1 (1983): p. 89–90;

18. D. Russell Humphreys *Proceedings of the First International Conference on Creationism*, volume II, "Reversals of the Earth's Magnetic Field During the Genesis Flood," Robert E. Walsh, Christopher L. Brooks, and Richard S. Crowell, editors, (Pittsburgh, PA: Creation Science Fellowship,1986), p. 113–123.

19. R.T. Merrill and N.W. McElhinney, *The Earth's Magnetic Field* (London: Academic Press, 1983); Humphreys, "Reversals of the Earth's Magnetic Field During the Genesis Flood," p. 113–123. What is "fossil" magnetism? The clay used to make pottery contains mineral grains that are slightly magnetic. When the clay is baked, the grains' magnetic field imprint at the time is "locked in" or fossilized. The strength of the magnetic field was not affected by field reversals. The sun

A stronger magnetic field is significant because the magnetic field partly shields the earth from the influx of cosmic rays,[20] which change nitrogen atoms into radioactive carbon-14 atoms. So a stronger magnetic field in the past would have reduced the influx of cosmic rays. This in turn would have reduced the amount of radiocarbon produced in the atmosphere. If this were the case, the biosphere in the past would have had a lower carbon-14 concentration than it does today.

The best estimates indicate that the earth's magnetic field was twice as strong only 1,400 years ago and possibly four times as strong 2,800 years ago. If this is true, the earth's magnetic field would have been much stronger at the time of the Flood, and the carbon-14 levels in the biosphere would have been significantly smaller.

So if you mistakenly assume that the radiocarbon levels in the atmosphere and biosphere have always been the same as they are today, you would erroneously estimate much older dates for early human artifacts, such as post-Babel wooden statuettes in Egypt. And that is exactly what conventional archaeology has done.

The Effect of More Carbon in the Pre-Flood Biosphere

An even more dramatic effect on the earth's carbon-14 inventory would be the destruction and burial of all the carbon in the whole biosphere at the time of the Flood. Based on the enormous size of today's coal beds, oil, oil shale, and natural gas deposits, and all the fossils in limestones, shales, and sandstones, a huge quantity of plants and animals must have been alive when the Flood struck. It is conservatively estimated that the amount of carbon in the pre-Flood biosphere may have been many times greater than the amount of carbon in today's biosphere.[21]

---

also regularly experiences field reversals without loss of strength in the magnetic field. Robert E. Walsh and Christopher L. Brooks, editors, *Proceedings of the Second International Conference on Creationism*, volume 2, "Physical Mechanism for Reversal of the Earth's Magnetic Field During the Flood," by D. Russell Humphreys (Pittsburgh, PA: Creation Science Fellowship, 1990), p. 129–142.

20. R. Ervin Taylor, Austin Long, and Renee S. Kra, editors, *Radiocarbon after Four Decades: An Interdisciplinary Perspective*, "Radiocarbon Fluctuations and the Geomagnetic Field," by Robert S. Sternberg (New York: Springer-Verlag, 1992), p. 93–116.

21. Robert H. Brown, "The Interpretation of C-14 Dates," *Origins* 6 (1979): p. 30–44; Glenn R. Morton, "The Carbon Problem," *Creation Research Society Quarterly* 20 no. 4 (1984): p. 212–219; H.W. Scharpenseel and Peter Becker-Heidmann,

We cannot yet know for certain how much radiocarbon (carbon-14) was in this pre-Flood carbon (a mixture of normal carbon-12 and carbon-14). Yet if the earth's atmosphere started to produce carbon-14 at the Fall, then many radiocarbon atoms could have been in the pre-Flood biosphere by the time of the Flood, about 1,650 years after creation. However, if there was a whole lot more normal carbon (carbon-12 or ^{12}C) in the pre-Flood biosphere, then the proportion of ^{14}C to ^{12}C would have been very much less than the proportion in today's biosphere.

So when scientists fail to account for so many more plants and animals in the lush pre-Flood biosphere and wrongly assume that plants buried in coal beds had the *same* proportion of carbon-14 as plants do today, then their radiocarbon dating would yield "ages" very much higher than the true Flood age of about 4,350 years.

A Prediction Fulfilled

Now if this model of the earth's past radiocarbon inventory is correct, then a logical prediction follows. Since all pre-Flood plants would have had the same low radiocarbon levels when they were buried, and they all formed into coal beds during that single Flood year, then those coal beds should all have the same low radiocarbon content.

They do! Samples from coal beds around the United States, ranging from Eocene to Pennsylvanian deposits, supposedly 40 to 320 million years old, all contain the same low radiocarbon levels equivalent to "ages" of 48,000 to 50,000 years.[22] This makes sense only if these coal beds were all formed out of pre-Flood plants during the year-long Flood, about 4,350 years ago. Carbon-14 dates of the same value are expected in creation theory and contrary to the expectations in conventional old-earth theory.

"Twenty-five Years of Radiocarbon Dating Soils: Paradigm of Erring and Learning," *Radiocarbon* 34 (1992): p. 541–549; Baumgardner, Snelling, Humphreys, and Austin, "Measurable ^{14}C in Fossilized Organic Materials: Confirming the Young Earth Creation-Flood Model," p. 127–147.

22. Baumgardner, "^{14}C Evidence for a Recent Global Flood and a Young Earth," p. 614–616; DeYoung, *Thousands . . . Not Billions: Challenging an Icon of Evolution, Questioning the Age of the Earth*, p. 45–62.

The "Puzzle" Is Being Solved

So the radiocarbon "puzzle" can be solved, but only in the biblical framework for earth history. Research is therefore underway to find a means of re-calibrating the radiocarbon "clock" to properly account for the Flood and its impact on dates for the post-Flood period to the present.

For example, conventional radiocarbon dating gives an age of "48,000 years" for a coal bed deposited during the Flood, about 4,350 years ago. This could be explained if the $^{14}C/^{12}C$ ratio at the time of the Flood was only 1/200th the ratio of the present world. If scientists assume the ratio is 200 times greater than it really was, then their radiocarbon age estimate would be exaggerated by 43,650 years.[23]

In reality, calculations (described above) have led to estimates that the pre-Flood biosphere may have had more than 100 times the carbon-12 as the present earth. Using this information, we may be able to calculate how much carbon-14 was actually on the early earth at the Flood. This, in turn, would allow us to develop a proper interpretation of all carbon-14 dates.

Once the research is completed, one exciting benefit is that it should be possible to begin more accurately dating any archaeological artifact within the true chronology of history found in God's Word.

---

23. These numbers are calculated in terms of half-lives, discussed earlier. If the modern ratio is 200 times greater than the ratio at the Flood, the error ends up being 7.618 carbon-14 half-lives, or 43,650 years!

Chapter 12

Radioactive Dating of Rocks?

Dr. Andrew A. Snelling

❦❦❦❦❦❦❦❦❦❦❦❦❦❦❦❦❦❦❦

Most people today think that geologists have proven the earth and its rocks to be billions of years old by their use of the radioactive dating methods. Ages of many millions of years for rocks and fossils are glibly presented as fact in many textbooks, the popular media, and museums.

For decades, the biologists have boldly proclaimed that, whereas we cannot observe today one type of creature evolving into a totally different type of creature, "Time is the hero of the plot. . . . Given so much time, the 'impossible' becomes possible, the possible probable, and the probable virtually certain. One has only to wait: time itself performs the miracles."[1]

Yet few people seem to know how these radiometric dating methods work. No one even bothers to ask what assumptions drive the conclusions. So let's take a closer look at these methods and see how reliable they really are.

Atoms — Basics We Observe Today

Each chemical element, such as carbon and oxygen, consists of atoms unique to it. Each atom is understood to be made up of three basic parts. The nucleus contains protons (tiny particles each with a single positive

---

1. George Wald, "The Origin of Life," *Scientific American* 191, no.2 (1954): p. 48.

electric charge) and neutrons (particles without any electric charge). Orbiting around the nucleus are electrons (tiny particles each with a single electric charge).

The atoms in each chemical element may vary slightly in the numbers of neutrons within their nuclei. These slightly different atoms of the same chemical element are called isotopes of that element. However, while the number of neutrons varies, every atom of any chemical element always has the same number of protons and electrons. So, for example, every carbon atom contains six protons and six electrons, but the number of neutrons in each nucleus can be six, seven, or even eight. Therefore, carbon has three isotopes, which are specified as carbon-12, carbon-13 and carbon-14 (figure 1).

Radioactive Decay

Some isotopes of some elements are radioactive; that is, they are unstable because their nuclei are too large. To achieve stability, these atoms must make adjustments, particularly in their nuclei. In some cases, the isotopes eject particles, primarily neutrons and protons. (These are the moving particles which constitute the radioactivity measured by Geiger counters and the like.) The end result is stable atoms, but of a *different* chemical element (not carbon) because these changes have resulted in the atoms having *different* numbers of protons and electrons.

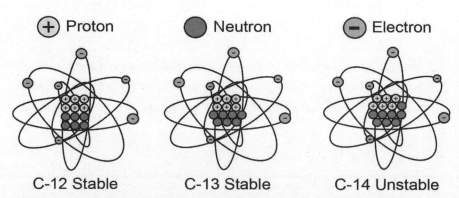

Figure 1. Comparison of stable and unstable atoms of the element carbon. They have six protons in their nuclei and six electrons orbiting their nuclei, which gives carbon its chemical properties. It is the number of neutrons in their nuclei that varies, but too many neutrons make the nuclei unstable, as in carbon-14.

This process of changing the isotope of one element (designated as the parent) into the isotope of another element (referred to as the daughter) is called radioactive decay. Thus, the parent isotopes that decay are called radioisotopes. Actually, it isn't really a decay process in the normal sense of the word, like the decay of fruit. The daughter atoms are not lesser in quality than the parent atoms from which they were produced. Both are complete atoms in every sense of the word. Rather, it is a transmutation process of changing one element into another.

Geologists regularly use five parent isotopes as the basis for the radioactive methods to date rocks: uranium-238, uranium-235, potassium-40, rubidium-87, and samarium-147. These parent radioisotopes change into daughter lead-206, lead-207, argon-40, strontium-87, and neodymium-143 isotopes, respectively. Thus, geologists refer to uranium-lead (two versions), potassium-argon, rubidium-strontium or samarium-neodymium dates for rocks. Note that the carbon-14 (or radiocarbon) method is not used to date rocks, because most rocks do not contain carbon.

Unlike radiocarbon (^{14}C), the other radioactive elements used to date rocks — uranium (^{238}U), potassium (^{40}K), rubidium (^{87}Rb), and samarium (^{147}Sm) — are not being formed today within the earth, as far as we know. Thus it appears that God probably created those elements when He made the original earth.

Chemical Analyses of Rocks Today

Geologists must first choose a suitable rock unit for dating. They must find rocks that contain these parent radioisotopes, even if they are only present in minute amounts. Most often, this is a rock body, or unit, which has formed from the cooling of molten rock material (called magma). Examples are granites (formed by cooling under the ground) and basalts (formed by cooling of lava flows at the earth's surface).

The next step is to measure the amounts of the parent and daughter isotopes in a sample of the rock unit. This is done by chemical analyses in specially equipped laboratories with sophisticated instruments capable of very good accuracy and precision. So, in general, few people quarrel with the resulting chemical analyses.

However, it is the interpretation of these chemical analyses of the parent and daughter isotopes that raises potential problems with these radioactive dating methods. To understand how geologists "read" the age of a rock from these chemical analyses using the radioactive "clock," let's use the analogy of an hourglass "clock" (figure 2).

In an hourglass, grains of fine sand fall at a steady rate from the top glass bowl to the bottom. At time zero, the hourglass is turned upside-down so that all the sand starts in the top bowl. After one hour, all the sand has fallen into the bottom glass bowl. So, after only half an hour, half the sand should be in the top bowl and the other half should be in the bottom glass bowl.

Suppose now that a person, who did not observe when the hourglass was turned upside-down (i.e., time zero), wants to "read" this "clock." He walks into the room and notices that half the sand is in the top bowl, and half the sand is in the bottom bowl. Because he knows the rate at which the sand falls (a full bowl of sand all falls in one hour), and assuming all the sand started in the top bowl, he is able to calculate that the "clock" evidently started half an hour ago.

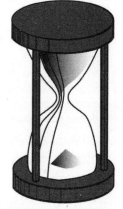

Reading the Radioactive "Clock"

The application of this analogy to reading the radioactive "clock" should be readily apparent. The sand grains in the top glass bowl (figure 2) represent atoms of the parent radioisotope (uranium-238, potassium-40, etc.). The falling of the sand grains

Figure 2. For more information, see page 134.

equates to radioactive decay, while the sand grains at the bottom represent the daughter isotope (lead-206, argon-40, etc.).

When a geologist today collects a rock sample to be dated, he has it analyzed for the parent and daughter isotopes it contains — for example, potassium-40 and argon-40. He then assumes all the daughter argon-40 atoms have been produced by radioactive decay of parent potassium-40 atoms in the rock since the rock formed. So if he knows the rate at which potassium-40 decays radioactively to argon-40 (i.e., the rate at which the sand grains fall), then he can calculate how long it has taken for the argon-40 (measured in the rock today) to form. Since the rock supposedly started with no argon-40 in it when it formed, then this calculated time span back to no argon-40 must be the date when the rock formed (i.e., the rock's age).

The radioactive methods for dating rocks are thus simple to understand. If one knows the rate of radioactive decay of a parent radioisotope in a rock (the sand falling rate in the analogous hourglass "clock" of figure 2), and how much daughter isotope is in the rock today (the quantity of sand at the bottom), then the age of the rock is the time it has taken for the daughter isotope to accumulate in the rock by radioactive decay of the parent radioisotope since the rock formed (since the hourglass "clock" was turned upside-down).

But what if the assumptions are wrong? For example, what if radioactive material was added to the rock (to the top bowl) or if the decay rates have changed since the rock formed?

The Necessary Assumptions

It is not readily apparent from the analogy with an hourglass that the reliability of the radioactive "clocks" is subject to three unprovable assumptions. After all, the reliability of an hourglass can be tested, for example, by turning the hourglass upside-down to start the clock, and by then watching the sand grains fall and timing it with a trustworthy clock. In contrast, no geologist was present when the rock unit to be dated was formed, to see and measure its initial contents. Nor has any geologist been present to measure how fast the radioactive "clocks" have been running in that rock unit through the millions of years that supposedly passed after the rock formed. Thus, there are three critical (but unprovable) assumptions every geologist must make when he dates a rock using the radioactive "clocks":

1. The conditions at time zero when the rock formed are, or can be, known.

2. The radioactive "clocks" in the rock have to be closed to any disturbances or outside interferences (from weathering or ground waters, for instance), that is, all the atoms of the daughter isotopes must have been derived by radioactive decay of atoms of the parent radioisotopes.

3. The radioactive decay rates of the parent radioisotopes must have remained constant through all the supposed millions of years since the rock formed, at the same slow rates we have measured today.

So let's now examine these in more detail.

Assumption 1: Conditions at Time Zero

No geologists were present when most rocks formed, so they cannot test whether the original rocks already contained daughter isotopes alongside their parent radioisotopes. In the case of argon-40, for example, it is simply assumed that none was in the rocks, such as volcanic lavas, when they erupted, flowed, and cooled. For the other radioactive "clocks," it is assumed that by analyzing multiple samples of a rock body, or unit, today it is possible to determine how much of the daughter isotopes (lead, strontium, and neodymium) were present when the rock formed (via the so-called isochron technique, which is still based on unproven assumptions 2 and 3).

Yet many lava flows that have occurred in the present have been tested soon after they erupted, and they invariably contained much more argon-40 than expected.[2] For example, when a sample of the lava in the Mount St. Helens crater (that had been observed to form and cool in 1986) was analyzed in 1996, it contained so much argon-40 that it had a calculated "age" of 350,000 years![3] Similarly, lava flows on the sides of Mt. Ngauruhoe, New Zealand, known to be less than 50 years old, yielded "ages" of up to 3.5 million years.[4] So it is logical to conclude that if recent lava flows of *known* age yield incorrect old potassium-argon ages due to the extra argon-40 that they inherited from the erupting volcanoes, then ancient lava flows of unknown ages could likewise have inherited extra argon-40 and yield excessively old ages.

There are similar problems with the other radioactive "clocks." For example, consider the dating of Grand Canyon basalts (rocks formed by lavas cooling on the earth's surface). In the western Grand Canyon area

2. Dr. Andrew A. Snelling, "Geochemical Processes in the Mantle and Crust," in Larry Vardiman, Dr. Andrew A. Snelling, and Eugene F. Chaffin, editors, *Radioisotopes and the Age of the Earth: A Young-Earth Creationist Research Initiative* (El Cajon, CA: Institute for Creation Research, and St. Joseph, MO: Creation Research Society, 2000), p. 123–304.

3. Steven A. Austin, "Excess Argon within Mineral Concentrates from the New Dacite Lava Dome at Mount St. Helens Volcano," *Creation Ex Nihilo Technical Journal* 10, no.3 (1996): p. 335–343.

4. Dr. Andrew A. Snelling, "'The Cause of Anomalous Potassium-argon 'Ages' for Recent Andesite Flows at Mt. Ngauruhoe, New Zealand, and the Implications for Potassium-argon 'Dating,' " in Robert E Walsh, editor, *Proceedings of the Fourth International Conference on Creationism* (Pittsburgh, PA: Creation Science Fellowship, 1998), p. 503–525.

are former volcanoes on the North Rim that erupted after the canyon it-self was formed, sending lavas cascading over the walls and down into the canyon. Obviously, these eruptions took place recently, after all the layers now exposed in the walls of the canyon were deposited. These basalts yield ages of up to 1 million years based on the amounts of potassium and argon isotopes in these rocks. But when the same rocks are dated using the rubidium and strontium isotopes, an age of 1,143 million years is ob-tained. This is the same as the rubidium-strontium age obtained for an-cient basalt layers deep below the walls of the eastern Grand Canyon.[5] How could both the recent and ancient lavas — one at the top and one at the bottom of the canyon, respectively — be the same age based on the same parent and daughter isotopes? One solution is that both the recent and earlier lava flows inherited the same rubidium-strontium chemistry — not age — from their same source, deep in the earth's upper mantle. This source already had both rubidium and strontium. To make matters even worse for the claimed reliability of these radiometric dating meth-ods, these same young basalts that flowed from the top of the canyon yield a samarium-neodymium age of about 916 million years,[6] and a ura-nium-lead age of about 2.6 billion years![7]

Assumption 2: No Contamination by Disturbances or Interferences

The problems with contamination, as with inheritances, are already well documented in the textbooks on radioactive dating of rocks.[8] Unlike the hourglass, where its two bowls are sealed, the radioactive "clocks" in rocks are open to contamination by gain or loss of parent or daughter

5. Dr. Andrew A. Snelling, "Isochron Discordances and the Role of Inheritances and Mixing of Radioisotopes in the Mantle and Crust," in Larry Vardiman, Dr. Andrew A. Snelling, and Eugene F. Chaffin, editors, *Radioisotopes and the Age of the Earth: Results of a Young-Earth Creationist Research Initiative* (El Cajon, CA: Institute for Creation Research, and Chino Valley, AZ: Creation Research Soci-ety, 2005), p. 393–524; Don B. DeYoung, "Radioisotope Dating Case Studies," in *Thousands . . . Not Billions: Challenging an Icon of Evolution, Questioning the Age of the Earth* (Green Forest, AR: Master Books, 2005), p. 123–139.
6. Ibid.
7. Steven A. Austin, editor, *Grand Canyon: Monument to Catastrophe* (Santee, CA: Institute for Creation Research, 1994), p. 123–126.
8. Gunter Faure and Teresa M. Mensing, *Isotopes: Principles and Applications*, third edition (Hoboken, NJ: John Wiley & Sons, 2005); Alan P Dickin, *Radiogenic Iso-tope Geology*, second edition (Cambridge, UK: Cambridge University Press, 2005).

isotopes because of waters flowing in the ground from rainfall infiltration and from molten rocks beneath volcanoes. Similarly, as molten lava rises through a conduit from deep inside the earth to be erupted through a volcano, pieces of the conduit wallrocks and their isotopes can mix into the lava and contaminate it. Because of such contamination, the less than 50-years-old lava flows at Mt. Ngauruhoe, New Zealand, yield a rubidium-strontium "age" of 133 million years, a samarium-neodymium "age" of 197 million years, and a uranium-lead "age" of 3,908 million years![9]

Assumption 3: Constant Decay Rates

Physicists have carefully measured the radioactive decay rates of parent radioisotopes in laboratories over the last 100 or so years and have found them to be essentially constant (within the measurement error margins). Furthermore, they have not been able to significantly change these decay rates by heat, pressure, or electrical and magnetic fields. So geologists have assumed these radioactive decay rates have been constant for billions of years. However, this is an enormous extrapolation of seven orders of magnitude back through immense spans of unobserved time without any concrete proof that such an extrapolation is credible. Nevertheless, geologists insist the radioactive decay rates have always been constant, because it makes these radioactive "clocks" work!

New evidence, however, has recently been discovered that can only be explained by the radioactive decay rates *not* having been constant in the past.[10] For example, the radioactive decay of uranium in tiny crystals in a New Mexico granite yields a uranium-lead "age" of 1.5 billion years. Yet the *same* uranium decay also produced abundant helium, but only 6,000 years' worth of that helium was found to have leaked out of those tiny crystals. This helium leakage is definitely more accurate as a dating method, because it is based on well-known physical laws. So this means that the uranium must have decayed very rapidly over the same 6,000 years

9. Dr. Andrew A. Snelling, "The Relevance of Rb-Sr, Sm-Nd and Pb-Pb Isotope Systematics to Elucidation of the Genesis and History of Recent Andesite Flows at Mt. Ngauruhoe, New Zealand, and the Implications for Radioisotope Dating," in Robert L. Ivey, Jr., editor, *Proceedings of the Fifth International Conference on Creationism* (Pittsburgh, PA: Creation Science Fellowship, 2003), p. 285–303; DeYoung, "Radioisotope Dating Case Studies," p. 123–139.
10. Vardiman, Snelling, and Chaffin, *Radioisotopes and the Age of the Earth*; DeYoung, *Thousands . . . Not Billions.*

that the helium was leaking. The rate of uranium decay must have been at least 250,000 times faster than today's measured rate, because the decay products (lead and helium) equivalent to 1.5 billion years of slow decay have in fact accumulated in only 6,000 years!

Thus, the necessary assumptions on which the radioactive "clocks" for the dating of rocks are based are unprovable. No geologists were there to test these clocks in the past, but they have been demonstrated, even by secular geologists, to be plagued with problems. Rocks may have inherited parent and daughter isotopes from their sources, or they may have been contaminated when they moved through other rocks to their current locations. Or inflowing water may have mixed isotopes into the rocks. In addition, the radioactive decay rates have not been constant. So if these clocks are based on faulty assumptions and yield unreliable results, then scientists should not trust or promote the claimed radioactive "ages" of countless millions of years, especially since they contradict the true history of the universe as recorded in God's Word.

So we have seen that even though the general principles of using radioisotopes to date rocks, and the chemical analyses involved, seem sound, anomalous and conflicting results are frequently obtained, as documented in the secular literature. Thus the claimed "ages" of many millions of years are totally unreliable.

Does this mean we should throw out the radioactive "clocks"? Surprisingly, they are useful! The general principles of using radioisotopes to date rocks are sound; it's just that the assumptions have been wrong and led to exaggerated dates. While the clocks cannot yield absolute dates for rocks, they can provide relative ages that allow us to compare any two rock units and know which one formed first. They also allow us to compare rock units in different areas of the world to find which ones formed at the same time. Furthermore, if physicists examine why the same rocks yield different dates, they may discover new clues about the unusual behavior of radioactive elements during the past.

Different Dates for the Same Rocks

Usually geologists do not use all four main radioactive clocks to date a rock unit. This is considered an unnecessary waste of time and money. After all, if these clocks really do work, then they should all yield the same

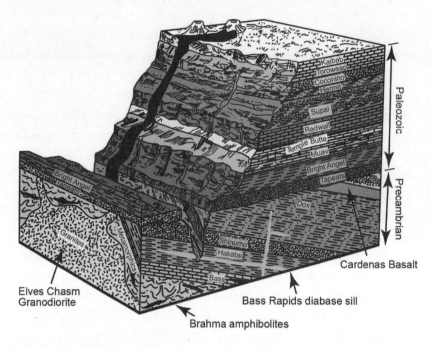

Figure 3. A geologic diagram to schematically show the rock layers exposed in the walls and inner gorge of the Grand Canyon and their relationships to one another. The deeper rocks were formed first, and the rock layers higher in the walls were deposited on top of them. The named rock units mentioned in the text are indicated.

age for a given rock unit. Sometimes though, using different parent radio-isotopes to date different samples (or minerals) from the same rock unit does yield different ages, hinting that something is amiss.[11]

Recent research has utilized all four common radioactive clocks to date the same samples from the same rock units.[12] Among these were

11. Thomas Oberthür, Donald W. Davis, Thomas G Blenkinsop, and Axel Höhndorf, "Precise U-Pb Mineral Ages, Rb-Sr and Sm-Nd Systematics of the Great Dyke, Zimbabwe — Constraints on Late Archean Events in the Zimbabwe Craton and Limpopo Belt," *Precambrian Research* 113 (2002): p. 293–305; Stephen B. Mukasa, Alan H. Wilson, and Richard W. Carlson, "A Multielement Geochrono-logic Study of the Great Dyke, Zimbabwe: Significance of the Robust and Reset Ages," *Earth and Planetary Science Letters* 164 (1998): p. 353–369; Jian-xin Zhao, and Malcolm T. McCulloch, "Sm-Nd Mineral Isochron Ages of Late Proterozoic Dyke Swarms in Australia: Evidence for Two Distinctive Events of Mafic Mag-matism and Crustal Extension," *Chemical Geology* 109 (1993): p. 341–354.
12. Snelling, "Isochron Discordances and the Role of Inheritances and Mixing of Radioisotopes in the Mantle and Crust," p. 393–524; DeYoung, "Radioisotope Dating Case Studies," p. 123-139.

four rock units far down in the Grand Canyon rock sequence (figure 3), chosen because they are well known and characterized. These were as follows:

1. Cardenas Basalt (lava flows deep in the east canyon sequence).

2. Bass Rapids diabase sill (where basalt magma squeezed between layers and cooled).

3. Brahma amphibolites (basalt lava flows deep in the canyon sequence that later metamorphosed).

4. Elves Chasm Granodiorite (a granite regarded as the oldest canyon rock unit).

Table 1 lists the dates obtained. Figure 4 graphically illustrates the ranges in the supposed ages of these rock units, obtained by utilizing all four radioactive clocks.

It is immediately apparent that the ages for each rock unit do not agree. Indeed, in the Cardenas Basalt, for example, the rubidium-strontium age is more than double the potassium-argon age, and the samarium-neodymium age is three times the potassium-argon age.

Nevertheless, the ages follow three obvious patterns. Two techniques (potassium-argon and rubidium-strontium) *always* yield younger ages than two other techniques (uranium-lead and samarium-neodymium). Furthermore, the potassium-argon ages are *always* younger than the rubidium-strontium ages. And often the samarium-neodymium ages are

Rock Unit	Ages (million years)			
	Potassium-argon	Rubidium-strontium	Uranium-lead	Samarium-neodymium
Cardenas Basalt	516 (±30)	1111 (±81)	–	1588 (±170)
Bass Rapids diabase sill	842 (±164)	1060 (±24)	1250 (±130)	1379 (±140)
Brahma amphibolites	–	1240 (±84)	1883 (±53)	1655 (±40)
Elves Chasm Granodiorite	–	1512 (±140)	1933 (±220)	1664 (±200)

Table 1. Radioactive ages yielded by four Grand Canyon rock units. (The error margins are shown in parentheses.)

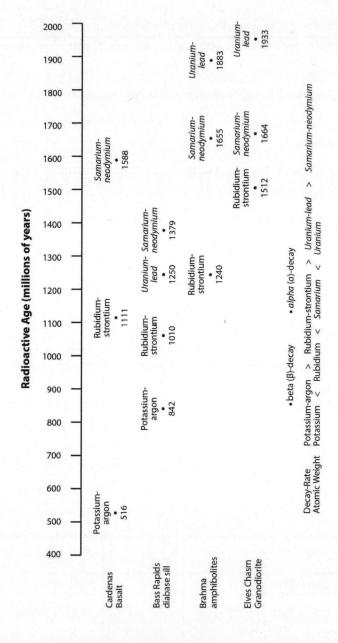

Figure 4. The comparative spread of ages for these four Grand Canyon rock units determined by the different radioactive methods on the same samples from these rock units. No two methods agree, and the ranges of ages enormous, well beyond the analytical errors inherent in all laboratory measurements. Indicated on the diagram are the two types of radioactive decay. The systematic patterns of ages obtained follow according to decay type, decay rate, and the atomic weights, suggesting an underlying physical cause for the acceleration of radioactive decay in the past.

younger than the uranium-lead ages.

What then do these patterns mean? All the radioactive clocks in each rock unit should have started "ticking" at the same time, the instant that each rock unit was formed. So how do we explain that they have each recorded different ages? The answer is simple but profound. Each of the radioactive elements must have decayed at different, faster rates in the past! In the case of the Cardenas Basalt, while the potassium-argon clock ticked through 516 million years, the rubidium-strontium clock must have ticked through 1,111 million years, and the samarium-neodymium clock through 1,588 million years. So if these clocks ticked at such different rates in the past, not only are they inaccurate, but these rocks may not be millions of years old!

But how could radioactive decay rates have been different in the past? We don't fully understand yet. However, the observed age patterns provide clues. Potassium and rubidium decay radioactively by the process known as beta (β) decay, whereas uranium and neodymium decay via alpha (α) decay (figure 4). The former *always* give younger ages. We see another pattern *within* beta decay. Potassium today decays faster than rubidium and *always* gives younger ages. Both of these patterns suggest something happened in the past inside the nuclei of these parent atoms to accelerate their decay. The decay rate varied based on the stability or instability of the parent atoms. Research is continuing.

Relative Ages

Look again at figure 3, which is a geologic diagram depicting the rock layers in the walls of the Grand Canyon, along with the rock units deep in the inner gorge along the Colorado River. This diagram shows that the radiometric dating methods accurately confirm the top rock layer is younger than the layers beneath it. That's logical, because the sediment making up that layer was deposited on top of, and therefore after, the layers below. So reading this diagram tells us basic information about the time that rock layers and rock units were formed relative to other layers.

Based on the radioactive clocks, we can conclude that these four rock units deep in the gorge (table 1) are all older in a relative sense than the horizontal sedimentary layers in the canyon walls. Conventionally the lowermost or oldest of these horizontal sedimentary layers is labeled early to middle Cambrian,[13] and thus regarded as about 510 to 520 million years old.[14] All the rocks below it are then labeled Precambrian and re-

---

13. Larry T. Middleton and David K. Elliott, "Tonto Group," in Stanley S. Beus and Michael Morales, editors, *Grand Canyon Geology*, second edition (New York: Oxford University Press, 2003), p. 90–106.
14. Felix M. Gradstein, James G. Ogg, and Alan G. Smith, editors, *A Geologic Time Scale 2004* (Cambridge, UK: Cambridge University Press, 2004).

garded as older than 542 million years. So, accordingly, all four dated rock units (table 1) are Precambrian (figure 3). And apart from the potassium-argon age for the Cardenas Basalt, all the radioactive clocks have correctly shown that these four rock units were formed earlier than the Cambrian, so they are *pre*-Cambrian. (But the passage of time between these Precambrian rock units and the horizontal sedimentary layers above them was a maximum of about 1,650 years — the time between creation and the Flood — not millions of years.)

Similarly, in the relative sense, the Brahma amphibolites and Elves Chasm Granodiorite are older (by hours or days) than the Cardenas Basalt and Bass Rapids diabase sill (figure 3). Once again, the radioactive clocks have correctly shown that those two rock units are older than the rock units above them.

Why then should we expect the radioactive clocks to yield relative ages that follow a logical pattern? (Actually, younger sedimentary layers yield a similar general pattern[15] — figure 5.) The answer is again simple but profound! The radioactive clocks in the rock units at the bottom of the Grand Canyon, formed during the creation week, have been ticking for longer than the radioactive clocks in the younger sedimentary layers higher up in the sequence that were formed later during the Flood.

Therefore, although it is a mistake to accept radioactive dates of millions of years, the clocks can still be useful to us, in principle, to date the relative sequence of rock formation during earth history. The different clocks have ticked at different, faster rates in the past, so the standard old ages are certainly not accurate, correct, or absolute. However, because the radioactive clocks in rocks that formed early in earth history have been ticking longer, they should generally yield older radioactive ages than rock layers formed later. So it is possible that relative radioactive ages of rocks, in addition to mineral contents and other rock features, could be used to compare and correlate similar rocks in other areas, to find which ones formed at the same time during the events detailed in Genesis, God's eyewitness account of earth history.

---

15. D. Russell Humphreys, "Accelerated nuclear decay: a viable hypothesis?" in Larry Vardiman, Dr. Andrew A. Snelling, and Eugene F. Chaffin, editors, *Radioisotopes and the Age of the Earth: A Young-Earth Creationist Research Initiative* (El Cajon, California: Institute for Creation Research, and St. Joseph, Missouri: Creation Research Society, 2000), p. 333–379.

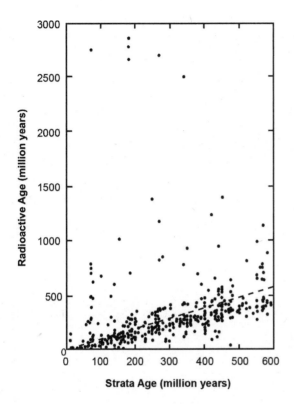

Figure 5. In general, the radioactive ages of rock layers match the ages for the strata according to their relative positions in the rock record. In this diagram the radioactive ages for rock units (vertical axis) are plotted against the strata ages determined by relative positions (horizontal axis). It can be clearly seen that often there is agreement, with the radioactive ages being in the right order according to the relative positions of the rock layers in the sequence. This is exactly what would be produced by an underlying systematic physical cause for accelerated radioactive decay.

Chapter 13

The Shroud of Turin — Was It in the Grave with Christ?

Bodie Hodge

⟨❋❋❋❋❋❋❋❋❋❋❋❋❋❋❋❋❋❋⟩

An amazing cloth shroud, about 14.3 feet (4 m) long and 3.7 feet (1 m) wide, first appeared in 1357 in France and is now stored in Turin, Italy (hence the name Shroud of *Turin*). The cloth has a realistic imprint that looks like a man's face (as well as a body) in a *negative image* style (think negative image in photography or photo software).

According to tradition, the shroud's image was miraculously formed upon the Resurrection as it covered Jesus' body in the tomb. Some people quote Matthew 27:59, Mark 15:46, and Luke 23:53 to justify the possibility of this miracle. These verses seem to indicate that a single cloth was used to wrap Jesus when He was taken off the Cross. But was this same cloth wrapped around Jesus' body when it was placed in the tomb? There will be more on this in a moment.

Claims, Controversy, and Caution

Some have claimed the shroud was actually in the possession of Thomas and Thaddeus Jude and was taken to Edessa (a town in the Middle East) soon after the Resurrection of Christ. How it arrived in France is a whole different question.

In modern times, there have been a number of experiments performed on the shroud. One of the most controversial was a Carbon-14

(C14) analysis. C14 can only give dates in the range of thousands of years and is very inaccurate due to the many assumptions involved.[1] By the way, it cannot give dates in the "millions of years" category, which is a common misconception (i.e., if the whole earth was C14, in one million years there would be none). People often use C14 on archeological things that were made of carbon (like nuts, cloth, etc.).

With the shroud being made of cloth, it was a C14 candidate. The results came out to be "medieval" (i.e., about 1,500 years ago), so many discounted the shroud. But later results showed that the piece used for dating was a sample of cloth used to repair the shroud, and hence "back to the drawing board." At any rate, a number of experiments and peer-reviewed papers have been published looking at various aspects (and such research should be commended, by the way).[2]

Before we get caught up in the details of "who says what" and "who concluded this" about this shroud found in France, we should go to the source material to get a proper foundation: and so we turn to the Bible. There have been a number of arguments for and against the authenticity of the Shroud of Turin.[3]

Does the Bible Say the Shroud of Turin Was in the Grave with Christ?

First, the Shroud of Turin is not mentioned by name in the Bible. Nor would we expect it to be. But as pointed out before, many have appealed to a large linen cloth that was used to take Christ's body from the Cross and was presumably buried with Him.[4]

After the Crucifixion, Jesus' body would have been bloody from Pilate's ordered whipping (Matthew 27:26), the crown of thorns (Matthew 27:29), and the nails driven into His hands and feet (Acts 2:23). More

---

1. Ken Ham, general editor, *New Answers Book 1* (Green Forest, AR: Master Books, 2006), p. 77–87.
2. Much of this information is common knowledge and found on numerous websites surrounding the Shroud of Turin such as www.shroud.com and http://shroudstory.wordpress.com/.
3. Norman Geisler, *Baker Encyclopedia of Christian Apologetics* (Grand Rapids, MI :Baker Books, 1999), p. 705–706.
4. Some may argue that it would have been another shroud altogether, but then they lose Luke 23:50–54, Mark 15:44–46, and Matthew 27:58–60 as support for their argument.

blood and water flowed from the spear wound in His side (John 19:34). So this cloth would have absorbed a lot of blood and was likely used to help initially clean the body of Christ. Now did this cloth remain on Jesus' body as it was carried to the grave? From a cursory look at the accounts in Matthew, Mark, and Luke, we might think so.

John, however, reveals more details (John 19:38–40).[5] Joseph of Arimathea took the body prior to its placement in the grave. Later Nicodemus joined him, applying about 75 pounds of spices and wrapping the body in strips of linen. To apply the spices, the caretakers must have removed the bloody linen covering Christ at the Cross. We have no reason to assume that they reused this single cloth. Instead, we would expect them to have followed Jewish customs of cleanliness to clean the body and use *fresh clean* linens to wrap the body.

Also, no Gospel author mentions a second single-cloth linen around Jesus's body — only a small cloth wrapped (denoted as a handkerchief) around Jesus' face and several other linen strips around the rest of his body (John 20:7). In fact, John indicates Lazarus was given the same kind of burial (John 11:43–44).

At Jesus' Resurrection, both John and Luke mention the strips of linen and the cloth on His face (Luke 24:12; John 20:3–7). They mention nothing else. From a biblical perspective, we have no reason to assume any other cloths were present in the tomb. We need to be careful not to impose our previously existing ideas about the shroud on the Bible, contrary to reasonable inferences, which is not the way to rightly divide the word of truth (2 Timothy 2:15). The Bible, when read carefully and in context, mentions no shroud in the *grave* cloths.

Doesn't the Bible Say There Was One Burial Shroud?

People have placed the shroud in the grave using Matthew 27:59, Mark 15:46, or Luke 23:53. They sometimes claimed this was the shroud that may have helped cover Jesus *along* with linen strips. Here are the verses:

---

5. See also, Mark Looy, "According to the Bible, It's not Shrouded in Mystery at All!" Answers in Genesis, http://www.answersingenesis.org/articles/2006/02/14/shrouded-in-mystery; Bodie Hodge, "Feedback: Testing the Shroud of Turin," June 5, 2009, Answers in Genesis, http://www.answersingenesis.org/articles/2009/06/05/feedback-testing-the-shroud-of-turin, Ken Ham and Bodie Hodge, Problematic Apologetics, *Answers* magazine, vol. 4, no. 2 (April–June 2009): p. 70–73.

He went to Pilate and asked for the body of Jesus. Then Pilate ordered it to be given to him. And Joseph took the body and wrapped it in a clean linen shroud and claid it in his own new tomb, which he had cut in the rock. And he rolled a great stone to the entrance of the tomb and went away (Matthew 27:58–60; ESV).

Pilate was surprised to hear that he should have already died.1 And summoning the centurion, he asked him whether he was already dead. And when he learned from the centurion that he was dead, he granted the corpse to Joseph. And Joseph bought a linen shroud, and taking him down, wrapped him in the linen shroud and laid him in a tomb that had been cut out of the rock. And he rolled a stone against the entrance of the tomb (Mark 15:44–46; ESV).

Now there was a man named Joseph, from the Jewish town of Arimathea. He was a member of the council, a good and righteous man, who had not consented to their decision and action; and he was looking for the kingdom of God. This man went to Pilate and asked for the body of Jesus. Then he took it down and wrapped it in a linen shroud and laid him in a tomb cut in stone, where no one had ever yet been laid. It was the day of Preparation, and the Sabbath was beginning (Luke 23:50–54; ESV).

These verses indicate there was a single cloth,[6] but was this the same cloth allegedly wrapping Jesus *in the grave*? The cloth that Matthew, Mark, and Luke mention is a clean linen cloth that wrapped Jesus' body when His body *came off the Cross*. At this point, Christ's body was severely bloody/messy with the Scriptures revealing the nail marks in the hands and feet (Acts 2:23), the beating he took prior to being put on the Cross (Matthew 27:26), the shoving of a crown of thorns into his head (Matthew 27:29), and the flow of blood and water from the spear (John 19:34). Therefore, this initial cloth, which was clean, *wouldn't be* after taking Jesus' body from the Cross. In essence, the linen was used for the first cleansing of the body. Therefore, the question becomes, did this linen cloth go directly from the Cross to the grave? As mentioned before, from a glance at these passages, it would appear so.

---

6. Strong's Number: 4616, *sindon*.

John offered clarity on this misconception as he gives more detail. So the passages in Matthew, Mark, and Luke were merely giving the highlights. Note that John says:

> After these things Joseph of Arimathea, who was a disciple of Jesus, but secretly for fear of the Jews, asked Pilate that he might take away the body of Jesus, and Pilate gave him permission. So he came and took away his body. Nicodemus also, who earlier had come to Jesus by night, came bringing a mixture of myrrh and aloes, about seventy-five pounds in weight. So they took the body of Jesus and bound it in linen cloths with the spices, as is the burial custom of the Jews. Now in the place where he was crucified there was a garden, and in the garden a new tomb in which no one had yet been laid. So because of the Jewish day of Preparation, since the tomb was close at hand, they laid Jesus there (John 19:38–42; ESV).

John indicates that Joseph of Arimathea took the body away *prior to* entering the grave. Then Nicodemus joined him with about 75 pounds of spices of myrrh and aloes, and wraps the body in strips of linen. By applying the spices to the body, the previous linen *must have* been removed and there is no biblical indication that this linen was reused.

There is no reason to assume this "now dirty" linen was re-used to wrap the body of Christ. Also, there is no mention of another single-cloth linen used to wrap Christ's body — only a small burial cloth used to wrap the face of Jesus (John 20:7). The linens and burial cloth around the head were the biblical burial customs. Again, John records that Lazarus' grave clothes were nearly identical — strips of linen and a cloth around his face, but no extra linen shroud:

> When he had said these things, he cried out with a loud voice, "Lazarus, come out." The man who had died came out, his hands and feet bound with linen strips, and his face wrapped with a cloth. Jesus said to them, "Unbind him, and let him go" (John 11:43–44; ESV).

Since Lazarus could walk, his legs were not constrained by a large wrapped cloth about his body. This is further confirmation that a shroud was not wrapping the whole body, but strips do make sense. Recall that both John *and Luke* record at Jesus' Resurrection that there were strips of linen and the burial cloth that wrapped the face. They mention nothing else.

> Peter, however, got up and ran to the tomb. Bending over, he saw the strips of linen [othonia in Greek] lying by themselves, and he went away, wondering to himself what had happened (Luke 24:12; ESV).

> So Peter went out with the other disciple, and they were going toward the tomb. Both of them were running together, but the other disciple outran Peter and reached the tomb first. And stooping to look in, he saw the linen cloths lying there, but he did not go in. Then Simon Peter came, following him, and went into the tomb. He saw the linen cloths lying there, and the face cloth, which had been on Jesus' head, not lying with the linen cloths but folded up in a place by itself. (John 20:3–7; ESV).

There is no cause to appeal to the strips of linens miraculously bonding together (which I did have one person appeal to in a letter). There is no reason to assume there were any other cloths present in the tomb. To do so would be to take ideas *to* the Bible and not derive deductions *from* the Bible. In other words, this would be taking man's ideas as a greater authority than God (i.e., a form of humanism).

Stevenson and Habermas argue that ancient Jewish sources (Essene burial procedures and *Code of Jewish Law*) reveal that a large cloth *was* used in the burial. They further argue that *othonia* (usually translated as "strips of linen") refers to *all* the grave clothes . . . as in Luke 24:12 including these other cloths (handkerchief around the face and the shroud.)[7]

If *othonia* referred to all the grave clothes, then why didn't John use this term the same way? Instead, John used this term but it excluded some grave clothes (e.g., the separate facial burial cloth that was not counted among the strips of linen). This is found in John 20:6–7, where the handkerchief was *not* lying with the strips of linen, whereas Luke mentions

---

7. Kenneth Stevenson and Gary Habermas, *Verdict on the Shroud* (Ann Arbor, MI: Servant Books, 1981), p. 48–49. Much of this book discusses some fascinating aspects and research of the Shroud of Turin.

that the linens (*othonia*) were together — which can indeed be the strips of linen, but cannot be *all* the grave clothes as argued by Stevenson and Habermas. It may be too much to assume that this word (*othonia*) was in reference to anything but the strips of linen.

From a biblical viewpoint, there was virtually no possibility of a blood-ridden, dirty, unclean, shroud of linen used to bury the Son of God, especially in light of Jewish burial customs based on high levels of cleanliness. And the Scriptures do not mention any other such linen in the grave with Christ.

Could the Shroud of Turin have been the initial cloth used to take Christ from the Cross (just not used as the grave clothes)?

Since there are obvious problems with a biblical shroud being in the grave with Christ, one must turn to other options. Whatever happened to the shroud that covered Jesus initially to clean him? The Bible doesn't say. It belonged to Joseph of Arimathea but it is possible that Nicodemus took it. Did this cloth get into the hands of Thomas and Thaddeus Jude and finally make its way to Liray, France? We simply don't know.

Any grave clothes of Christ should have been laced heavily with burial spices, of which the Shroud of Turin has none. But if the Shroud of Turin was this initial cloth used to clean Christ, then we would expect it to be absent of spices, which were added later after this linen was removed. Was the Shroud of Turin used to clean Christ when His body was removed from the Cross? I would leave open the possibility but even so, we can never be certain. But it is intriguing.

Conclusion

The Bible reveals no large *burial* cloth when Christ was buried. Instead, strips of linen and a head cloth are repeatedly mentioned. So one should not be dogmatic about the Shroud of Turin being *in the grave* with Christ.

Is it possible that the Shroud of Turin was the linen used to remove Christ from the Cross? It is possible, but again we cannot be sure (of course, this would refute the common claim that the image was made at the Resurrection in the grave). Is the Shroud of Turin an interesting item with some fascinating features? No doubt! Should it be studied? No doubt!

Even then, there are more questions than answers. Many doubt the authenticity of the Shroud since its public awareness came at a time in medieval Europe when the forging of "sacred relics" became commonplace. Using oil paint on glass and using light to expose it to linen can make an image very similar to that found on the Shroud.[8]

It is not the purpose of this chapter to look at all Shroud-related questions, but in all speculative things exercise caution and realize that the existence of God and the truthfulness of the Bible have little if anything to do with the Shroud of Turin.

---

8. http://www.shadowshroud.com/, accessed 5/16/2012, specifically images and process explanation: http://www.shadowshroud.com/images.htm

Chapter 14

Chronology Wars?

Larry Pierce

❀❀❀❀❀❀❀❀❀❀❀❀❀❀❀❀❀❀

Have you ever wondered how the early history of Egypt and other ancient nations fits within biblical history? You're not alone. In the centuries before Christ, a war broke out to see which nation had the oldest pedigree, whether real or invented. Just as an arms race raged between the super-powers in the 1960s, so an age race raged among the ancient civilizations in the centuries before Christ's birth. Each claimed to have the oldest history. While some writers seemed interested in the truth, others were playing a game to see who could spin the biggest and most convincing yarn about the antiquity of their nation.

Greece's history supposedly went back 1,800 years; Egypt's, 11,000 years; and Babylon's, a whopping 730,000 years.[1]

In the first centuries after Christ, Christians like Eusebius (the "father of church history") tried to reconstruct an accurate world chronology, reconciling the Bible with pagan chronologies, but with little success. The ancient king lists had been so doctored that it proved impossible to sort out the truth. Ever since, Christians and non-Christians have been trying to make sense of ancient chronologies, with equal frustration.

---

1. In this chapter, unless noted otherwise, references cite paragraph numbers in *Newton's Revised History of Ancient Kingdoms* (Green Forest, AR: Master Books, 2009). These numbers are from paragraphs 193–194.

Isaac Newton to the Rescue

No less a person than Isaac Newton, sometimes called "the greatest mind of all time," dabbled in this topic throughout his life. He eventually collected his thoughts into a book, *The Chronology of Ancient Kingdoms Amended* (1728), published a year after he died.

Though he did not have the advantage of modern archaeology, Newton was so well read in the classical Greek and Latin writers that he was able to detect serious problems in the dating of ancient records before 700 B.C. His basic claims are solid:

- God's Word is correct in every detail, including its history, so it must be our starting point (par. 410–415).

- Except for the Bible itself, the other histories of early nations were not recorded until well after the events had passed (par. 483–484). For example, the first historian to write about ancient Egypt (apart from Moses) was Herodotus (c. 484–425 B.C.).

- Most records of early history were lost or distorted as a result of repeated foreign invasions (par. 517).

- Ancient peoples were not averse to making big assumptions to fill in the gaps (par. 193).

Newton alludes to the Persian invasion of Egypt as an example. In 525–523 B.C. the Persians under Cambyses invaded Egypt and destroyed most of the historical records that the Assyrians and other previous nations had missed. The Egyptian priests were left to reconstruct most of their history from memory, and their efforts were not without guile.

Newton explains, "After Cambyses had carried away the records of Egypt, the priests were daily feigning new kings, to make their gods and nation look more ancient" (par. 517). When Herodotus visited Egypt in the mid-fifth century B.C., the priests had constructed a list of 341 Egyptian kings reigning some 11,340 years! Even Herodotus was dubious.

Fishy Figures

Newton points out that except for biblical history, early historians did not use absolute dates until around 250 B.C. Before that time, they usually marked time by the reign of kings. The Greeks, Romans, and Egyptians assumed that an average of three kings reigned for every century, and they pigeonholed dates accordingly (par. 204).

Newton asked himself, "Is this reasonable?" He then analyzed the dynasties of a dozen other known kingdoms, such as the English monarchs. To his surprise the average reign was only 18 to 20 years, about half of what ancient pagan historians had claimed. Even in biblical times, the kings of the Southern Kingdom ruled an average of a little over 21 years each, while those of the Northern Kingdom reigned about 17 years each.

Newton was particularly interested in Greek history because the Greeks were the first to record their history, and they connected many events to the Olympiads, which were held every four years. By pinning down important dates in Greece's history, such as Jason's expedition with the Argonauts, Newton believed he could easily connect this fixed date to events in other countries.

Applying what he learned about the average length of a king's reign, half of Greece's recorded history before 700 B.C. evaporated! For example, the Trojan War and Argonaut expedition were much more recent than is usually assumed, Newton argued. He also found that other king lists, such as the list of Roman kings, had exaggerated the length of their reigns, and so the lists should be cut in half. Newton then proceeded to look at the histories of other nations, such as Egypt, rejecting any fictitious names or mythological eras. By his reckoning, based on the information available in his day, he calculated that only 22 names reflected real kings in ancient Egypt (par. 486).

Putting Together the Pieces

As Alexander's empire splintered into warring kingdoms, each competed to spin the biggest yarn. Few historical accounts have survived from authors who lived before Alexander the Great (356–323 B.C.) led his Greek army across the "known world," conquering the former domains of Babylonia/Assyria/Persia, Egypt, and India. Older histories are sometimes quoted by later authors, but the works themselves do not survive. So we must rely on the later authors.

The problem is that as Alexander's empire splintered into warring factions ruled by his generals, each kingdom had a vested interest in promoting its own history.

Manetho's History of Egypt

A veritable "cottage industry" of fabricated histories flourished after Alexander's death. Possibly most famous of these new historians was Manetho (third century B.C.), who lived in Egypt. He recorded a long series of Egyptian dynasties that the priests told him about. But his history shared little in common with what Herodotus had recorded two hundred years earlier.

Two centuries after Manetho, a Greek historian named Diodorus Siculus wrote a new version of Egyptian history. He ignored the dynasties of Manetho and reduced the number of Egyptian kings back down to only a handful of men, as Herodotus had done. But he also rejected Herodotus and other older writers "who deliberately preferred to the truth the telling of marvelous tales and the invention of myths for the delectation [delight] of their readers."[2]

What a mess! Newton rejected the work of Manetho and tried instead to reconcile the histories of Diodorus and Herodotus. While he acknowledged that other kings' names in Manetho's list might be confirmed, he believed the final list would be nowhere near as long as Manetho's (par. 515).

Berossus's History of Babylonia

Over the centuries, the priests in Babylon had produced their own fabulous lists of kings, along with many myths. Using these sources, a Babylonian astronomer named Berossus wrote a three-book History of Babylonia (c. 290–278 B.C.). His version of Babylonian history includes legendary kings from creation to the mythical Babylonian flood, spanning hundreds of thousands of years.

Greek Histories of Various City-States

The jealous city-states of Greece also got into the war of histories. Since Greece did not have historical records of its ancient kings, as Egypt and Babylon did, they began to make them up. For example, the "historian" Castor of Rhodes (first century B.C.) invented early dates for the Greek gods and made up a long list of kings, beginning with Aegialeus,

---

2. Diodorus Siculus, *Library of History*, Book 1, p. 69; http://penelope.uchicago.edu/Thayer/E/Roman/Texts/Diodorus_Siculus/1D*.html.

the supposed founder of Sicyon. Argos invented its own king Inachus, and Athens got a king named Ogyges.[3]

The Lesson for Today

This confusion about ancient chronology has profound implications for us today. The ultimate goal in studying ancient dates, obviously, is accuracy; and accuracy demands that the dates coincide perfectly with Scripture.[4]

Yet today almost all dating of ancient history is based on a foundation of sand, not the rock of Scripture. Modern secular historians have a deep bias against Scripture, and they interpret history with a "hermeneutic of suspicion," as Egyptologist James K. Hoffmeier writes.[5] Even theologians sometimes try to expand the chronologies in Genesis 5 and 11 to accommodate the supposed history of other ancient cultures. The biblical text is assumed to be inaccurate right out of the gate.

Isaac Newton had the right approach. Nothing in ancient history (when properly understood) can possibly conflict with biblical history. As archaeologists continue to make exciting new discoveries, we have nothing to worry about. God's eyewitness record is 100 percent true and reliable, the only sure starting point for studying the time-line of human history.

---

3. "Perhaps to match the Orientals, Greek writers manufactured genealogical tables which traced the pedigree of famous Greek cities to remote antiquity" (ref. 2, p. 451). On the first kings of Greek city-states, see ref. 2, p. 464–468, 474. See also ref. 1, par. 383.
4. The effort to reconcile ancient secular chronologies is extremely complex, and many questions remain unsolved. Several scholars are trying to piece together an accurate chronology that matches Scripture, though with varying levels of success, including John Bimson's *Redating the Exodus and Conquest* and David Rohl's *A Test of Time: The Bible from Myth to History*. However, all attempts to reconstruct Egyptian history based on Manetho's fictious king lists are doomed to failure, no matter how well intentioned.
5. See his book, *Israel in Egypt: The Evidence for the Authenticity of the Exodus Tradition* (New York: Oxford University Press, 1996), p. 4.

Chapter 15

Has Noah's Ark Been Found?

Bodie Hodge

❧❧❧❧❧❧❧❧❧❧❧❧❧❧❧❧❧❧❧❧

Introduction

As with many questions, there are always debates, and the questions surrounding the search for Noah's ark are no different. However, one debate most people are probably *somewhat* familiar with, or have at the very least considered, is "Has Noah's ark been found?" There is actually much more to this than meets the eye. As we delve into this topic, some other questions arise:

Where exactly does the Bible say the ark landed?

Is there any other ancient literature on this subject that could help?

Where are the mountains of Ararat?

What can we gather from the geology of Mt. Ararat?

Entire volumes could be written on this subject of the ark, and some have been written already. However, the aim here is to provide some concise answers to the best of our ability to the many questions about the ark in an overview format. And the best place to start is with the Bible.

Biblical Data

The Bible gives some information about the ark:

- Its overall dimensions were 300 by 50 by 30 cubits (Genesis 6:15). Using the short or common cubit (~18 inches), it would have been about 450 feet long; or using a longer royal cubit (~20.4 inches), it would have been around 510 feet long.[1]

- It was made of wood (gopher)[2] — Genesis 6:14.

- It was covered with pitch inside and out — Genesis 6:14.

- The ark had rooms — Genesis 6:14.

- It had three decks — Genesis 6:16.

- The ark had a covering — Genesis 8:13.

- It had a window (Hebrew: *tsohar,* which means "noon"), which was finished to a cubit from above (think of something like a "ridge vent" on houses today for ventilation and lighting) and could be opened and shut (though Noah did not open it until 40 days after they landed on the mountains of Ararat — Genesis 6:16, 8:6.

- The ark was made/fabricated, and done so with godly fear — Genesis 6:14–15, 6:22; Hebrews 11:7.

- One of its purposes was to house land-dwelling, air-breathing animals during the Flood with a male-female pair from each of the representative kinds[3] of the unclean animals and seven individuals (or pairs — the meaning is debated) of the clean animals

1. Bodie Hodge, "How Long Was the Original Cubit?" *Answers* magazine (April–June 2007): p. 82, http://www.answersingenesis.org/articles/am/v2/n2/original-cubit.
2. Scholars have debated whether this was a particular type of wood or a means of processing wood (similar to the process of making plywood or pressed wood). Many ancient ships of antiquity had intricate wood that had been processed to make it stronger and more durable. Was that technology passed down through Noah and his sons? It is possible.
3. It is important to note that a kind is not necessarily what we know today as a "species." For more information, see Georgia Purdom and Bodie Hodge, "What Are 'Kinds' in Genesis?" in *The New Answers Book 3*, Ken Ham, editor (Green Forest, AR: Master Books, 2010), p. 39–48.

(likely three breeding pairs of these clean animals, as well as sacrificial individuals for after the Flood) — Genesis 6:20, 7:2–3, 7:21–23, 8:20.

- Eight people survived on the ark: Noah, Shem, Ham, Japheth, and their respective wives — Genesis 7:7, 7:13; 1 Peter 3:20; 2 Peter 2:5.

- It had a door which was likely in the center deck as implied by the wording "lower, second, and third decks"; that is, one deck was lower than the door — Genesis 6:16.

- The Lord shut the door to the ark from the outside (and it is probable that it too was sealed with pitch like the rest of the ark; otherwise, the rest of the pitch was pointless with these untreated seals) — Genesis 7:14, 16.

- The unrighteous sinners who did not go on the ark did not realize their doom, even up to the day that Noah boarded the ark — Matthew 24:38; Luke 17:27

- The ark was lifted off the ground by or on the 40th day of the Flood and then floated high above land surface on the waters — Genesis 7:17.

- It landed in the mountains of Ararat on the 150th day of the Flood (confirmed by calculating from Genesis 7:11 with a 360-day year) — Genesis 8:3–4.

- The ark survived the Flood, and Noah's family and the animals came out of the ark — Genesis 8:18–19.

- They had remained on the ark for 370 days (or 371, depending on whether half days are rounded as full days or not) — Genesis 7:11, 8:14–16.

- Noah's family left the ark and settled where there was fertile soil for Noah, who became a farmer — Genesis 8:19, 9:1, 9:20. This first settlement would have been in an east/west direction from Babel, the later place of rebellion — Genesis 11:2.[4]

---

4. There could be more information from the biblical text, but this should be a sufficient to give us the relevant highlights of ark information from the Bible.

Notice that very little information is given about the ark's resting place (simply "mountains of Ararat"). However, there are some deductions and inferences that can be made from the Scriptures, which leads to the debate over the ark's landing site.

Where Are the Mountains of Ararat?

If someone had asked me years ago which mountain Noah's ark landed on, my response would have been a naïve, "Mt. Ararat, of course, because that is what the Bible says." However, a reading of Genesis 8:4 reveals no such thing. Instead, the text says the "mountains of Ararat," which refers to a range of mountains, not a specific mountain.

And this raises an important point. Christians always need to check information with the Scriptures. Let God be the authority, rather than man, on any subject. Believers know Noah's ark existed, and they can be certain of that because of God's Word, regardless of whether or not any remains of the ark are found. The all-knowing God says in His Word that the ark existed. There is no greater authority on this subject to whom one can appeal.

So where are the mountains of Ararat? The mountains of Ararat form a mountain range named after the Urartu people who settled in that region after the dispersion event at the Tower of Babel. In Hebrew, Ararat and Urartu are even spelled the same way. Hebrew does not have written vowels, so both are essentially spelled *rrt*.

Josephus, a Jewish historian living about 2,000 years ago, said that Armenia was made up the descendants of Hul through Aram and Shem.[5] Armenia is the *later name* of the region of Urartu/Ararat, which is a specific part of the Armenian highlands. So it is understandable why Josephus used the later name, whereas Moses used the earlier name.

When Moses wrote Genesis around 1491–1451 B.C.,[6] he had been educated in Egypt as royalty (and he had been inspired by the Holy Spirit), so it is to be expected that he understood the geography of the peoples in the Middle East. In fact, other Bible writers like Isaiah and Jeremiah,

5. Bodie Hodge, "Josephus and Genesis Chapter Ten," Answers in Genesis, http://www.answersingenesis.org/articles/aid/v4/n1/josephus-and-genesis-chapter-ten#fnList_1_1.
6. James Ussher, *The Annals of the World*, Larry and Marion Pierce, editors (Green Forest, AR: Master Books, 2003), p. 39–47.

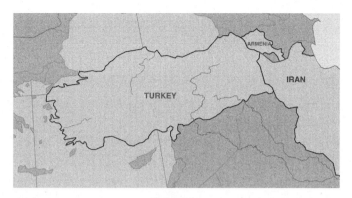

Figure 1

who lived well after Moses but well before Josephus, were also familiar with the Ararat land and people:

> Now it came to pass, as he was worshiping in the house of Nisroch his god, that his sons Adrammelech and Sharezer struck him down with the sword; and they escaped into the land of Ararat. Then Esarhaddon his son reigned in his place (Isaiah 37:38).

> Set up a banner in the land, blow the trumpet among the nations! Prepare the nations against her, call the kingdoms together against her: Ararat, Minni, and Ashkenaz. Appoint a general against her; cause the horses to come up like the bristling locusts (Jeremiah 51:27).

This ancient region is basically in the eastern part of modern-day Turkey, Armenia, and western Iran (see figure 1).

The Debate Over Which Mountain

One of the most heated debates on this subject, though, is over which specific *mountain* the ark landed on within the mountain range. Of course, the Bible does not say the ark landed on a specific mountain, but this is inferred. It is possible it landed in a lower area within the mountains of Ararat. However, the two most popular sites are:

Mt. Ararat (Agri Dagh)
Mt. Cudi (or Cudi Dagh; Cudi sounds like "Judi")

Both are denoted in figure 1.

Many ark landing sites have been proposed over the years. One that has been rejected as a geological formation by most scholars in recent years is the Durupinar or Akyayla site in Turkey, near the Iran and Turkey border. That site consists of something akin to a boat-shaped feature that is readily recognizable (think of a football field-sized "footprint" in the shape of a boat).[7]

Other sites that have attained some popularity but have been largely rejected by archaeologists and researchers are Mt. Salvalon and Mt. Suleiman in Iran. It is unreasonable for these mountains to be included in the region of Ararat. There are other problems associated with them, too.[8]

Ararat

Key verses in the Scriptures need to be consulted before proceeding:

> Then the ark rested in the seventh month, the seventeenth day of the month, on the mountains of Ararat. And the waters decreased continually until the tenth month. In the tenth month, on the first day of the month, the tops of the mountains were seen (Genesis 8:4–5).

The tops of the surrounding mountains were seen 74 days after the ark landed in the mountains of Ararat. This gives the impression that the mountain the ark landed on was much higher than the others. So the obvious choice is Mt. Ararat, which today towers excessively over all the other mountains in the region.[9]

Mt. Ararat is a large volcano that extends to a height of 16,854 feet! This is higher than any mountain in the 48 contiguous United States (Alaska does have a few mountains that are taller). Lesser Ararat (also known as Little Ararat) is another volcano that stands adjacent to Mt.

---

7. Dr. Andrew Snelling, "Special report: Amazing 'Ark' Expose," *Creation ex nihilo*, Sept. 1, 1992, p. 26–38, http://www.answersingenesis.org/articles/cm/v14/n4/special-report-amazing-ark-expose.
8. Gordon Franz, "Did the BASE Institute Discover Noah's Ark in Iran?" Associates for Biblical Research, February 16, 2007, http://www.biblearchaeology.org/post/2007/02/Did-the-BASE-Institute-Discover-Noahs-Ark-in-Iran.aspx#Article.
9. This does not take into account the fact that some mountains of the region may have been raising and lowering during this transitional period of the Flood (Psalm 104:8–9).

Ararat and is 12,782 feet high, which is similar in height to a number of impressive peaks in the Rocky Mountains in the United States.

Many say that if the ark landed on Mt. Ararat, then it would have taken another two and one-half months for the water to reveal other surrounding mountain peaks. This seems logical. In fact, this is one reason some scholars argue that Mt. Ararat is the resting place for the ark.

Nevertheless, this is not the main reason why the search for the ark has focused on Ararat. The primary reason is because of the eyewitness accounts of ark sightings in recent times. B.J. Corbin wrote a book on the search for Noah's ark, which is helpful to anyone wanting to find out the details of various expeditions on Ararat. The book also discusses Mt. Cudi, the other proposed site. In the preface of the second edition, Corbin states:

> The only major reason to consider Mount Ararat is because of the few documented eyewitnesses. . . . There is a number of intriguing statements from individuals who indicate that there may be a barge-like or boat-like structure high on modern day Mount Ararat. These statements are really the primary basis for the search on Mount Ararat.[10]

Corbin, who has also been involved in the ark search on Ararat, confirms that the primary reason to for the search on Ararat is because of the eyewitness accounts. There have been quite a few accounts, including many reputable people in the 20th century, and in the preface to his book Corbin documents these as well. Furthermore, Ararat is covered with ice and glaciers all year, so this is an ideal hiding place (i.e., more difficult to locate) for an ark.

Even in some older literature, such as in the writings of Byzantine historian Philostorgius in the 5th century, Ararat was suggested as the ark's landing site. After the 13th century A.D., more sources affirm this mountain as the landing site.[11]

Considering the scriptural basis of the highest mountain, the eyewitness accounts, and the historical sources, why would anyone look elsewhere for the landing site?

---

10. B.J. Corbin, *The Explorers of Ararat* (Long Beach, CA: Great Commission Illustrated Books, 1999), p. 8.

11. Richard Lanser, "The Case for Ararat," *Bible and Spade* (Fall 2006): p. 114–118.

The Debate Gets Heated

On the other side of the debate there are some objections to consider. First, even with all the eyewitness accounts of purportedly seeing something like the ark on Ararat, there has never been anything of substance ever found or documented to prove the ark landed on Ararat.

Also, the Bible does not explicitly say that it was *only* due to the water's recession (which all sides agree is indeed a factor) as to why mountaintops were seen. The text says, "the tops of the mountains were seen" (Genesis 8:5). This involves two things, water level (1) *and* visibility (2).

This second factor that is often overlooked is the conditions that may affect visibility. The warmer ocean water (which is expected from the Flood with continental shifting, rising basalts from the mantle, and possibly some nuclear decay would surely generate heat and volcanism) gives off vapors and mists that form low-lying fog and clouds. Hence, visibility would likely be rather low. Genesis 8:5 may well be discussing the state of visibility and atmospheric condition regarding clouds and fog from the heated ocean just as much at it discusses water level.

One way or another, this passage (Genesis 8:5) cannot be so easily used to affirm a landing spot on the highest peak. It *may* still be the highest peak but one cannot be dogmatic. Another factor needs to be considered here too. If it were the highest peak, what was the highest peak *at this time*?

One common objection is that if the ark landed at such a high altitude, how did the animals get off the ark and make their way down from this deadly mountain? And how did man and the animals at that high altitude survive all that time without sufficient oxygen after striking ground (day 150) until being called off the ark (day 370)? Oxygen tanks would not be necessary when floating on the surface of the water, because oxygen percentages are based on sea level (about 21 percent at sea level). If the ark were at 16,000 feet above sea level, then when the water receded oxygen would be a requirement because serious problems can occur due to lack of oxygen at altitudes over 12,000 feet.[12]

---

12. It is possible that this volcano was much smaller originally, and later post-Flood eruptions are what caused it to become so large and so high. But if this were the case, eruptions should have burnt the wooden vessel to oblivion, so no remains of the ark should ever be found on Ararat. It is possible that petrification of the wood could take place at such temperatures; however, being coated in pitch,

Another oft-used argument is that pillow lavas should be found on Mt. Ararat if it formed underwater. For those unfamiliar with pillow lavas, they are formed when a volcanic eruption occurs underwater. The lavas that come in contact with water cause it to harden quickly in masses that look "like a pillow."[13]

Mt. Ararat and lesser Ararat: volcanoes with their respective flows on top of the foothills.

Some believe there may possibly be some pillow lavas on Ararat, as reported by Corbin[14] and through observation attributed specifically to Clifford Burdick. However, if this volcano was formed in the Flood before day 150 when the ark ran aground, then such pillow lavas should have extensively covered it. But this is not the case. Rather, there is a severe lack of evidence that this mountain was ever covered by water. There are some pillow lavas on Ararat at very high altitudes (e.g., 14,000 feet),[15] but the same characteristic features of pillow lavas also form when lavas meet ice and snow, which may be a better explanation of these specific pillow lavas at high altitudes on Ararat where it is capped in snow and ice.[16]

Another argument must also be considered: Mt. Ararat and Lesser Ararat are volcanoes. They have been identified as having been formed after the Flood because they sit on top of fossil-bearing sediment from the Flood.[17] Classed as Pleistocene rock, Ararat is regarded by most creation researchers as post-Flood continuous with the Ice Age that followed the

---

which is typically rather flammable, and being made of seasoned dry wood, it makes more sense that the ark would be burned in the presence of volcanic heat, not petrified.

13. There are also other underwater geological evidences that should be present such as interbedded water-deposited volcaniclastics and pyroclastics, but these do not cover the mountain either.

14. Corbin, *The Explorers of Ararat*, p. 326.

15. Ibid., p. 326.

16. "Ararat," NoahsArkSearch.Com, http://www.noahsarksearch.com/ararat.htm.

17. Y. Yilmaz, Y. Güner, and F. Şaroğlu, "Geology of the Quaternary Volcanic Centres of the East Anatolia," *Journal of Volcanology and Geothermal Research* 85 (1998): p. 173–210.

Flood.[18]

By this argument, these volcanoes *did not exist* at the time the ark landed. When viewing these volcanoes from above, one can readily see the lava and volcanic flow from the volcanoes *overlaying* the foothills and plains that make up part of the region of the mountains of Ararat. From the account of Scripture, the mountains of Ararat were made by day 150 of the Flood (Genesis 8:4) and the ark landed on day 150 of the Flood (Genesis 8:4), so these volcanoes had to come *after* both the mountain formation and ark landing to have their volcanic flows sitting aloft on the foothills of the mountains of Ararat today.[19]

Furthermore, fossils are readily found within the mountains of Ararat, but they are rare or absent entirely on Mt. Ararat. Some claim to have found some, but there is no documentation for *in situ* (in their original place) fossils on Ararat. The layers on Ararat are volcanic, not sedimentary.

Cudi

The other potential mountain that has long been proposed is Mt. Cudi. Habermehl has reviewed the search for Noah's Ark.[20] Though Answers in Genesis does not agree with all of Habermehl's assertions,[21] she does pro-

---

18. For more on the post-Flood Ice Age see Michael Oard, "Where Does the Ice Age Fit?" in *The New Answers Book 1*, Ken Ham, editor (Green Forest, AR: Master Books, 2006)..

19. It is possible these volcanos were smaller at the time of the Flood and further eruptions have covered or destroyed any remains of the ark at the previous height of the mountains, but if this were the case, the ark did not come to rest on Ararat as we know it, nor would we know if it were taller than any other mountain in the range at that time.

20. Anne Habermehl, "A Review of the Search for Noah's Ark," in *Proceedings of the Sixth International Conference on Creationism*, Dr. Andrew A. Snelling, editor (Pittsburg, PA: Creation Science Fellowship; Dallas, Texas: Institute for Creation Research, 2008), p. 485–502.

21. As one example, she holds the position that Noah and his family settled rather close to the ark and hence uses Genesis 11:2 as a basis to relocate Babel to an east-west direction of the ark landing site. Many scholars have pointed out the fallacy in this east-west direction, as this is in reference to Noah's first settlement after the Flood (see footnote 7 or Adam Clarke's Commentary on Genesis 11:2). Noah's initial settlement is unknown, but it was a place that was fertile enough to farm. Noah and his family were also able to live in tents. One cannot assume this was essentially still at the ark landing site as Noah and his immediate family were told to come off the ark (Genesis 8:16) and fill the earth (Genesis 9:1.) It was not until Noah had (in some cases) great, great, great, great grandsons that the

vide a thorough review of evidences and arguments regarding Ararat and Cudi.

Crouse and Franz point out that this mountain has gone by various names such as Judi, Cardu, Quardu, Kardu, Ararat, Nipur, Gardyene, and others.[22] Cudi, being in the mountains of Ararat region, also sits in a "specified" range of mountains known as the Gordian, Kurdish, Gordyene, and others. This is important to know, as many ancient sources say the ark landed on this specific portion of the mountains. Both Ararat and Cudi are in the basic region of where the Urartu lived, but whereas Ararat is referred to in some early literature (5th century at the earliest) as the ark's landing site, Mt. Cudi is referred to as the landing site in many more and far earlier sources.

In *Bible and Spade*, there were cases presented for Ararat (Lanser) and for Cudi (Crouse and Franz), along with other pertinent articles on the subject.[23] Crouse and Franz did an extensive historical review referring to numerous ancient and modern sources that point to Cudi. These include direct and indirect allusions to Cudi from Jewish (e.g., Josephus, Targums, Book of Jubilees, and Benjamin of Tudela), Christian (e.g., Theophilus of Antioch of Syria, Julius Africanus, Eusebius, and several others), pagan (e.g., Berossus and *The Epic of Gilgamesh*), and Muslim sources (e.g., Koran [Qur'an], Al-Mas'udi, Zakariya ibn Muhammad al Qazvini).

Cudi is much lower in elevation, being about 6,800 feet high, so it would not have been so difficult to herd animals down the mountain, there would have been no problems with low oxygen levels, and this mountain is not a volcano that is resting upon the top of the mountains of Ararat (like volcanic Ararat is). But it was easily in a place where pieces could be looted or taken as relics. According to Crouse and Franz, the Muslims claimed to have taken the last of the major beams for use in a

---

rebellion occurred at Babel. Also, why live in tents when there is a huge wooden mansion to live in (i.e., the ark) or, at the very least, wood enough to build a proper shelter? Furthermore, Noah had his pick of the new world, so why remain at or near the rough mountainous area of the ark landing site and not find a place to start a new beginning, especially somewhere suitable for farming?

22. Bill Crouse and Gordon Franz, "Mount Cudi — True Mountain of Noah's Ark," *Bible and Spade* (Fall 2006): p. 99–111, http://www.biblearchaeology.org/publications/bas19_4.pdf.

23. Ibid.

mosque.[24]

The legends and lore associated with this mountain still persist in the area as well. Christians, Jews, Muslims, and others still came together for a yearly celebration in honor of the sacrifices made by Noah after the Flood as recorded by a historian nearly 100 years ago (W.A. Wigram).[25] There is even a place on Cudi that is the traditional landing spot of the ark on a particular ridge. So is this the absolute landing site? We simply do not know.

Conclusion

Has Noah's ark been found? The obvious answer is that people would not be asking this question if Noah's ark really had been found! It would likely be the find of a lifetime.

Both Ararat and Cudi have had their share of popularity over the years. And both have strong supporters on their side. When viewing the evidence through the lenses of Scripture, the more logical choice is that of Cudi, not modern-day, volcanic Mt. Ararat that sits on top of fossil-bearing sediment from the Flood.

But would we be dogmatic that Cudi was the landing spot? Not at all. The Bible simply does not say, and though many ancient sources point to Cudi, these sources are not absolute, while Scripture is. The fact is that there has been no indisputable evidence of Noah's Ark having been found anywhere (outside of Scripture, which itself is sufficient proof that the ark existed, as there is no greater authority on any subject than God). But is such external evidence needed? Not at all.

To summarize, there was so much more that could have been discussed, but with such limitations, a brief overview of the debate is the best that can be hoped for in a single chapter of a book. My hope is that this brief introduction will encourage you to learn more about the subject, and that you will give glory to God when doing so. Much more research

24. One also has to consider the amount of deterioration the wooden vessel underwent over 4,350 years. If kept frozen or in a dry, arid climate, a wooden ark could last quite a long time. However, in mid-temperate areas with alternating wet-dry conditions, it should not last long at all (think of a barn in the Midwest; one must work hard to keep such a thing for even 200 years). Being coated with pitch helps, but even that is not a perfect preservative. A perfectly engineered ark would have the pitch's usefulness end at the end of the Flood (~370 days).

25. Habermehl, "A Review of the Search for Noah's Ark."

on the topic of the ark's landing site needs to be done, be it on Ararat, Cudi, or other places.

Would undisputed evidence of the ark be of value? Absolutely. But is it necessary for one's faith? Not in the least. So do not forget this point: the Bible is true, and Christ is who He says He is regardless of whether anyone finds the remains of the ark or not.

Further Reading:

1. Bible and Spade Debate: http://www.biblearchaeology.org/publications/bas19_4.pdf.

2. B.J. Corbin, *The Explorers of Ararat* (Long Beach, CA: Great Commission Illustrated Books, 1999).

3. Noah's Ark Search website: http://www.noahsarksearch.com/.

4. Rick Lanser of the Associate for Biblical Research has published a four-part series on the group's website entitled "The Landing-Place of Noah's Ark: Testimonial, Geological and Historical Considerations," parts 1–4, available here: http://www.biblearchaeology.org/category/flood.aspx.

I would like to extend a special thanks to Dr. Andrew Snelling for his guidance on this chapter.

Chapter 16

What about Theophanies (Appearances of God) in the Old Testament?

Tim Chaffey

❀❀❀❀❀❀❀❀❀❀❀❀❀❀❀❀❀❀❀

Introduction

It has become increasingly popular for skeptics to make claims similar to the following: Christianity is a new religion started by Jesus or His followers about 2,000 years ago. The objection may be worded as follows: "There are plenty of religions in the world that are much older, so what gives you the right to say that Christianity is the right one?"

How would you answer this question? There are several approaches you could use. For example, the antiquity or newness of a belief system does not determine its truthfulness. So the entire argument is illogical. Nevertheless, the objection does raise an interesting question. Was God concerned with teaching humanity the truth prior to sending Jesus to the earth? This article will explore an intriguing concept in the Bible that dismantles the basic premise of this skeptical claim.

What Is a Theophany?

Many readers are confused by certain Old Testament passages that speak of God appearing to certain individuals. Since the Bible claims that no one can see God and live (Exodus 33:20), how could God appear to these people? Before explaining what took place in these passages, let's take a look at two of these accounts.

Abraham:

Then the LORD appeared to [Abraham] by the terebinth trees of Mamre, as he was sitting in the tent door in the heat of the day. So he lifted his eyes and looked, and behold, three men were standing by him; and when he saw them, he ran from the tent door to meet them, and bowed himself to the ground, and said, "My Lord, if I have now found favor in Your sight, do not pass on by Your servant" (Genesis 18:1–3).

Jacob:

Then Jacob was left alone; and a Man wrestled with him until the breaking of day. Now when He saw that He did not prevail against him, He touched the socket of his hip; and the socket of Jacob's hip was out of joint as He wrestled with him. . . . And He said, "Your name shall no longer be called Jacob, but Israel; for you have struggled with God and with men, and have prevailed."

Then Jacob asked, saying, "Tell me Your name, I pray."

And He said, "Why is it that you ask about My name?" And He blessed him there.

So Jacob called the name of the place Peniel: "For I have seen God face to face, and my life is preserved" (Genesis 32:24–30).

Many theologians refer to the appearances of God in these passages, and others like them, as "theophanies" (Greek: *theos* = "God" + *phaino* = "appear") or "Christophanies." So these words mean "appearances of God" and "appearances of Christ," respectively.

The Old Testament also mentions "the Angel of the LORD"[1] on several occasions. For example, this "Angel" appeared to Manoah's wife to tell her that she would give birth to Samson.

---

1. It should be noted that the phrases "the Angel of the LORD" and "an angel of the Lord" appear in the Old Testament and New Testament, respectively. One should not automatically assume that these necessarily refer to the same individual. Notice the use of the definite article and that LORD is in "small caps" in the first phrase, indicating that this is "the Angel of YHWH" (as the Hebrew reveals). The former usually refers to a theophany, while the latter often simply refers to one of the angels (Acts 7:30, which references the Old Testament, is a clear exception). Some Bible translations attempt to assist the reader in distinguishing between the two terms by capitalizing "Angel" when referring to "the Angel of the LORD"; however, they are often inconsistent in their capitalizations because it is often difficult to know if the term is being used generally or specifi-

And the Angel of the LORD appeared to the woman and said to her, "Indeed now, you are barren and have borne no children, but you shall conceive and bear a son. Now therefore, please be careful not to drink wine or similar drink, and not to eat anything unclean. For behold, you shall conceive and bear a son. And no razor shall come upon his head, for the child shall be a Nazirite to God from the womb; and he shall begin to deliver Israel out of the hand of the Philistines."

So the woman came and told her husband, saying, "A Man of God came to me, and His countenance was like the countenance of the Angel of God, very awesome; but I did not ask Him where He was from, and He did not tell me His name (Judges 13:3–6).

Christians generally agree that the above passages and many others that mention "the Angel of the LORD" are appearances of the pre-incarnate Christ (Christ before He came in the flesh).[2] Let's take a look at some of the characteristics of this "Angel" as given in the various passages.

- The "Angel" is referred to with masculine pronouns (Genesis 16:13; Judges 6:21).
- He is identified as God (Judges 6:11, 14; Zechariah 12:8).
- He performed miracles (Judges 6:21; 13:20).

---

cally. For example, the New King James Version often capitalizes "Angel of the LORD" (מַלְאַךְ־יהוה / mal'ak YHWH), such as in Genesis 16:7 and 22:11. But in some cases the translators chose not to capitalize "angel" (e.g., 2 Samuel 24:16; 2 Kings 19:35).

2. Since the term "angel" often refers to a messenger, it is possible that some uses of "the Angel of the LORD" refer to normal angels rather than one specific "Angel" — the pre-incarnate Christ. A text note in the NET Bible explains why some people do not view these appearances as theophanies. After explaining that the term simply means "messenger of the LORD," the editors of the NET Bible wrote, "Some identify the angel of the LORD as the pre-incarnate Christ because in some texts the angel is identified with the LORD himself. However, it is more likely that the angel merely represents the LORD; he can speak for the LORD because he is sent with the LORD's full authority. In some cases the angel is clearly distinct from the LORD (see Judg 6:11–23). It is not certain if the same angel is always in view. Though the proper name following the noun "angel" makes the construction definite, this may simply indicate that a definite angel sent from the LORD is referred to in any given context. It need not be the same angel on every occasion. Biblical Studies Press, The NET Bible First Edition, (Biblical Studies Press, 2006), Genesis 16:7.

- Gideon and Manoah thought they would die because they saw the "Angel" face to face (Judges 6:22; 13:22).
- The "Angel" accurately foretold future events (Judges 13:3).
- His name is "wonderful" (Judges 13:18; cf., Isaiah 9:6).
- He destroyed 185,000 soldiers of the Assyrian army in one night (2 Kings 19:35).[3]

While angels have occasionally performed some of these actions, such as miracles and prophecy, there are clear examples when "the Angel of the Lord" cannot be viewed as a normal angel. He is occasionally identified as God, accepted worship, and at least two people who saw Him thought they would die for seeing Him face to face. These same attributes and activities are clearly attributed to God elsewhere in Scripture.

There are a few other statements to consider. In Zechariah 3:1–2, "the Angel of the Lord" is distinguished from Yahweh because He talks to Yahweh. John 1:18 states, "No one has seen God at any time. The only begotten Son, who is in the bosom of the Father, He has declared Him." So man has only seen the Son of God, not the Father or the Holy Spirit. Also, the "Commander of the army of the Lord" (Joshua 5:14) is likely the same individual as "the Angel of the Lord." Joshua saw this "Commander" holding a sword, and He accepted Joshua's worship, something the holy angels refuse to do (Revelation 19:10, 22:8–9). Finally, "the Angel of the Lord" does not make any appearances after the birth of Christ in the New Testament, although the risen Jesus did appear to Saul on the road to Damascus (Acts 9:1–6, 22:6–10, 26:14–19; 1 Corinthians 9:1, 15:8).

These truths have led many students of Scripture to conclude that "the Angel of the Lord" in the Old Testament is none other than Christ Himself. He is called God, given attributes of God, seen by people, worshiped, and distinguished from the Father and Spirit. So rather than undermining the uniqueness and importance of Christ, theophanies affirm the uniqueness of Jesus. They also show the intimacy of God with His creation, unlike the distant god of deism that some people incorrectly associate with the God of the Bible.

Some Christians believe another theophany occurred in the fiery furnace when Nebuchadnezzar claimed to see four men walking in the midst

---

3. For more information on these and other theophanies, please see http://www.answersingenesis.org/articles/nab2/is-jesus-god.

of the fire. According to the NKJV, Nebuchadnezzar said that "the form of the fourth is like the Son of God" (Daniel 3:25). This may seem like an obvious reference to Jesus, and it may have been Him, or it may have been an angel. Nebuchadnezzar definitely saw a fourth being in the furnace, but we need to remember that at this point he was a pagan king trying to explain things from his polytheistic perspective. His words are recorded in Aramaic, and he called the fourth person in the furnace a בַּר־אֱלָהִין (bar 'elahin), which is literally translated as "a son of the gods." This literal translation is included in a textual note in the NKJV. For these reasons, we cannot be certain that this was a theophany.

Besides making for an interesting Bible study, the appearances of Christ in the Old Testament confirm the fact that He existed prior to the Incarnation, just as He plainly stated: "Most assuredly, I say to you, before Abraham was, I AM" (John 8:58). The fact that Jesus is the Creator also demonstrates His existence prior to His first advent (John 1:1–3; Colossians 1:16).

Some people have claimed that Jesus is Michael the archangel. For example, the founder of the Jehovah's Witnesses, Charles Taze Russell, used the notion that Jesus and Michael are the same individual to claim that Jesus is a created being, rather than the Creator of all beings.

Some Christians have also linked Jesus and Michael. John Calvin and Matthew Henry made similar connections in their respective commentaries on Daniel 12:1–4. However, unlike the Jehovah's Witnesses, neither believed Jesus to be a created being. Rather, they believed that Michael was another name for the "Angel of the LORD." This position is not without its problems. For example, in Daniel 10:13, Michael is called "one of the chief princes."[4] Jesus is not just one of a group; He is the only begotten Son of God.

Why Would God Do This?

There are several reasons why Jesus went through this process. He did it to fulfill prophecy. In Genesis 3:15, God prophesied that the Seed of the woman would crush the head of the serpent, and Isaiah 7:14 also contains a prophecy of the virginal conception of Immanuel (literally "God with

---

4. The phrase "one of the chief princes" can be translated from the Hebrew in a few different ways, although the majority of popular translations (KJV, NKJV, NASB, ESV, NET, NIV) agree on using "one of the chief princes." The YLT calls Michael the "first of the chief heads." If the latter is a better rendering then it may lend stronger support to Calvin's and Henry's positions.

us"). He also came in the flesh so that He could sympathize with humanity. Hebrews 4:15 states, "For we do not have a High Priest who cannot sympathize with our weaknesses, but was in all points tempted as we are, yet without sin."

Of course, one of the major reasons Jesus became a man was to save us from our sins. Hebrews 10:4 states, "For it is not possible that the blood of bulls and goats could take away sins." This chapter goes on to reveal that the Levitical priests repeatedly offered the same sacrifices that could never take away our sins. Instead, these sacrifices served to *cover* the sins of the people. In order for our sins to be *removed* (i.e., *forgiven*), we needed the blood of a perfect man.

> By that will we have been sanctified through the offering of the body of Jesus Christ once for all. . . . But this Man, after He had offered one sacrifice for sins forever, sat down at the right hand of God, from that time waiting till His enemies are made His footstool. For by one offering He has perfected forever those who are being sanctified (Hebrews 10:10–14).

By being conceived in Mary, Jesus took on human flesh so that He could be our "kinsman-redeemer" (Ruth 3:12; NIV).[5] As a literal descendant of Adam, Jesus could be the perfect sacrifice for the sons of Adam. He died, was buried, and bodily rose from the dead in fulfillment of Old Testament Scripture (1 Corinthians 15:3–5). He died and rose again to give life to those who are descendants of Adam (the one who brought sin and death into the world) and who repent of their sins and trust in Jesus Christ as Savior and Lord (1 Corinthians 15:21–22). Not only was He one of us, but also Jesus perfectly fulfilled the Law and offered Himself as a lamb without blemish (Hebrews 9:14; 1 Peter 1:19). By living a sinless life, He also provided the perfect example of obedience for us to follow. And by His perfect life and death in the flesh, He broke the power of Satan (Hebrews 2:14).

How Did Old Testament Saints Recognize a Theophany?

By the time of Genesis 18, God had already appeared to Abraham on at least two occasions (Genesis 12:7, 17:1) and spoken to him in some way several other times (Genesis 12:1, 13:14, 15:1). It is reasonable to conclude

---

5. For a good discussion on the kinsman-redeemer concept, please see: http://www. abideinchrist.com/messages/lev25v25.html, Accessed February 6, 2012.

that in Genesis 18 God appeared in the same form as before so that Abraham would recognize Him. Indeed, when he saw the Lord and the other two "men" (angels), Abraham ran out to Him and bowed down.

Of course, this pushes the question back to an earlier time. How did Abram (Abraham) recognize God the first time He appeared to him? The Bible does not tell us this, but based on the many other theophanies discussed earlier, we know that the person usually recognized "the Angel of the LORD" soon after seeing Him. The very first theophany may have occurred when God pronounced the Curse. Remember, after Adam and Eve sinned and sewed fig leaves together, they "heard the sound of the LORD God *walking* in the garden in the cool of the day" (Genesis 3:8, emphasis added).[6] The implication is that God appeared in physical form since they heard Him *walking* in the garden prior to confronting Adam and Eve.

Throughout Scripture, God conveyed His message to man through various means. He gave Joseph, Pharaoh, and Nebuchadnezzar dreams that foretold future events. He also used visions to communicate with Daniel, Ezekiel, John, and others. In many places, we are simply told that "God said" or "the word of the LORD came to" a certain individual. In these instances, it is possible that a theophany took place and God spoke face to face with the individual. It is also possible that God audibly communicated with people without physically appearing to them, as was apparently the case with Elijah when God used "a still small voice" to speak to His prophet (1 Kings 19:12–13).

Of course, without the Bible specifically telling us if God took on the appearance of a man to speak with people, we can only speculate. Regardless of why God chose this method at times, we know that He effectively communicated His message to the recipient when He appeared.

Do Theophanies Blur the Line Between Angels and Humans?

Hebrews 13:2 states, "Do not forget to entertain strangers, for by so doing some have unwittingly entertained angels." Some commentators

---

6. Many people have claimed that, prior to sinning, Adam and Eve used to walk with God in the garden. While this may have happened, the Bible never makes this claim. Instead, it tells us that they heard God walking in the garden *after* they had sinned. Others may have literally "walked with" the Lord such as Enoch (Genesis 5:24), Noah (Genesis 6:9), or even these cases with Abraham, who dined with Him (Genesis 18). However, the phrase "walked with" is likely an idiom referring to the close relationship Enoch and Noah had with the Lord.

link this passage to Abraham in Genesis 18; however, Abraham did not "unwittingly" entertain angels. He was fully aware that at least one of his guests was supernatural. There were others in the Bible who seemed to have been unaware that they were entertaining angels or "the Angel of the LORD" (e.g., Lot in Genesis 19:1–2 and Gideon in Judges 6:11–24).

Some may view these incidents as blurring the line between humans and angels, but there are clear distinctions. Angels are spiritual beings (Hebrews 1:13–14), while humans have flesh and bones along with a spiritual component (Luke 24:39; Acts 17:16). Angels, at least some of them, can take on human form when God allows it, but humans are incapable of taking on an angelic form. Hebrews quotes Psalm 8:4–6, which reveals that man has been made "lower than the angels." Angels are certainly more powerful than humans and are aware of many things that we don't know.

However, there are some ways in which man has the advantage over angels. First Peter 1:12 tells us that there are things "angels desire to look into" — namely, things pertaining to the message of salvation. In fact, only humans can receive salvation because Jesus became a descendant of Adam and only descendants of Adam can be saved. Jesus didn't take on the nature of angels to die for them (Hebrews 2:16).

So even though an angel may be able to take on the form of a man through some supernatural ability or power, an angel cannot actually become a descendant of Adam. Rebellious angels cannot be saved, but rebellious humans can be saved if they repent of their sins and place their faith in Christ alone to save them.

The Bible also tells us that Satan and many of these rebellious angels are engaged in efforts to deceive humanity (Ephesians 6:10–13; 2 Corinthians 11:14–15), so we must exercise discernment and "test the spirits" (1 John 4:1–3; Galatians 1:6–9) to determine whether or not the messages we hear are in line with Scripture — especially the gospel.[7] Remembering that we are actually in a spiritual battle with masters of deception should cause us to be even more diligent in studying the Scriptures to make sure we are following the one true Christ instead of "false christs" (Matthew 24:24).

---

7. The phrase "test the spirits" may not necessarily mean that we are literally dealing with "spirits" (i.e., angels), but that the messages we are to test ultimately have a spiritual origin and need to be compared to God's Word.

Conclusion

The theophanies in the Old Testament offer an interesting solution to the question posed at the beginning of this chapter. God has always been interested in teaching humanity the truth. From the very beginning, God set forth certain instructions for Adam and Eve. Later, He communicated to Enoch, Noah, Abraham, Isaac, Jacob, and others. He gave Moses and the Israelites the Law at Mt. Sinai. Throughout the Old Testament, God sent prophets to His people to warn them to turn from their sinful ways and to inform them about God's plans.

The New Testament shows Jesus as the ultimate revelation of the Father. In fact, He told Philip, "He who has seen Me has seen the Father" (John 14:9). Those who were able to listen to Jesus were learning from God Himself. Certainly that would have been an incredible opportunity in the first century. However, the theophanies demonstrate that God had an intimate care and concern for His people during Old Testament times, too, and that He occasionally interacted with them in a very personal way.[8]

False religions have been around since shortly after the Fall, but the true faith has existed since God made man on day 6, and He has never left Himself without witness in this world.

---

8. This is true even if some of the events described in the article were merely angelic appearances rather than theophanies. These angels would have been sent by God to accomplish His purpose in communicating God's Word to mankind.

Chapter 17

What about Annihilationism and Hell?

Bodie Hodge

❊❊❊❊❊❊❊❊❊❊❊❊❊❊❊❊❊❊❊❊❊❊

In today's culture, there are a growing number of people who believe in God and yet reject the reality of hell. They adopt a position that says that God is "too loving" to punish someone in hell, especially for eternity.

In doing so, they may develop an annihilationist position: essentially, unsaved people cannot go to heaven, and *they believe* they cannot go to hell, so they are left with the position that unsaved people are simply annihilated and never punished or potentially put in a state of unconsciousness so they do not feel the punishment. There are variations to this, but more on this in a moment.[1]

For several biblical reasons (which will be discussed shortly), Answers in Genesis rejects annihilationism, which is found in "Section 3: Theology," point eleven of our Statement of Faith. Our rejection of annihilationism was not placed in our Statement of Faith on a "whim," but as a result of diligence in scriptural study. The point on annihilationism states the following:

---

1. This is not to be confused with the Roman Church's position of purgatory, an idea that originates in the minds of men about a second chance between earth and heaven. People who hold to annihilationism still adhere to Scriptures like Hebrews 9:27 that say we die once, and then after this is the judgment, as opposed to dying once and then being offered a second chance in purgatory.

Those who do not believe in Christ are subject to everlasting conscious punishment, but believers enjoy eternal life with God.[2]

Much of the debate surrounding a literal hell stems from arguments over the way some may *perceive* God as opposed to what God says in His Word. So this becomes a biblical authority issue (due to a battle over a *god* of one's own making versus the God of the Bible). In this chapter, the 66 books of the Bible are used as the authority, rather than human emotion, which tends to fuel this debate the most.

What Is Annihilationism?

Many would say that annihilationists believe that hell is not real. But this is not entirely fair to say, as many annihilationists would agree that hell is real. It is better to say that annihilationists believe that hell is not a place for the unsaved to spend eternity. They distinguish this by saying that hell is indeed reserved for the devil and his fallen angels (where they will spend eternity), but not for sinful, unrepentant, unsaved man. Rather, this position holds that the unsaved will be annihilated (cease to exist) or at the very least will be made unconscious of the pain, but they will not go to hell to be in torment for all eternity.

Those who hold to the annihilationist view do get one thing right: hell *was* created for the devil and his angels (Matthew 25:41), likely since the devil's rebellion occurred immediately before mankind's Fall into sin.[3] But in this same passage it says *people* will be there as well. And keep in mind, just because it was created for the devil and his angels does not mean that others could not be put there.

There are variations of annihilationists' positions, too. Some hold that people *will* go to hell, but only for a short time, and then God releases them (e.g., non-eternal; perhaps even heaven afterward?). However, this would not be a true annihilationist position but something more akin to a hypothetical purgatory. And that is not the focus of this chapter.

Some say an unsaved person goes to hell for a short time, and then they are annihilated. Others argue that hell itself will be annihilated after

---

2. "The AiG Statement of Faith," Answers in Genesis, http://www.answersingenesis.org/about/faith.

3. Bodie Hodge, *The Fall of Satan* (Green Forest, Arkansas: Master Books, 2011), pp. 53-57.

a certain point so it no longer exists. Still others say there is no hell at all, and that fallen man (as well as Satan and his fallen angels) will be annihilated immediately. People who take this view liberally interpret "reconciliation" in 1 Corinthians 15:28. There are certainly other variations beyond these but this short introduction to annihilationism should suffice to get us started.

Is Hell a Reality?

The reality of hell must be addressed first. Hell is discussed throughout the Bible. Jesus speaks extensively about hell and heaven, so that should settle the issue that both are real places. The Greek word for hell is *gehenna*. And there are several passages where these are used, including in the gospel of Mark:

> If your hand causes you to sin, cut it off. It is better for you to enter into life maimed, rather than having two hands, to go to **hell,** into the fire that shall never be quenched — where "Their worm does not die, And the fire is not quenched." And if your foot causes you to sin, cut it off. It is better for you to enter life lame, rather than having two feet, to be cast into **hell,** into the fire that shall never be quenched — where "Their worm does not die, And the fire is not quenched." And if your eye causes you to sin, pluck it out. It is better for you to enter the kingdom of God with one eye, rather than having two eyes, to be cast into **hell** fire — where "Their worm does not die, And the fire is not quenched" (Mark 9:43–48, emphasis added).

Other passages that use this Greek word are Matthew 5:22, 5:29–30, 10:28, 18:9, 23:15 and 33; Luke 12:5; and James 3:6. This is not to be confused with the word *hades,* which has connotations of hell (Luke 16:19–31) but means "grave," "death," and "depths." The Hebrew word *sheol* is likely a counterpart to hades, since its definition is "grave," "underworld," and "pit" with connotations of hell.[4]

---

4. There is also the Greek term *tartaroo,* which also refers to hell, but is specifically used in conjunction with fallen angels. Since this term is used only once in the Bible (2 Peter 2:4), it may be more difficult to ascertain its full meaning or range of meanings. Regardless, according to the passages above, hell is a reality.

Is Hell an Eternal Conscious Punishment?

Next, the Bible never states that punishment in hell is temporary; on the contrary, punishment in hell is described as "everlasting destruction" (2 Thessalonians 1:9). This is significant because the primary reason for denying that punishment in hell is eternal often *does not come* from the Bible but from the proposition, "How can a loving God condemn people to eternal hell?" That proposition implies that God is not cruel and would not dare judge in such a fashion; i.e., God is perfect in love, forgiveness, and grace. But the theology then lends that God is not perfect in justice, judgment, or eternal decree.

But again, this view of God does not come from the Bible. The Bible teaches something different: a crime against an infinite and eternal Creator demands an infinite and eternal punishment (eternity in hell). This is why the Son (Jesus Christ), who is the infinite and eternal God, could take on such a punishment from the Father who is the infinite and eternal God.[5]

Is such an eternal punishment discussed in the Bible? Consider Daniel:

> And many of those who sleep in the dust of the earth shall awake, some to everlasting life, some to shame and everlasting contempt (Daniel 12:2).

In both cases, the same terminology is used of those who will inherit everlasting life and those who will inherit everlasting contempt. The Hebrew word for contempt here is *deraówn* and means "aversion" and "abhorrence," both of which indicate extreme feelings such as loathing and dislike. And the passage makes it clear that they will be conscious ("awake") during this time. The New Testament echoes this teaching in John 5:28–29:

> Do not marvel at this; for the hour is coming in which all who are in the graves will hear His voice and come forth — those who have done good, to the resurrection of life, and those who have done evil, to the resurrection of condemnation.

---

5. Interestingly, it is possible to do functions mathematics with infinites. For example, 1 infinity minus 1 infinity equals zero. So in an abstract sense, one infinite punishment that mankind deserves minus one infinite satisfaction of that punishment by the Son equals 0. In other words, Christ's substitutional atonement was sufficient for salvation.

In this passage, "resurrection of life" is contrasted with "resurrection of condemnation," giving equal duration to both; this is very similar to Daniel 12:2. Basically, the grave will give up its dead and they will be judged for eternal life or eternal judgment. Even Paul confirms such a resurrection and judgment of the just and unjust will take place (Acts 24:14–16).

Also with regard to the duration of punishment in hell, consider Christ's own words:

> Then He will say to those on his left, "Depart from Me, you cursed, into the eternal [*aionios*] fire prepared for the devil and his angels: For I was hungry and you gave Me no food; I was thirsty and you gave Me no drink; I was a stranger and you did not take Me in, naked and you did not clothe Me, sick and in prison and you did not visit Me." Then they also will answer Him, saying, "Lord, when did we see You hungry or thirsty or a stranger or na- ked or sick or in prison, and did not minister to You?" Then He will answer them, saying, "Assuredly, I say to you, inasmuch as you did not do it to one of the least of these, you did not do it to Me." And these will go away into everlasting [*aionios*] punishment, but the righteous into eternal [*aionios*] life (Matthew 25:41–46).

Jesus made it clear that hell is not annihilation but instead an eternal conscious punishment. Punishment in hell is contrasted with life once again in this passage, meaning that if the punishment is not everlasting or eternal, then neither is life. What would this say about the character of a loving God who promises to give eternal life and yet does not? It is better to trust the Scriptures that there is an eternal punishment and in the same way that a good and loving God rewards those who have received Him with eternal life.

The Greek word meaning "eternal" in this passage *(aionios)* is the same word used to describe the eternality of God Himself in other pas- sages such as Romans 16:26; 1 Timothy 1:7; Hebrews, 9:14, 13:8; and Rev- elation 4:9. So to make the claim that the term *eternal* does not necessar- ily mean eternal to those being punished has serious repercussions, such as inadvertently calling into question the eternality of God. Paul in one of his letters reaffirms this teaching of Christ:

These will pay the penalty of eternal destruction, away from the presence of the Lord and from the glory of His power (2 Thessalonians 1: 9; NASB).

John and Jude also speak of everlasting punishment, be it for angels or others ("forever and ever, no rest, punishment of eternal fire"):

Then another angel, a third one, followed them, saying with a loud voice, "If anyone worships the beast and his image, and receives a mark on his forehead or on his hand, he also will drink of the wine of the wrath of God, which is mixed in full strength in the cup of His anger; and he will be tormented with fire and brimstone in the presence of the holy angels and in the presence of the Lamb. And the smoke of their torment goes up forever and ever; they have no rest day and night, those who worship the beast and his image, and whoever receives the mark of his name" (Revelation 14:9–11; NASB).

And angels who did not keep their own domain, but abandoned their proper abode, He has kept in eternal bonds under darkness for the judgment of the great day, just as Sodom and Gomorrah and the cities around them, since they in the same way as these indulged in gross immorality and went after strange flesh, are exhibited as an example in undergoing the punishment of eternal fire (Jude 1:6–7).

When we look at the Bible, it should be clear that the biblical understanding of hell is an eternal conscious punishment, not annihilation.

As an additional note, some believe that since such a punishment exists, God is responsible for it. However, there is no need for such a punishment until *after* Satan's and man's sin against Him. Originally, God made a perfect world (Genesis 1:31; Deuteronomy 32:4). It was because of man's actions that death and sin entered the world. It is because of man's actions against a perfect God that such an eternal punishment in hell even exists (Genesis 3; Romans 5).[6] Therefore, blaming God for such a place as hell is not warranted. The blame should be directed at sinful man, sinful Satan, and sinful angels.

---

6. Satan did sin first, but he did not have *dominion* over the world — Adam and Eve did (Genesis 1:26–28). When they sinned, then their dominion fell. This is why sin affected the world when Adam ate of the tree, not when Satan sinned. However, Satan's sin, even though it would have been prior to Adam, did require punishment, and hence, hell is his final destination.

There are other Greek words that discuss eternal punishment. The root word for the eternal torment in Revelation 14:11 is *basanizo*. It means "grievous pains" and "torment." It is used to describe labor pains in Revelation 12:2, and the centurion's servant in Matthew 8:6, who is "dreadfully tormented."

Revelation 14:10–11 speaks of the punishment as having no rest day or night from it:

> He himself shall also drink of the wine of the wrath of God, which is poured out full strength into the cup of His indignation. He shall be tormented with fire and brimstone in the presence of the holy angels and in the presence of the Lamb. And the smoke of their torment ascends forever and ever; and they have no rest day or night, who worship the beast and his image, and whoever receives the mark of his name.

There will be no stop to the pain for all eternity. For the punishment from an infinite God is an infinite punishment. This is all the more reason to witness to all people, who are our relatives through Adam and Noah. Consider John 3:36:

> He who believes in the Son has everlasting life; and he who does not believe the Son shall not see life, but the wrath of God abides on him (NKJV).

How can this wrath from an eternal God be satisfied, when the people in hell are not equal to God? Because they are not, this wrath will continue for all eternity. Consider the words of Scripture regarding Judas: "The Son of Man indeed goes just as it is written of Him, but woe to that man by whom the Son of Man is betrayed! It would have been good for that man if he had not been born" (Matthew 26:24).

If the punishment were merely annihilation or an unconscious torment, then it *would* be as though the person were never born. But this is not the case for Judas, for Scripture says the opposite.

What about Proverbs 12:7, which says the wicked will be "no more"? The answer is simple enough when read in context (Proverbs 12:5–7):

> The thoughts of the righteous are right, but the counsels of the wicked are deceitful. The words of the wicked are, "Lie in wait

for blood," but the mouth of the upright will deliver them. The wicked are overthrown and are no more, but the house of the righteous will stand.

The context is clearly speaking of the wicked *on earth*, their actions *here* and their judgment *here*, not their eternal judgment, which occurs after death (Hebrews 9:27).[7]

The point is that God makes it clear in Scripture that the wicked will be punished eternally, and they will be conscious of it. When people try to make the argument that God will reduce this punishment's duration or cause people to be annihilated, it does not come from Scripture but from arbitrary opinions.

Is Reconciliation Salvation?

Some have argued that reconciliation in the Bible is essentially salvation (e.g., Colossians 1:20). Reconciliation is *not* salvation nor is it a temporal ending of punishment. The Bible never equates reconciliation with salvation.

"Reconciliation of all" means that there will be a change for all: all will change to know who Christ is. This change happens to believers when they are saved (since we had a mind of sin but now have the mind of the Spirit), but it also happens to unbelievers, *but after* they die — but by then it is too late for them. They *will* bow the knee, confess to God, and know that God is God, and they will be reconciled unto that (Isaiah 45:23; Romans 14:11; Philippians 2:10), but they will still have to endure the punishment because it is too late for them at judgment.

Some have tried to use John 12:32 to argue for a form of reconciliation as well. When Jesus says, "And I, if I am lifted up from the earth, will draw all peoples to Myself," He is not saying all people will be saved, but that all peoples *will be drawn*. This is confirmed by other passages of Scripture (e.g., John 6:44; Colossians 1:23). Other debates aside, what it shows is that no one has an excuse (Romans 1:20). All peoples have been drawn, but if they do not receive the Lord Jesus as their Savior, they retain

---

7. Some have also tried to use Psalm 37:10 to defend an annihilationist view, but again the context is in reference to what is occurring on earth and the actions of the wicked on earth. This is not speaking of an eternal state but of affairs on earth. The wicked shall be cut off and be no more on earth — and then they will face eternal judgment.

the wrath of God (John 1:12, 3:36).

Is Hell Complete Separation from God?

One aspect of this argument is that hell is complete separation from God, and since something cannot exist outside of God, it must be annihilated. Many Christians use the term "separation from God" as a nice way of saying "hell." But it needs to be clarified because it is only partially accurate — it is not a *complete* separation.

When man sinned against God in the Garden of Eden, death and suffering came into the creation (Genesis 3; Romans 8). Essentially, sin became a point of separation between man and God. We were separated from God to a certain degree; death, which is the result of sin (e.g., Genesis 2:17, 3:19; Romans 5:12), and eternal death (for unbelievers, Satan, and fallen angels), which has its final culmination in hell, is seen by some as *absolute separation* from God.

However, this is not exactly a *complete* separation, as even hell will be not be able to escape the fact that all things are being upheld by Christ (Hebrews 1:3). The wrath of God will abide on those in hell (John 3:36), so even God will have a direct influence there. Hell will not be annihilated, but will be sustained for all eternity.

To be clear, there is separation (Matthew 13:49, 25:32; Hebrews 7:26), but it is better to understand this "separation" as an absolute separation *from God's goodness and love,* not a complete separation from existence. In other words, those in hell will not receive God's goodness but rather the punishment they deserve. Christians will not experience this separation from God's love and goodness (Romans 8:35).[8]

Conclusion: Image of God

In conclusion, the last point of discussion I want to address is that man is made in the image of God. Unlike a plant or an animal, man is made special and unique, having the breath of God inserted into him from God to Adam (Genesis 1:26–27, 2:7); from Adam to Eve (Genesis 3:21–25); and from them to all of us (Genesis 9:6).

---

8. Consider the rich man and Lazarus of which Jesus spoke (Luke 16:19–31). Upon death, there was a great chasm or gulf that existed between the two, so that the rich man, who was in torment, could not pass through to the other side.

Can God simply cease to exist? No. It would be contrary to His nature of being absolute life, from which all life and existence stem. Bearing the image of God, we too are eternal beings (not to be confused with infinite beings). We will live on: either in heaven with God and His goodness, or in hell, separated from God's goodness and love and having the wrath of God abiding on us for all eternity.

Do you see why it is important to witness to people, to see them saved? Such a punishment is not what anyone would want to endure.

The Lord is not slack concerning His promise, as some count slackness, but is longsuffering toward us, not willing that any should perish but that all should come to repentance (2 Peter 3:9).

Chapter 18

How Can I Use Hell in Evangelism?

Ray Comfort

❦❦❦❦❦❦❦❦❦❦❦❦❦❦❦❦❦❦❦

Till "Hell" Freezes Over

I dropped an old John Wayne movie into my DVD player to try and kill two hours on a flight from Denver to Los Angeles. The movie didn't last very long. Within a few minutes, the Duke had said, "As sure as [expletive deleted]." Someone else said, "I'll be [expletive deleted]," and another fellow told someone to "Go to [expletive deleted]!" The inappropriate use of Hell should shock a Christian, but, sadly, they are commonplace in today's secular society — even among many children's television shows and books!

If Hell didn't exist, neither would my efforts at evangelism. I would instead spend my time enjoying my passion — surfing. But that's something I have set aside until, figuratively, the "surfer will lie down with the shark" (Isaiah 11:6). In the meantime, I will spend my time "warning every man . . . that we may present every man perfect in Christ Jesus" (Colossians 1:28).

The world must be told that they are in danger of being sent, like livid lightning, into a terrible place called Hell. Eternal justice hovers over their every move like an electro-magnet above a metal anvil (see John 3:36). They are enemies of God in their minds through wicked works, and every time they sin they are storing up wrath that will be revealed on the Day of Wrath (see Colossians 1:21 and Romans 2:5–11).

You may have noticed my small pet peeve. It's the use of a small *h* when talking about Hell. It's a very real place, and, like "new york" or "los angeles," it should be noticeable when it isn't given respect as such.

Hell is more than a bad day at the office or something we give the enemy. Hell is real, horrific, everlasting, and it's waiting for the criminals, sinners, who have violated God's perfect law.

Yet, there are learned pulpiteers who say that Hell isn't eternal (e.g., annihilationists), or they say that it's merely symbolic of the grave, or simply a place where trash was burned outside of Jerusalem. But their "trash-talk" is a very "grave mistake," and such an error is rooted in violation of the second of the Ten Commandments.

The Subtle Sin

The making of a graven image (commonly called "idolatry") is an extremely subtle sin, but I believe that it's the tap-root of all sin. It sounds strange nowadays to even talk about it because we are beyond the irrationality of cutting down trees and shaping idols for family worship.

Instead, we shape an idol in our minds — one to suit ourselves — and he's not made of wood or of stone. He's made of the stuff of the place of imagery—the imagination. He's a divine butler who is supposed to come running at our beck and call when we thirst for pleasure or have a problem that needs solving. Modern idolaters cling to the erroneous image that God is all-loving and absolute kindness, but not really an absolutely just God. So, He would *never* create Hell. And they are right. Their god would never create Hell because he couldn't. He doesn't exist! He's merely a creation of the imagination of a sinful mind.

Even the foolishness of atheism is rooted in idolatry. An atheist will often gather an image of a god in his mind — made up of "harsh and unfair" judgments of the Old Testament.[1] The image is tyrannical and offensive, and one that he therefore throws away in disgust. And so he should, because the god that he "doesn't believe in," doesn't exist. But in tossing his god away, he feels justified with his own viewpoint that *nothing created everything*. In his own mind, he now has good reason to sin his wicked heart out. Idolatry dissipates the fear of the Lord.

---

1. Bodie Hodge, "Isn't the God of the Old Testament evil, harsh and downright mean?" in Ken Ham, editor, *The New Answers Book 3*, (Green Forest, AR: Master Books, 2010), pp. 347–356.

What Not to Fear

Jesus said, "And do not fear those who kill the body but cannot kill the soul. But rather fear Him who is able to destroy both soul and body in hell" (Matthew 10:28). Look at His words. He said not to be fearful when someone comes at you with a sharpened knife to cut your throat; or threats of suicide bombers; or when a wild-eyed madman holds the cold steel of a gun barrel at your face, and screams that he's going to blow your brains out! Not fearful? *Who in his right mind wouldn't be?*

But Jesus is saying that such a terrifying scenario of being murdered *is nothing compared to falling into the hands of judgment of Almighty God.* How many of us do actually fear God and can say with the Psalmist, "My flesh trembles for fear of You" (Psalm 119:120)?

A wise man once said, "Most, I fear God. Next, I fear him who fears Him not." A man who has no fear of God will lie to you, steal from you, and even kill you . . . if he thinks he can get away with it. That's why America had over 400,000 murders between 1990 and 2010 — four hundred thousand — and that doesn't count the millions of babies who are murdered through abortion! Think of it — in just 20 years, we created a mountain of dead bodies the size of four Super Bowl crowds stacked on top of each of other. That's what happens when a country loses the fear of the Lord and creates its own false image of its Creator. It becomes one nation under a delusion about God.

Down through the ages, Israel's bloody and tragic history reveals that she continually forsook God and His laws, strayed into idolatry, lost the fear of God, gave herself to sexual and other sins, and then came under the judgment of God. We must learn from this.

Why the Silence?

I believe that the blame for the loss of the fear of God and His just judgment lies primarily at the feet of the pulpits of modern America. Many contemporary preachers have degenerated into motivational speakers, parroting the gospel as a means *of gain* or *of success* in *this* life. Few ache with horror at the thought of an everlasting Hell, and so few plead with humanity to flee its terrible flames and run to Jesus. The double tragedy is that these preachers have reproduced after their own kind and filled our pews with complacency.

Preaching that avoids the mention of Hell traces itself back to the neglect of God's moral Law (the Ten Commandments) and an abandoning of God's Word as the authority. If the Law is neglected, the exceeding sinfulness of sin isn't understood (Romans 7:13). The Law brings the knowledge of sin and shows it to us in its true nature (Romans 3:19–20). Paul said that without the Law he didn't even know what sin was (Romans 7:7). So when the Law is overlooked, mankind is left in the dark about his moral condition. If you don't believe me, ask any unrepentant sinner if he thinks he's a good person, and you will think that you are talking to an incarnation of a cross between Mother Theresa and Mahatma Ghandi.[2]

Again, without the Law to give us light (see Proverbs 6:23) we are left thinking that we are morally good. We may have some weaknesses, but we are only human. From that thinking comes the unspoken conclusion in many pulpits: *God is harsh and unjust to send anyone but Hitler and a few other nasty folks, to Hell.* Hence, the deafening silence on the subject. It's hard to justify Hell when an all-loving God is preached.

But the deleterious consequence of a Law-less and unbiblical gospel presentation goes even deeper than producing apathy. It causes a shallow understanding of Christ's blood shed on the Cross. And so the prodigal returns home — not to become a servant, but because he wants more money from his father; *because he never understood that his desires were for pig food.* Unrepentant, sin-loving people fill churches as tares among the wheat and as goats grazing among the sheep. "Good fish" and "bad fish" swim together, deceived by their sins because we have failed to do what Jesus did — use the Law to awaken them with the knowledge of sin (see Mark 10:17). We haven't imitated Paul (as he told us to), when he said, "You who preach against stealing, do you steal? You who say that people should not commit adultery, do you commit adultery?" (Romans 2:21–22). Instead of emulating Paul and reasoning with sinners about sin, righteousness, and judgment so that they tremble, we have consoled them with nice words and fair speeches. Who is going to be broken considering the sacrificial payment made on his behalf if he isn't told he has broken the Law?

---

2. If you don't talk to sinners because you have isolated yourself into the cozy cocoon of a Christian environment, watch the movie *180* and you will see a nasty, "black-hating," "Jew-hating," neo-Nazi, venomous, atheist, saying, "I hate America," and in the next breath saying, "Don't you think it's strange that God would send a nice guy like me to Hell?"

But when the Ten Commandments are unmasked and our sin is seen in its terrible reality, the Cross becomes a glorious pardon from the hopeless dismay of the gallows. The Law thundered our just condemnation of death and Hell, but God, who is rich in mercy, gave us life and Heaven.

Deluded Ramblings

If sinners die in their sins, they will be ripped from their graves and cast into the lake of fire. In doing so, God is doing that which is right, just, and good (Revelation 21:8). Such talk sounds like the ramblings of a depraved mind, until we think for a moment. Think about a town in the old West during the 1840s. It's filled with the lawlessness of rape and murder. The local council gathers and decides to bring in ten sharpshooting U.S. Marshalls to clean up the town. Think now — who is going to cringe at the thought of justice? Only the criminals. Who is going to rejoice when justice is done? Only the good people of the town. And so we should cringe at the thought of Judgment Day, *because we are criminals* in the eyes of a holy God. Look at what the Scriptures tell us about the day when God judges the world in righteousness:

> Let the rivers clap their hands; let the hills be joyful together before the LORD, for He is coming to judge the earth. With righteousness He shall judge the world, and the peoples with equity (Psalm 98:8–9).

Creation will clap with great joy when Hitler gets justice. It will be "joyful together before the Lord" when *every* murderer gets what is coming to him. But divine justice won't stop there. It *craves* righteousness, and will grind to powder with absolute and severe diligence every rapist, thief, fornicator, adulterer, and liar. And it won't stop there. It will search the inward parts and root out every hate-filled, lust-filled son and daughter of Adam and give them justice. It will judge the thoughts and intents of the heart, and even every idle word that a man speaks (Matthew 12:36). What a fearful thing to fall into the hands of the living God! But on that day righteousness, justice and truth will shine like the noonday sun.

When Men Speak Well of You

I was preaching in the open air recently at a local university and began by asking my 60-or-so listeners if they thought that they were good people. Then I went through the spirituality of the Ten Commandments, showing that God sees lust as adultery (Matthew 5:27–28) and hatred as murder (1 John 3:15). I spoke of the reality of Judgment Day, the surety of Hell for all who die in their sins, and the sobriety of personal eternal salvation. Then I preached the love of God in Christ — that God was rich in mercy, that He had provided a Savior and defeated death, and that each person must repent and trust in Christ alone to be saved.

As I got down from my soapbox, a student stood to his feet and began to preach. He said that I was wrong to condemn people, and that's not what Jesus did. He said that God was loving and kind, and that He wanted to bless sinners, adding, "He wants you to believe in yourself, and to know that one day any of you could rise to become the president!" The crowd applauded his encouraging words, no doubt confirming to him that he had said the right thing. Charles Spurgeon called such a preacher a "murderer."

> Ho, ho, sir surgeon, you are too delicate to tell the man that he is ill! You hope to heal the sick without their knowing it. You therefore flatter them; and what happens? They laugh at you; they dance upon their own graves. At last they die! Your delicacy is cruelty; your flatteries are poisons; you are a murderer. Shall we keep men in a fool's paradise? Shall we lull them into soft slumbers from which they will awake in hell? Are we to become helpers of their damnation by our smooth speeches? In the name of God we will not.[3]

Remove Hell from our message and you rip the beating heart out of the body.

Many years ago I knew an elderly woman whose life had been made miserable by a biker. Unbeknown to him, she was standing on a sidewalk when he started his massive machine, and its loud noise burst her eardrum. For years after that incident she had a screaming inside of her head that never stopped, and she was continually asking for prayer and pleading for help. The biker never knew what he did. He simply started his bike and drove off.

3. Charles Spurgeon, "Coming Judgment of the Secrets of Men," http://www.spurgeon.org/sermons/1849.htm, accessed May 7, 2012.

Such is the case of those who preach a Law-less gospel. They unwittingly cause great damage to Christianity. In a book (that can be freely read online) called *God Has a Wonderful Plan for Your Life*[4] you will find statistics that will make you want to scream for a lifetime. Law-less preaching has inoculated millions to the truth of the gospel, but the tragic results of unbiblical evangelism will only be *fully* realized in eternity.

Many preach the gospel unaware that the gospel is the arrow and the Law is the bow. It is the Law that gives the arrow of the gospel its thrust. It gets across the point that we are in danger, and that we desperately need a Savior.

Again, Spurgeon gives us light:

> Lower the Law, and you dim the light by which man perceives his guilt. This is a very serious loss to the sinner, rather than a gain; for it lessens the likelihood of his conviction and conversion. . . . I say you have deprived the gospel of its ablest auxiliary [most powerful weapon] when you have set aside the Law. You have taken away from it the schoolmaster that is to bring men to Christ . . . they will never accept grace till they tremble before a just and holy Law. Therefore the Law serves a most necessary and blessed purpose and it must not be removed from its place.[5]

How then do we convince a godless world that Hell exists? Simply by opening up the Law as Jesus did. Show sinners that God considers lust to be adultery and hatred to be murder, and the Holy Spirit will faithfully use the "work of the Law" to do His wonderful work (see Romans 2:14–15). Stir the conscience so that it does its God-given duty. Explain that if God is good He must punish sin, and then appeal to reason by asking what sort of judge would be considered good if he didn't do all he could to see that justice is done? Reason as Paul did with Felix — until there is trembling (Acts 24:25).

Let Holy Scripture be your guide as you paint the character of God on the canvas of the human heart, and, with the help of the Holy Spirit, you will see sinners work out their own salvation with "fear and trembling." Few souls will be swift to answer Him when there's no threat of the terrible

---

4. www.freeWonderfulBook.com, accessed May 7, 2012.
5. Charles Spurgeon, "The Perpetuity of the Law of God," http://www.angelfire.com/va/sovereigngrace/perpetuity.spurg.2.html, accessed May 7, 2012.

swift sword of judgment. Nor will they have jubilant feet if they don't hear that there will be "trampling out the vintage where the grapes of wrath are stored."

Depraved Indifference

Do you have a deep concern for the salvation of this wicked world? When, then, did you last mention Hell, or plead with a sinner to repent and trust the Savior? Or are you busy feeding yourself at the rich man's table while Lazarus lies at the gate, covered in sores? Do you care about the fate of the lost? Do you love your neighbor as yourself? Did you know that if you let another person die when you have the ability to save him, criminal law says that you are guilty of the crime of "depraved indifference"? What a perfect choice of words: *depraved* means that it's about as low as you can get, and *indifference* means that you couldn't care less.

It seems that much of the professing church could be guilty of the crime of depraved indifference. Bill Bright, in his book *The Coming Revival*, said that only 2 percent of the contemporary church in America regularly share their faith with others. The modern church is too busy feeding itself and quietly whispering, "World, go to Hell . . . I couldn't care less." We have a sinful world that doesn't know what sin is, doesn't see that they are in danger of damnation in Hell, and boldly uses Hell and damnation in an inappropriate way. God help them. God help us.

Chapter 19

The Importance of the Reformation

Dr. Carl J. Broggi

Introduction

For those who don't know, the Reformation was a split within the church. In fact, it was a much-needed split that had been building for centuries and finally happened.

The Reformation brought truth out of error and light out of darkness. Since the establishment of the Christian Church with Christ and the Apostles, there has been no greater single event that has taken place in the Church than the Reformation that began to rapidly unfold in the 16th century.[1] It was the fulfillment of a wonderful promise Jesus Christ made to the Apostle Peter and to all Christians when He said, "I will build My church, and the gates of Hades shall not prevail against it" (Matthew 16:18).

In the Bible, "gates" are symbolic of authority and power in the same way a gate is the key to the stronghold of a city — he who controls the gates are the ones in power and authority. For a Hebrew person, the city gate meant the same thing that city hall means to people in the Western world. Important business was transacted at the city gate.[2]

---

1. There was a prior split between the eastern and western churches around A.D. 1000, but the Protestant Reformation was essentially a "shot heard round the world!"
2. Deuteronomy 16:18, 17:8; Ruth 4:11.

When the Lord Jesus promised that He would build His Church and that the "gates of Hades" would not overpower it, He was picturing His victory over the organized power of Satan and death. Christ made a promise to His people that by His own death and Resurrection He would "storm the gates" and conquer death, so that death and Satan would not be victorious.[3]

The Reformation is a powerful illustration of Christ keeping His promise to His people. The Reformation sought to restore true Bible-based Christianity in a day that was mired in superstition, corruption, unbiblical ideas, and legalism.

Getting Started with a Reformation

When we think of the Reformation, it is important for us to remember that it did not happen all at once or that there was ever a time when Christ's Church had been extinguished. Since the day the Church began on Pentecost, Christ has always had His people.[4] When the Church first began they met in homes and in public spaces[5] and eventually in buildings by about the mid-third century. Beginning with the coming of the Holy Spirit, God has always had His people meeting in various places.

However, there was a time in human history when the organized, visible Church had become so corrupt that individuals within the Church sought to reform it — get it back to the authority of the Word of God. We typically refer to these individuals as "reformers." They included such people as John Knox, John Calvin, Heinrich Bullinger, Philip Malanchthon, Thomas Cranmer, Hugh Lattimer, and many others.

It is difficult to pinpoint with precision when the winds of reform began to blow; however, one might find opposition toward Rome and a love for the Scriptures as early as the 8th century and onward with groups

---

3. 1 Corinthians 15:50ff; Hebrews 2:14–15.
4. The ability to trace one's church back to the "first church" is an argument used by Roman Catholics along with the Greek Orthodox and a number of Protestant denominations. The Church, which began on the Day of Pentecost, is recorded for us in the New Testament with its growth, doctrine, and practices. Being able to trace a church's roots back to the "first church" is nowhere in Scripture given as a test for being the true church. What are given are repeated comparisons between what false teachers teach and what the first church taught, as recorded in the Bible. God has always had His "true church," even in the darkest time of human history.
5. The New Testament speaks of a large church in Jerusalem meeting together in a public space (e.g., the outer court of the temple in Acts 2:46), and by smaller groups in houses (e.g., the house of Mary, mother of Mark, in Acts 12:12).

such as the Paulicians, the Bogomils, and the Beghards. Later in the 12th and 13th centuries names such as the Albigensians and the Waldensians appeared in the regions of southern France and northern Italy. However, if a single figure rises to the forefront leading the charge in the early centuries, one might see it in the person of the Oxford scholar John Wycliffe, who has been aptly called, "the morning star of the reformation."

We might begin the story of Luther and his 95 Theses on the door of the Castle Church in Wittemburg in 1517 as an echo of Galatians 4:4, "when the fullness of the time had come." A corrupted papacy, the declension of monasticism, and the decay of scholastic thought coupled with the invention of the printing press and the publication of the Greek New Testament were all contributors to the tsunami of ideas which deluged the Romish system of indulgences and penance and merit and oppression.

The customary act of nailing a thesis to a church door to challenge the locals to a theological debate was, in our language, God's timing for the "straw to break the camel's back." Almost simultaneous to reformation in Germany, the change came to Switzerland, and then following in England, Scotland, France, and Holland, and in other European nations.

The product of more recent scholarly studies has brought to light the huge movement in Europe, sometimes called the "Left Wing" or the "Second Front" of the reformation. More commonly referred to collectively as "The Anabaptists," these included groups such as the Mennonites, the Moravians, the Hutterites, the Hugenots, and others. This can be summed up in the words of Swiss reformer Ulrich Zwingli who stated, "The struggle against the catholic party was but child's play when compared to the struggle that was erupting on the Second Front."[6]

However, the acount of Martin Luther and his collision with the Roman hierarchy is in some ways typical and is well worth telling because he was probably the most famous and best known of all the reformers. He was born in Eiselben, Germany, on November 10, 1483, and he grew up in a very poor family. Through great sacrifice, his father sent him to law school where he distinguished himself as one of the best students at the University of Eufurt. It was there that he was exposed to the Scriptures for the first time when in the library he discovered a copy of the Latin Bible.

---

6. Lenard Verduin, "The Reformers and Their Stepchildren," http://gospelpedlar. com/articles/Church%20History/stepchildren.html.

In 1505, through the sudden loss of a close friend and then through a near-death experience in a violent storm, Luther gave up the study of law to begin the study of theology. He was in search of inner peace. He was fearful of his spiritual state, wondering what would happen if, as his friend, he had suddenly died in that fierce thunderstorm. This led to his becoming an Augustinian monk in 1505.

Though Luther's life had been touched when he read the Latin Bible in law school, like the Ethiopian eunuch he needed help in understanding the Scriptures.[7] At this time in his life, Luther did not understand the significance of Christ's death and Resurrection. He sought favor with God through prayer and fasting, good deeds, and doing penance. He did not realize that he could be forgiven through faith in Christ. When found unconscious in his room from exhaustion in trying to serve God, Johann von Staupitz, the head Augustinian monk, witnessed to Luther of Christ's love. He encouraged him to find forgiveness through Christ's blood and to love Christ because Christ first loved him.[8] But Luther did not understand and was afraid of God and of His Son Christ.

In May of 1507, he was ordained as a priest, and in 1508 he was asked to become a professor at the University of Wittenberg. While serving at the university, Luther had the opportunity in 1510 to visit Rome where he expected to find godly priests, bishops, and cardinals. Instead he found a corrupt church . . . men who were living in opulence (wealth and riches) and priests who did not even believe what they were teaching the people. This, coupled with his pilgrimage on his knees up the "holy stairs" where he hoped to find forgiveness, left Luther confused and he did not understand why he was unable to find any peace.[9]

---

7. The Scriptures can be understood at face value, but often God uses a Spirit-filled Christian to help the unbeliever understand (e.g., Philip explained the Scriptures to the Ethiopian eunuch in Acts 8:26–35).
8. Johann von Stauptiz was the vicar of the German Observant Augustinian Friars who was deeply concerned for Luther because of his sickly state. He is an example of a true believer who served at that time in the organized Church.
9. There is in Rome, a flight of white marble steps called the *Scala Sancta*, which means, "holy stairs." It is claimed that Jesus climbed these very stairs when He went from Pilate's judgment hall to Calvary. It is said that an angel moved them from Jerusalem to Rome. In Luther's day, the priests in Rome told the people that whoever went up these stairs on his knees would have all his sins forgiven. So Luther went up these stairs on his knees, praying and kissing each step, but he found no peace for his soul.

God was preparing Luther to find forgiveness through faith in Jesus Christ.

In the two years that followed, Luther was studying and lecturing on the Book of Romans. Somewhere in this time frame, around 1515, he was meditating on Romans 1:17 and his life was wondrously changed. The phrase, "The just shall live by faith" brought personal assurance to him that he was accepted by God — through faith alone.

He wrote in his introduction to his commentary on Romans, "I felt myself to be reborn and to have gone through open doors into paradise." He realized for the first time that salvation was not something he needed to achieve (by works), but something he needed to receive. Luther's life was radically and forever changed. He was now eager to obey God, not to *earn* salvation, but because he had found salvation on the basis of Christ's death and Resurrection. Luther knew that the simple message of God's grace through His Son's sacrifice needed to be proclaimed.

The need to change or "reform" the Church became very apparent to him when he witnessed Johann Tetzel selling indulgences in his city of Wittenberg. An indulgence was a piece of paper, signed or stamped with the pope's name, which guaranteed that all sins past, present, and even future, would be forgiven at death. For a small fee, purgatory could be avoided and immediate entrance into heaven would be obtained. Purgatory was a theoretical place where Roman Catholics believed souls were "purged" and cleansed.[10] A popular slogan of the day became, "When the coin in the coffer rings, the soul from Purgatory springs."[11] The money collected from the sale of indulgences was used to help rebuild St. Peter's Cathedral in Rome and also to foster a luxurious lifestyle for the pope and clergy.

This whole course of events led Martin Luther to attach his famous 95 Theses to the church door of Wittenberg on October 31, 1517. His

---

10. The Roman Catholic doctrine of purgatory remains to this day. It is argued that nearly all persons must undergo further cleansing or "purging" before they may enter heaven. The Roman Catholic Church also teaches that those who are still alive here on earth can "bring comfort and alleviation to those in purgatory by 'masses, prayers, almsgiving, and other pious works' " (*The Teaching of Christ — A Catholic Catechism for Adults*, Sunday Visitor Publishing Division, 1991 — an officially stamped catechism for Roman Catholics).

11. Luther directly addressed Tetzel's sale of indulgences in his "95 Theses," for theses #27 reads, "There is no divine authority for preaching that so soon as the penny jingles into the money-box, the soul flies out" [of purgatory].

assertions stated how he felt the Roman Catholic Church had deviated from the clear teaching of Scripture.[12] To post a document on a door was a common academic practice of that day. Since it was posted on the door of the Catholic Church, it served as an invitation to debate. Luther's assertions challenged a number of different practices and doctrinal positions of the Roman Catholic Church. This document was originally posted in Latin, the language of the scholar, but it was soon translated in nearly every European language. The common people soon understood how Luther was challenging the established Church. This document was used by God to start the Reformation. Luther, and others like him, knew the corruption in the Church needed to end and that the truth of God's Word needed to be proclaimed. Since a number of priests and clergy like Luther were "protesting" the established Church headquartered in Rome, this movement came to be known as the "Protestant Reformation."

So what were some of the central doctrines of the Protestant Reformation? What did Luther and the other reformers believe?

While it is true that with time a number of the reformers differed among themselves over certain doctrinal issues subsequently dividing them into different denominations, there was still doctrinal unity over what they considered to be essential non-negotiable doctrines.[13] Those non-negotiable doctrines that they believed to be essential to the health of the true Church revolved around the *solas* of the reformation. The Latin word *sola* means "alone" or "only" in English. There were five *solas* during the reformation that represented the foundational doctrines of this movement. It is impossible to understand the importance of the Reformation without understanding these five central truths.

Sola Scripture: Scripture Alone

Sola scriptura is the teaching that the Bible is the only inspired, inerrant, and authoritative Word of God. The Reformers believed that when the

---

12. The official name of what is commonly referred to as the "95 Theses" is "The 95 Theses on the Power and Efficacy of Indulgences," highlighting the issue that originally motivated Luther to write this document.

13. Luther, Zwingli, and Calvin differed over such issues as the meaning and role of the sacraments and the relationship of the Church to the state. With time, the reformers broke into different groups, including the Lutherans, the Presbyterians, the Puritans, and Anglicans. But on the essential doctrines necessary to believe for salvation they were in full agreement.

Bible speaks, we can speak and where it is authoritative, we can be authoritative, because *Scripture alone* is the only source for Christian doctrine. Furthermore, they taught that since all Christians were "priests of God," the Scripture is accessible to all and ultimately can be understood by all.[14]

Without dismissing the importance of a contextual, historical, literal interpretation of Scripture, Martin Luther and other Protestant Reformers opposed the idea that only those in Church leadership could understand the Bible correctly. For Luther, there were many practices in the Roman Catholic Church that went either beyond the realm of Scripture or were in direct contradiction to Scripture.

They understood the truth that everything that an individual or church believes is based on something. The Reformers believed that in the final analysis, all teaching either originated with God or it originated with man. Therefore, the only sure and certain litmus test for truth was *sola scriptura*.

Sola Gratia: Grace Alone

Sola gratia is the belief that salvation is not something that can be earned or merited by a person's good deeds, but is based on God's unmerited favor. This was indeed the clear teaching of both Christ and the apostles.[15]

When the Apostle Paul defended salvation by grace to the Galatian Christians who had been infiltrated with false teachers he wrote, "I do not set aside the grace of God; for if righteousness comes through the law, then Christ died in vain" (Galatians 2:21; also see Romans 5:15). We could paraphrase Paul's words of salvation by grace alone by simply saying, "If a person could achieve a righteous standing before God by what he does, then there was no need for the death of Christ."

Clearly, the plain teaching of the Bible is that Christ's death was according to the preordained plan of God.[16] The Lord Jesus taught that His

14. This is commonly referred to as "the priesthood of the believer," based on passages like 1 Peter 2:9–10. The priesthood of all believers implies the right and duty of the Christian laity not only to read the Bible in their own language, but it also opposes the idea that only the clergy can exclusively serve as mediators between God and the people.

15. Luke 18:9–17; John 3:14–16; Acts 26:18; Romans 3:21–5:1; 1 Corinthians 1:30; Galatians 2:15–16; Ephesians 2:8–9; Philippians 3:1–9; Colossians 1:20; Titus 3:3–7; Hebrews 10:5–10; 1 Peter 1:18–19; 1 John 4:9–10; Revelation 5:9–10.

16. The Old Testament clearly illustrated and prophesied this truth in passages like Genesis 22, Psalm 22, and Isaiah 53, while the New Testament plainly stated this truth in passages like Acts 2:23, 3:18 and 4:27–28.

life would not be taken from Him, but that He would give it (John 10:17–18). The manner in which the Crucifixion unfolded demonstrated that Christ voluntarily gave His life as complete and total payment for sin (John 18). The Reformers understood this to be the free and unmerited grace of God.

The unearned favor of God is described in Paul's letter to the Romans when he states, "And if by grace, then it is no longer of works; otherwise grace is no longer grace" (Romans 11:6). And so, Paul can write in his letter to Titus that we are "justified by His grace" and not by our deeds (Titus 3:7). For the Reformers salvation, as revealed in the Bible, from beginning to end is the work of God. Because God acts alone to save the sinner, *sola gratia* is one of the five fundamental beliefs of reformation theology.

Sola Fide: Faith Alone

Sola fide is the teaching that our salvation can only be received on the basis of our faith in Christ. The Reformers never grew weary of teaching that our salvation is by grace alone through faith alone.

Luther, Calvin, Zwingli, and others all referred to *sola fide* as the "material principle," because it involves the very "matter or substance" of what a person must understand and believe in order to be saved. They taught that if a person thought salvation could be received apart from faith alone in Christ's death and Resurrection, he could not be saved.

The teaching of faith alone flows from the doctrine of grace alone. Because salvation is completely based on God's grace alone, then it must be received by faith alone. Of course, this plain truth is found in hundreds of passages throughout the Bible. When the Apostle Paul wrote to the Ephesians he said, "For by grace you have been saved through faith, and that not of yourselves; it is the gift of God, not of works, lest anyone should boast" (Ephesians 2:8–9).[17]

Because the organized church of the 16th century taught that man could merit salvation or be justified partly by the things he did, the Reformers emphasized sola fide.[18] They emphasized that good works could

---

17. See also Romans 5:1–2 and Acts 26:18.
18. The issue of debate concerned how a person could be saved or justified. Justification is the act of God by which he declares sinners to be righteous by what Jesus Christ accomplished. It comes to the individual not by anything he or she might do but by "faith alone" (*sola fide*).

not save, or even help save, but that good works were only the evidence and fruit of genuine conversion.[19]

Only by placing complete faith and trust in the death and Resurrection of Christ could a person find true salvation. To put it differently, the Roman Catholic Church in Luther's day taught that faith *and* good works produced justification. This teaching was in contradistinction from the Reformers who emphasized that faith alone in Christ yielded justification *and that good works would follow*. In other words, in Catholic theology, righteous works are considered, in addition to faith in Christ, as a partial basis for salvation.

In biblical theology, in Reformation theology, good works are seen as the *result and evidence* of someone who has placed their trust in Christ alone. Justification by faith alone is what the reformers understood as *sola fide*.

Solus Christus: Christ Alone

Since Scripture alone is the final authority for determining what we are to believe (*sola scriptura*), the Reformers taught that justification comes from God's grace alone (*sola gratia*) and is ours through faith alone (*sola fide*). But the reason they taught we can be declared forgiven and clean in God's sight by grace through faith is due to the work of Christ alone (*solus Christus*).[20]

During the time of Martin Luther, the medieval church obviously spoke about Christ. A church that failed to do so could hardly claim to be even nominally Christian.[21] However, the Roman Catholic Church had added many human achievements to Christ's work, so that it was no longer possible to say that salvation was entirely by Christ.

The Reformers understood that to deny the sufficiency of Christ's death, burial, and Resurrection as able to save without works was heretical. To do so was to be guilty of preaching a "different Jesus" (2 Corinthians 11:4). The axiom *solus Christus* was an affirmation that because of

---

19. Ephesians 2:10; Titus 1:15; Titus 2:13–14
20. Sometimes in a more popular form this *sola* is written as *sola Christa*, but since Latin is a case language it is properly written *solus Christus*.
21. A nominal Christian is someone who is Christian in name only but who has not experienced genuine conversion to Christ. Such a person may be religious but not born-again, which is necessary to enter the kingdom of God (John 3:1–8).

Christ's sinless life and substitutionary death, nothing could be added to what He as the resurrected Lord accomplished in order for us to be saved. They believed any "gospel" that either denies or fails to acknowledge this truth is a different gospel, a false gospel, which subsequently is powerless to save anyone (Galatians 1:6–9).

The Reformers understood when the Lord Jesus, who had never sinned, became "sin for us" by bearing our sin "in His own body on the cross," the guilty repentant sinner could be declared righteous on that basis alone (2 Corinthians 5:21; 1 Peter 2:24). On the Cross, our guilt and shame for failing to keep God's commandments was laid on Christ, so that when we come to God through faith in Jesus, we are credited with His righteousness.

For the Reformers, because the death of Christ paid for all our sin in full and finished all the demands God had against us (John 19:30; Hebrews 10:10–14), there is no need to find an ongoing sacrifice in a religious service, in the communion table, or in seeking help through clergy, saints, or Jesus' mother.

Solus Christus emphasizes that because Christ alone saves, there is only one mediator between God and man and that mediator is Christ Himself (1 Timothy 2:5; Acts 4:12; John 14:6). In addition, since Christ's death and Resurrection was a complete and full payment for our sins, the Reformers understood that all true Christians are "believer priests" without any need for a human priest to offer a sacrifice on our behalf.

The only sacrifice that Christians or clergy can offer today, as a royal priesthood, is not to shelter us from God's wrath, but to be given out of gratitude for being delivered from God's wrath.[22] *Solus Christus* was the Reformation call to faith in Christ as the sole mediator between God and man.

Soli Deo Gloria: To God Alone Be the Glory

Each of the great *solas* is summed up in the fifth Reformation motto: *soli Deo gloria*, meaning, "to God alone be the glory." The Reformers believed that the organized Church of the day gave honor and glory to man

---

22. The Bible speaks of sacrifices forgiven people make including the giving of yourself (Romans 12:1–2), your temporal treasures (Philippians 4:17–18), your verbal witness (1 Peter 2:9–10), your praise (Hebrews 13:15), and your good deeds (Hebrews 13:16).

because in the popular theology of that day man contributed to and helped earn his salvation. They believed that the popes and clergy and the canonized saints robbed the glory that belonged to God alone.

Reformers taught that no one should ever exalt man, but God alone, since God is the author of salvation from start to finish. *Soli Deo Gloria* is precisely what the Apostle Paul expressed in Romans 11:36 when he wrote, "to [Him] be glory forever. Amen." The Reformers believed that all of life is to be lived to the glory of God and that the chief end of man is to glorify God.

The glory of God became the great and all-consuming goal of the men and women who helped to reform the organized Church that had become corrupted. A man-centered religion could only produce man-centered admiration. But Christ-centered faith could only produce people who were interested in giving God praise and honor and glory.[23] So it is not surprising to find the redeemed in heaven saying, "Amen! Blessing and glory and wisdom, thanksgiving and honor and power and might, be to our God forever and ever. Amen" (Revelation 7:12).

Luther's Excommunication

In the year 1521, Martin Luther was excommunicated from the Catholic Church by Pope Leo X and declared a heretic. A death warrant was issued giving anyone freedom to kill him. God gave Luther protection in a castle owned by Prince Frederick of Saxony. It was there that he produced a translation of the Bible in the German language that the common man could read.

Twelve years after Luther posted his "95 Theses" to the church door in Wittenberg, a movement of reform had grown so large that the word "Protestant" became the popular word used to describe those people who stood behind Luther's protests against the Catholic Church.

The Reformation was important because it brought tens of thousands of people back to the Bible as their final authority. As men and women searched the Scriptures, they discovered that salvation was by grace alone, through faith alone, on the basis of Christ alone, such that God alone should receive all the glory.

---

23. The glory of God runs all the way through the Scripture. For a sampling of New Testament verses see Romans 11:33–36; 1 Corinthians 10:31; Ephesians 3:21; 1 Peter 4:11; 2 Peter 3:1; Revelation 1:6.

Martin Luther, and many like him, laid the foundation for the Reformation that changed the course of history for centuries to come. Christ's promise to His people that He would "storm the gates of Hades" by conquering death was being realized in a fresh way. The Reformation is a powerful illustration of Christ keeping His promise to His people. Oh that God would give a modern day Reformation to His Church.

Chapter 20

Were Adam and Eve
Real People?

Dr. Georgia Purdom

❧❀❀❀❀❀❀❀❀❀❀❀❀❀❀❀❀❀❀❀❀

The historicity of Adam and Eve is one of the most debated issues in modern Christianity. There are many who simply do not believe Adam and Eve existed, even within the Church! You may be wondering how this can be. Let me explain. . . .

Many liberal Christian scholars have concluded that genetics has disproven the Genesis account of Adam and Eve.[1] Francis Collins, director of the National Institutes of Health and founder of Biologos, a liberal Christian organization that promotes theistic evolution (meaning that God used evolution and millions of years to create the universe and everything in it), states,

> As noted previously, studies of human variation, together with the fossil record, all point to an origin of modern humans approximately a hundred thousand years ago, most likely in East Africa. Genetic analyses suggest that approximately ten thousand ancestors gave rise to the entire population of 6 billion humans on

---

1. A liberal Christian may be a believer in Christ (if they have received the Jesus of Scripture as their Lord and Savior and believe God raised Him from the dead), but they have taken many "liberties" with the text of Scripture. In many cases, they simply do not believe what is written in the Bible, especially Genesis.

the planet.[2]

Karl Giberson, author, former professor, and former vice-president of Biologos, and Francis Collins write,

> Based on what we know today about both science and the ancient world of the Hebrews, it is simply not reasonable to try to turn the brief comments in Genesis into a biologically accurate description of how humans originated.[3]

Kathryn Applegate, program director for Biologos, and Darrel Falk, president of Biologos and professor of biology at Point Loma Nazarene University, state,

> All science can say is that there was never a time when only two people existed on the earth: it is silent on whether or not God began a special relationship with a historical couple at some point in the past.[4]

Some scholars do not believe that the existence of a literal Adam and Eve is crucial to Christian doctrines of the Fall and redemption. William Dembski, college professor and Senior Fellow with Discovery Institute Center for Science and Culture, writes,

> The theodicy [defense of God's goodness in view of the existence of evil] developed in this book is certainly compatible with a literal Adam and Eve. But it does not require a literal Adam and Eve. What it does require is that a group of hominids, however many, had their loyalty to God fairly tested; moreover, on taking the test, they all failed.[5]

Others believe that the Genesis account of the creation of man and the Fall may be allegorical. Francis Collins states,

> The real dilemma for the believer comes down to whether

2. Francis S. Collins, *The Language of God* (New York: Free Press, 2006), p. 207.
3. Karl W. Giberson and Francis S. Collins, *The Language of Science and Faith* (Downers Grove, IL: Intervarsity Press, 2011), p. 206.
4. Darrel Falk and Kathryn Applegate, "NPR's Adam and Eve Story," August 10, 2011, http://biologos.org/blog/nprs-adam-and-eve-story.
5. William Dembski, *The End of Christianity* (Nashville, TN: B & H Publishing, 2009), p. 146.

Genesis 2 is describing a special act of miraculous creation that applied to a historic couple . . . or whether this is a poetic and powerful allegory of God's plan for the entrance of the spiritual nature (the soul) and the Moral Law into humanity.[6]

Peter Enns, author, former professor, and Senior Fellow of Biblical Studies for Biologos, in an interview for *Christianity Today* reveals,

To [Peter] Enns, a literal Adam as a special creation without evolutionary forebears is "at odds with everything else we know about the past from the natural sciences and cultural remains." As he reads the early chapters of Genesis, he says, "The Bible itself invites a symbolic reading by using cosmic battle imagery and by drawing parallels between Adam and Israel."[7]

In summary, these scholars believe that the initial human population was about 10,000 people (evolved from ape-like ancestors) who lived over 100,000 years ago, that the existence of a literal Adam and Eve is not vital to Christian doctrine, and that the Genesis account of creation and the Fall may be allegories representing "higher" spiritual truths or a symbolic representation of the nation of Israel.

So what is the truth? Does the Bible teach the existence of a literal Adam and Eve and is it essential to Christian doctrine? Does modern genetics "disprove" their existence? Let's take a closer look at both the theological and scientific aspects of this issue to discover the answers to these questions.

Christian Doctrine and Adam and Eve

Scripture Teaches the Existence of a Literal Adam and Eve

Genesis 1 and 2 clearly describe Adam and Eve as literal historical people. Adam was created first from the dust of the ground (Genesis 2:7) and Eve was then created from a rib taken from Adam's side (Genesis 2:18). They were distinct creations from the animals and were created in God's image (Genesis 1:26–27). Adam was placed in the Garden of Eden to work it and take care of it (Genesis 2:15), and Adam and Eve were given dominion over all living things (Genesis 1:28). Adam was com-

---

6. Collins, *The Language of God*, p. 207.
7. Richard N. Ostling, "The Search for the Historical Adam," *Christianity Today* (June, 2011): p. 26.

manded by God not to eat from the tree of knowledge of good and evil and was told that if he disobeyed he would die (Genesis 2:17). Adam and Eve were joined in marriage by God (Genesis 2:24) and told to be fruitful and multiply and fill the earth (Genesis 1:28). Only *living* human beings can work, rule over, obey, marry, have children, and die!

Other Bible authors also reveal their belief in the existence of a literal Adam and Eve. Job (31:33) refers to Adam trying to cover his sin (Genesis 3:7). Paul (1 Corinthians 15:45, 47–49) writes about man (referring to Adam) being a living being and made from dust (Genesis 2:7, 3:19). In 2 Corinthians 11:3, Paul warns the Corinthian church not to be deceived as Eve was deceived by the serpent (Genesis 3:6). Acts 17:26 states that every nation is made of one blood. This is only possible if Genesis 3:20, which says that the woman was named Eve because she was the "mother of all living," refers to a real life Eve.

Paul affirms the sequence of creation — Adam first, then Eve — in 1 Corinthians 11:8–9, 12 and 1 Timothy 2:13–14. He subsequently builds church doctrine on this basis, teaching that men are to be the spiritual leaders of the Church. The creation sequence is also vital to Paul's teaching on leadership and submission in marriage, which is a symbol of the relationship between Christ and the Church (Ephesians 5). If the creation sequence of Adam and Eve is not literal and historical, then the doctrines that Paul builds off it are meaningless — even his calling Jesus "the last Adam" (1 Corinthians 15:45)!

Jesus affirms the existence of a literal Adam and Eve in Matthew 19:4–5 (also Mark 10:6–8) when He quotes Genesis 1:27 and 2:24 as the institution of the first marriage. If Adam and Eve were merely allegories, then so was their marriage. This would certainly not provide Jesus with a foundation for real-life marriage since as an allegory their marriage would represent something different.

Adam is also mentioned in several genealogies. In Genesis 5:1–5, it is written that Adam had sons and daughters, was 130 years old when Seth was born, and died at 930 years old. These ages only have relevance if they are referring to a literal person. First Chronicles 1:1–27 traces Abraham's genealogy beginning with Adam, and Jude 1:14 references "Enoch, [as] the seventh from Adam", who prophesied. Not many question the historicity of Enoch and Abraham, and yet they think Enoch and Abraham's great, great . . . grandfather was likely not a real person.

Luke 3:23–38 traces Jesus' genealogy back to Adam. This is significant because Jesus was the Seed of Eve promised in Genesis 3:15 that would bruise or crush Satan's head. Few question that Jesus was a real person, but then how can He be the promised *physical Seed* if His great, great . . . grandmother is an allegory?

It is clear from Scripture that the Bible's authors and Jesus Himself believed in the existence of a literal and historical Adam and Eve.

The Existence of a Literal Adam and Eve Is Essential to the Christian Doctrines of Sin and Salvation

Oddly enough, atheists understand the vital relationship between the historicity of Adam, Eve, and original sin to the purpose of Christ. On a website promoting their Christmas campaign, the organization American Atheists stated:

> Chances are, if you're reading this, you don't believe in the fable of Adam and Eve and the talking snake. . . . You probably don't believe that Adam literally ate a fruit, resulting in God expelling him and Eve out of the idyllic Garden of Eden.
>
> In other words, you know that's a myth.
>
> Right so far? So if Adam and Eve and the Talking Snake are myths, then Original Sin is also a myth, right? Well, think about it. . .
>
> • Jesus' major purpose was to save mankind from original sin.
>
> Then they continue,
>
> • Without Original Sin, the marketing that all people are sinners and therefore need to accept Jesus falls moot.
>
> No Adam and Eve means no need for a savior. . . . No Fall of man means no need for atonement and no need for a Redeemer. You know it.[8]

The atheists understand the foundational importance of a literal Adam and Eve committing original sin to the purpose of the death and Resurrection of Jesus Christ. That is why they attack Genesis so much!

Paul understood this essential link between Adam and Christ and

---

8. American Atheists Christmas Campaign, http://atheists.org/content/christmas. See also Georgia Purdom, "American Atheist Christmas Campaign," Answers in Genesis, http://blogs.answersingenesis.org/blogs/georgia-purdom/2010/12/21/american-atheist-christmas-campaign/.

discussed it in Romans 5:12, 14–19 and 1 Corinthians 15:21–22, 45–49. Paul's emphasis on this connection is not surprising since his audience was mainly Greeks. They did not know the Bible or have an understanding of it as the Jewish people did.

In order for them to understand their need for Christ, Paul had to take them back to Genesis so they would know what sin is (disobedience to God) and why all people are sinners (because they are descendants of Adam and Eve who committed the first sin). This allowed the Greeks to come to a realization of their sinful state and their need of salvation from their sins through Christ.

The historicity of Adam and Eve lies at the very heart of the gospel message. If Adam is not a historical person who sinned, as stated in Genesis, and we are not all sinners as a result, then Jesus died for nothing! A.B. Caneday, professor of New Testament Studies and Biblical Theology at Northwestern College, writes,

> If Paul holds and advocates wrong beliefs concerning Adam's origin and historicity, how is he to be trusted doctrinally, since the doctrines he affirms and teaches are entirely inseparable from biblically stated origins and historicity.
>
> The one man, Adam, as a historic person is integral both to humanity's impaired dominion and subjection to death and sin bound up in his disobedience and to the proclamation of God's gracious gift of righteousness that restores dominion in life through the obedience of one man, Jesus Christ (cf. Rom 5:17).[9]

Scripture makes clear that the existence of a literal Adam and Eve is foundational and essential to the gospel of Jesus Christ.

Modern Genetics and Adam and Eve

Did Mitochondrial Eve and Y Chromosome Adam Live 100,000+ Years Ago?

Mitochondrial Eve and Y chromosome Adam are supposedly some of our earliest ancestors. Mitochondrial Eve is proposed as the great, great . . . grandmother of us all and lived approximately 200,000 years

---

9. A.B. Caneday, "The Language of God and Adam's Genesis and Historicity in Paul's Gospel," *Southern Baptist Journal of Theology* 15 (2011): p. 26–59.

ago.[10] Y chromosome Adam is proposed as the great, great . . . grandfather of us all and lived approximately 142,000 years ago.[11] They were two people among larger populations of people of their time whose DNA survived and exists in every woman and/or man today. Clearly this does not refer to one couple specially created by God in the Garden of Eden only 6,000 years ago.[12]

Mitochondrial and Y chromosome DNA are useful in studies of human populations because they are passed with very little change from one generation to the next. Mitochondrial DNA is used to trace maternal lineages since it is only passed from mother to children (fathers do not contribute mitochondrial DNA to their children). Y chromosome DNA is used to trace paternal lineages since it is only passed from the father to male children (females do not have a Y chromosome).

Small differences in the mitochondrial and Y chromosome DNA over time serve as a "molecular clock" that assists in determining how long ago our ancestors lived. However, a molecular clock is not an independent measure of time and is based on assumptions about the past. For evolutionary scientists, this includes assumed evolutionary relationships (i.e., chimps and humans share a common ancestor), assumed mutation rates (i.e., rates do not vary over time), and assumed accuracy of radiometric dating of rock layers and, thus, fossils.

If the assumptions are wrong, then the molecular clock will not give accurate dates. From a biblical perspective, there are obvious problems with these assumptions, but even evolutionary scientists acknowledge that molecular clocks are extremely suspect. In an article entitled, "Reading the Entrails of Chickens: Molecular Timescales of Evolution and the Illusion of Precision," the authors state,

> Despite their allure, we must sadly conclude that all divergence

---

10. Krzysztof A. Cyran and Marek Kimmel, "Alternatives to the Wright-Fisher Model: The Robustness of Mitochondrial Eve Dating," *Theoretical Population Biology* 78 (2010): p. 165–172.

11. Fulvio Cruciani et al., "A Revised Root for the Human Y Chromosomal Phylogenetic Tree: The Origin of Patrilineal Diversity in Africa," *The American Journal of Human Genetics* 88 (2011): p. 814–818.

12. If we tally up the genealogies in the Bible from Adam to Christ, we only get about 4,000 years, and a great many chronologists have done this. That chronology places Adam and Eve only about 6,000 years ago (Christ was about 2,000 years ago from today).

estimates [used to calibrate molecular clocks] discussed here are without merit. Our advice to the reader is: whenever you see a time estimate in the evolutionary literature, demand uncertainty.[13]

Creation scientists who have studied mitochondrial and Y chromosome DNA have concluded that due to the low levels of variation (few differences) in DNA from many different people groups around the world that a very short time has passed between modern humans and our ancestors.[14] Time frames proposed by evolutionists would result in much greater differences in the DNA than is observed. This confirms the biblical chronology of only a few thousand years between humanity today and Adam and Eve.

Interestingly, people in different geographic locations have differences in mitochondrial and Y chromosome DNA (called haplotypes) that appear specific to certain populations. Creation scientists are actively studying these clusters of differences to shed light on possible migration routes following the dispersion of people at the Tower of Babel.

Was the Initial Human Population Composed of 10,000 Individuals?

Evolutionary scientists have shown in mathematical simulations that to achieve the genetic diversity of modern humans the starting initial population would need to be greater than two people. Most estimates put the number around 10,000.[15] However, as discussed previously, these studies are based on assumptions about the past. For evolutionary scientists, this includes assumed evolutionary relationships, assumed mutation rates, and assumed generation times (the time between parents and offspring does not vary). They are arbitrarily assuming evolutionary processes to try to prove evolutionary processes, which is a fallacy.

If the assumptions are wrong, then the mathematical simulations will

---

13. Dan Graur and William Martin, "Reading the Entrails of Chickens: Molecular Timescales of Evolution and the Illusion of Precision," *Trends in Genetics* 20 (2004): p. 80–86.

14. Robert Carter, Dan Criswell, and John Sanford, "The 'Eve' Mitochondrial Consensus Sequence," in *Proceedings of the Sixth International Conference on Creationism*, A. A. Snelling, editor (Pittsburgh, PA: Creation Science Fellowship and Dallas, TX: Institute for Creation Research, 2008), p. 111–116.

15. John H. Relethford, "Genetics of Modern Human Origins and Diversity," *Annual Review of Anthropology* 27 (1998): p. 1–23.

not give an accurate initial population size necessary to generate today's human genetic variation. In fact, the genetic evidence is consistent with human DNA being "young" and the human race beginning with a very small starting population (the Bible tells us the starting population was two people!).

The International HapMap project endeavors to study a select group of DNA similarities and differences between humans known as single nucleotide polymorphisms (SNPs).[16] The SNPs are believed to be representative of the genome (total human DNA) such that what is true for them would be true for the whole genome. These studies and others have shown that the difference in DNA between any two humans is amazingly low . . . only 0.1 percent.[17]

Reflecting on this very low percentage, some scientists posited, "This proportion is low compared with those of many other species, from fruit flies to chimpanzees, reflecting the *recent* origins of our species from a *small* founding population" (emphases mine).[18] They also stated, "[Certain genetic estimates] tell us that humans vary only slightly at the DNA level and that only a small proportion of this variation separates continental populations."[19]

These findings are consistent with the Bible's history that humans were created several thousands years ago; in other words, a short amount of time has passed, so there is little genetic variation. It also gives us support regarding the dispersion of the human population at Babel into groups that migrated and were largely isolated from other groups. Specific genetic differences became prominent in these groups on separate continents and remains in these populations today.

In addition, many places in the human genome that vary (like the SNPs) occur in only two versions.[20] For example, approximately 50 percent of the world's population has "version A" and 50 percent has "version B." This is consistent with a founding population of only two people!

Other versions such as "C" and "D" are restricted to specific popula-

---

16. International HapMap Project, http://hapmap.ncbi.nlm.nih.gov/.
17. Lynn B. Jorde and Stephen P. Wooding, "Genetic Variation, Classification and 'Race'," *Nature Genetics* 36 (2004): S28–S33.
18. Ibid.
19. Ibid.
20. "Genome Variations," Genome News Network, http://www.genomenewsnetwork. org/resources/whats_a_genome/Chp4_1.shtml.

tions in certain geographical locations. These likely represent "private mutations" that occurred in populations that became isolated from each other following the Babel dispersion. The findings of the HapMap Project and other studies will be invaluable to creation scientists studying migration routes and post-Babel populations.

In comparing various models for understanding human genetic variation, a group of evolutionary scientists compared the favored serial founder model (out of Africa model of human origins) to several others including a model they named the "instantaneous divergence model."[21] They define this latter model as all populations diverging at the same time in the past. Of course, this sounds strikingly similar to what occurred at the Babel dispersion in the Middle East; however, the scientists believe it is historically "implausible."

Their results showed that the genetic "predictions" of the instantaneous divergence model are consistent with observed human genetic variation! The scientists concluded, "Thus, although a serial founder model is supported by the analysis, many alternatives cannot be excluded."[22] Once again, genetic evidence is consistent with biblical history.

The answer to our original question, "Does modern genetics disprove the existence of a literal Adam and Eve?" is a definitive no. Instead, modern genetics is consistent with a starting population of two people only a few thousand years ago as described in Genesis.

Conclusion

The debate surrounding the historicity of Adam and Eve is not only an attack on the truthfulness and authority of Genesis but also an attack on the gospel and the clarity, truthfulness, and authority of all of God's Word. Richard Phillips, senior minister at Second Presbyterian Church in Greenville, South Carolina, sums it up well when he states,

> Can the Bible's theology be true if the historical events on which the theology is based are false? The hermeneutics behind theistic evolution are a Trojan horse that, once inside our gates,

---

21. Michael DeGiorgio, Mattias Jakobsson, and Noah A. Rosenberg, "Explaining Worldwide Patterns of Human Genetic Variation Using a Coalescent-based Serial Founder Model of Migration Outward from Africa," *PNAS* 106 (2009): p. 16,057–16,062.
22. Ibid.

must cause the entire fortress of Christian belief to fall.[23]

Scripture and science are clear that Adam and Eve are literal, historical people. This fact is important to the truthfulness and authority of Genesis, the gospel, and all of Scripture.

---

23. Richard N. Ostling, "The Search for the Historical Adam," *Christianity Today* (June 2011): p. 22–27.

Chapter 21

The "Missing" Old Testament Books?

Brian H. Edwards

(❀❀❀❀❀❀❀❀❀❀❀❀❀❀❀❀❀❀❀

Introduction

How come the Bible is missing so many books? Why did the Jews and then the Church exclude these other ancient works about God? How can Christians be sure their books are the right ones? These sorts of questions are becoming increasingly popular among today's skeptics. Corresponding to these questions are the claims that a handful of books were rejected that should have been included in the Bible's Old Testament.

Christians must be prepared to deal with the skeptical assaults on the Word of God. This chapter will address the notion that the Old Testament should have included other ancient Jewish writings and will explain to believers how to respond appropriately to these attacks.

Israel's Bible

The Jewish Scriptures are a collection of books fixed in its number, divine in its origin, and authoritative in its claims. Throughout Israel's history there was little doubt as to which books belonged and which did not. They did not number or order them in the same way as our Old Testament, but the same books were there. This is known to us as the *canon* (a word meaning "measure" or "rule") of the Old Testament.

There is no convincing reason to doubt that each of the books was written close to the time of its history — the first five at the time of Moses, the historical records close to the period they record, the psalms of David during his lifetime, and the prophets written at the time they were given. The theory that many of the books of the Old Testament were not compiled until sometime in the fifth century B.C. to bolster the courage of the Jews in exile rests on assumptions without foundation.[1]

Josephus (A.D. 37–100), the Jewish historian who helped lead the revolt against the Roman occupation before his capture, clearly stated in his defense of Judaism that, unlike the Greeks, the Jews did not have many books: "For we have not an innumerable multitude of books among us, disagreeing from and contradicting one another [as the Greeks have] but only twenty-two books, which contain the records of all the past times; which are justly believed to be divine." Those 22 are exactly the same as our 39 because many books, including the two books of Samuel, Kings, and Chronicles and the 12 "Minor Prophets," are counted as one book each. Since they were believed to be from God, Josephus claimed "no one has been so bold as either to add anything to them, to take anything from them, or to make any change in them."[2]

Philo (c.25 B.C.–A.D. 50), a Hellenistic Jewish philosopher, similarly commented that the Jews "have never altered one word of what was written by him [Moses], but would rather endure to die ten thousand times than to do any thing in opposition to his laws and to the customs which he established."[3]

The well-established tradition that Ezra around 400 B.C. collected the accepted books and had them accurately copied is confirmed by many scholars and is in line with the view expressed in the Talmud and other Jewish writings. The New Testament scholar John Wenham concluded, "There

1. A view taken, for example, by Pfeiffer and Barclay. William Barclay, *The Making of the Bible* (London: Lutterworth Press, 1965), p. 17; and Israel Finkelstein and Neil Silberman, *The Bible Unearthed — Archaeology's New Vision of Ancient Israel and the Origin of Its Sacred Text* (New York: The Free Press, 2001). The vast majority of liberal scholars also adopt a post-exilic date for the authorship of the Old Testament.
2. Josephus, "Against Apion," in William Whiston, trans., *The Works of Josephus* (Peabody, MA: Hendrickson, 1987), I.8.42.
3. Eusebius, often called the father of church history, preserved these words attributed to Philo. Philo, "Hypothetica: Apology for the Jews" in C.D. Yonge, translator, *The Works of Philo: Complete and Unabridged* (Peabody, MA: Hendrickson, 1995), p. 743.

is no reason to doubt that the Canon of the Old Testament is substantially Ezra's canon, just as the Pentateuch was substantially Moses' canon."[4]

Lost Books of the Old Testament

Scattered throughout the Old Testament are references to records that apparently would fill out the details of biblical events and lives: the *Book of Jasher* is mentioned in Joshua 10:13 and 2 Samuel 1:18; the *Book of the Wars of the LORD* in Numbers 21:14; the *Chronicles of the Kings of Israel* and the *Chronicles of the Kings of Judah* in 1 Kings 14:19, 29, et al. (these could be 1 and 2 Chronicles in our Bible). In addition, reference is made to the *Book of the Acts of Solomon* (1 Kings 11:41), the *Chronicles of King David* (1 Chronicles 27:24), the *Records of Samuel the Seer* (probably 1 and 2 Samuel), the *Records of Nathan the Prophet*, the *Records of Gad the Seer* (1 Chronicles 29:29), the *Prophecy of Ahijah*, the *Visions of Iddo the Seer* (2 Chronicles 9:29). With the possible exception of those which may correspond to 1 Samuel, 2 Samuel, 1 Chronicles, and 2 Chronicles, none of the other books mentioned have survived, and we are therefore not in a position to discuss their content. Clearly, they were never intended to enter the canon of the Hebrew Scriptures as separate books, though they may have been used by some who compiled the biblical record.

The Apocrypha

When we turn from the Book of Malachi to the Gospel of Matthew, we have jumped over 400 years of biblical silence (other than prophetic pronouncements of events in this period like those found in Daniel 11). The Jews themselves acknowledged that throughout this time, there was no voice of the prophets in the land.[5] This is known as the "intertestamental" period — between the testaments. But there were other books to fill the gap. In particular, 14 (15 if the Prayer of Jeremiah is included separately from Baruch), known as the Apocrypha, explain some of the history and ideas of the Jewish people from this time and are a mixture of history and legend, fact and fantasy, poetry, and apocalyptic and wisdom literature.

---

4. John W. Wenham, *Christ and the Bible* (London: The Tyndale Press, 1972), p. 134.
5. The apocryphal book of 1 Maccabees records events from the time of the Jewish revolt led by Judas Maccabeus against Syrian occupation in the second century B.C. The writer of this book acknowledged that God was not speaking to His people during this time. "So there was great distress in Israel, such as had not been since the time that prophets ceased to appear among them" (1 Maccabees 9:27, NRSV).

First Esdras follows the history of Judah from Josiah to the destruction of Jerusalem by Babylon in 587 B.C. and its rebuilding under the Persian kings; clearly the biblical books of Chronicles, Ezra, and Nehemiah are used, though there are interesting discrepancies between, for example, the genealogical records in Ezra 3 and Esdras 5. **Second Esdras** (the biblical Ezra) includes a series of visions that Ezra supposedly received revealing the future judgment of God upon the nations and the earth.

The story of **Tobit** recounts how this Jew was taken into exile at the time of the Assyrian conquest; he boasts of his adherence to the Levitical law and the story briefly traces his life and that of his son Tobias.[6] The book of **Judith** purports to take place in the time of "Nebuchadnezzar, king of the Assyrians."[7] By intrigue, Judith rescues her city from the Assyrian general Holofernes and becomes the heroine of the story. The **Book of Esther** adds six more chapters to the story of Esther that ends abruptly in the Bible. However, it places the story in the time of Artaxerxes rather than his father Xerxes (Ahaseurus in the Bible) and simply retells the account with different and often contradictory details. It includes a lengthy prayer of Esther and, unlike the biblical book, the name of God and the LORD appears frequently.

The **Wisdom of Solomon** and **Ecclesiasticus** are both wisdom literature that contain some helpful and truthful assessments of the vanity of the world and the value of godly living. **Baruch** was supposedly written by the scribe of Jeremiah (Jeremiah 36:4), although it may have been written as late as A.D. 100 to explain the destruction of Jerusalem. There are other books allegedly written by Baruch (e.g., 2 Baruch, 3 Baruch). The short **Song of the Three Holy Children** claims to be the song sung by the friends of Daniel as they walked in the fire (Daniel 3), while the **History of Susanna** is a

---

6. While posing as a human named Azariah, an angel named Raphael claims to be the son of one of Tobit's relatives named Hananiah (Tobit 5:4, 13, NRSV). While manifesting as a human may occasionally be necessary for an angel to fulfill its duties, lying about one's identity and heritage is certainly unbecoming of a holy angel. This is one of the reasons Protestants reject Tobit as being inspired by God.

7. Nebuchadnezzar was the king of Babylon, not of Assyria (Daniel 1:1). This mistake may have been made intentionally by the author. Many believe the book of Judith cryptically describes an event during the Greek's (Seleucid's) occupation of Israel in Maccabean times, but the names were deliberately changed to make it sound like a Jewish story from the times of their struggles with Babylon. Support for this idea is seen in the many parallels between General Holofernes in Judith and the Seleucid General Nicanor.

charming story of how Daniel rescued a vulnerable girl from the designs of two wicked judges. **Bel and the Dragon** adds to the story of Daniel and is set in the time of Cyrus of Persia; Bel is an idol which Daniel refuses to worship and the dragon, also worshiped, was blown up by Daniel. The short **Prayer of Manasses** is supposedly the repentant prayer offered by Manasseh of Judah when he was held captive in Babylon (see 2 Chronicles 33:12–13). Finally, the two books of **Maccabees** tell the history of the Maccabean revolt of Mattathias Maccabeus and his sons, led by Judas, against the Seleucids during the second century B.C. The second book of Maccabees includes stories of heroic suffering and martyrdom by the Jews.

The Apocrypha and Our Bible

It is generally agreed that most of these books were written during the second and first centuries B.C. (some may have been later) and therefore cannot be authentic accounts penned by Ezra or Daniel. Those that add to the biblical record, like the Book of Esther, were likely invented by the imagination of a keen writer, or by a Jew who did not have access to the Hebrew Scriptures but had heard the biblical stories and other traditions and wrote from memory.

These have never been considered as part of the Hebrew Scriptures. Philo quotes from or refers to all but five Old Testament books, with some 2,000 quotations from the Pentateuch alone, but he never quotes from the Apocrypha. Similarly, Josephus, the Jewish Council of Jamnia in the first century A.D., and the Jewish Talmud (a collection of biblical discussions and wise sayings of Jewish rabbis in the fourth century A.D.) were clear that the apocryphal books formed no part of the Hebrew Scriptures. For the Jews, therefore, Scripture as a revelation from God through the prophets ended around 450 B.C. with the close of the book of Malachi. They looked forward to a day when "a faithful prophet" should appear.[8]

On the other hand, most of the early translations of the Bible into English included the Apocrypha. The translation of John Wycliffe and his team in the 14th century interspersed the books throughout the Old Testament, though later translations placed them separately to avoid confusion. Coverdale's Bible (1535) was careful to point out that these books "are not judged among the doctors to be of like reputation with the other

---

8. *The Apocrypha*, 1 Maccabees 4:46 and 14:41.

scripture."[9] Even the *Geneva Bible* (1560) — so loved by the later Reformers, the Puritans, the Pilgrim Fathers, Shakespeare, Milton, Bunyan, and the Scots — included the Apocrypha between the Old and New Testaments, though with the firm advice that they are "not received by common consent to be read and expounded publicly in the Church, neither yet served to prove any point of Christian religion, save inasmuch as they have the consent of the other Scriptures called Canonical. . . ." However, they were considered useful for furthering our knowledge of history and "the instruction of godly manners."[10] From 1599, the *Geneva Bible* had abandoned the Apocrypha altogether. The *King James Version* (1611) added the Apocrypha at the end. By 1647 the Westminster Confession of Faith declared the Apocrypha to be no more than "human writings."[11]

Some have tried to find hints of the Apocrypha in the New Testament and claim this as evidence that the Apostles accepted it as part of their canon. Hebrews 1:3 *may* contain an allusion to the Wisdom of Solomon 7:26, where wisdom is described as "a reflection of eternal light, a spotless mirror of the working of God, and an image of his goodness." The "innumerable angels" (Hebrews 12:22; ESV) *may* reflect "the innumerable hosts of angels" described in 2 Esdras 6:3. However, the similarity of two words of a phrase is a very weak connection, especially when both possible allusions are of common ideas and words. Wenham points out that even if these are deliberate allusions, "On such grounds, allusions in modern religious literature would canonize *Hymns Ancient and Modern*."[12] Certainly the Apostles, even if they alluded to the Apocrypha, never once provide the source, whereas they almost always do when quoting from the Old Testament.[13]

In the fourth century, Athanasius (A.D. 296–373), the Christian leader at Alexandria, represented the widespread view of the churches across the Roman Empire and beyond when he distinguished between books that were canonical (clearly accepted as inspired Scripture), those that were

---

9. David Daniel, *The Bible in English* (Newhaven & London: Yale University Press, 2003), p. 187.
10. *The Geneva Bible* (1560), p. 386.
11. For a full discussion on the Apocrypha in early editions of English Bibles, see David Daniel, *The Bible in English* (Newhaven & London: Yale University Press, 2003).
12. Wenham, *Christ and the Bible*, p. 145.
13. For more on this see Brian H. Edwards, *Nothing but the Truth* (Darlington, England: Evangelical Press, 2006), p. 203–206.

edifying (they could be profitably read but were not regarded as Scripture), and those that should be avoided. Under the first heading, he listed precisely the 66 books of our Bible. He wrote, "I fear lest, as Paul wrote to the Corinthians, some few of the simple should be beguiled from their simplicity and purity, by the subtlety of certain men, and should henceforth read other books — those called apocryphal — led astray by the similarity of their names with the true books." Athanasius warned against those who "mix them up [the apocryphal books] with the divinely inspired Scripture."[14] By "apocryphal," Athanasius referred to both the Apocrypha and some of the books and letters pretending to be authored by an Apostle. He was the first to use the word *canon* to describe the collection of accepted books "handed down, and accredited as divine." Athanasius concluded: "Let no one add to these; let nothing be taken away from them."[15] He acknowledged that some of the books in the Apocrypha were allowed to be read in the churches, but they were "not received as canonical."[16]

Despite the words of Athanasius, some church fathers, including Augustine for some time, viewed the Apocrypha as canonical.[17] The Eastern Orthodox churches accept the Apocrypha as Scripture. At the Council of Trent (1546–1563), the Church of Rome officially added the Apocrypha to their canon — though they ascribe it as "deuterocanonical" (literally, "second canon," perhaps signifying that they carry slightly less status). The Council pronounced an anathema on all who disagreed.[18] Rome needed some of these books to support doctrines that

---

14. Athanasius' 39th Festal Epistle (A.D. 367) 2 & 3.
15. Ibid., p. 6.
16. Ibid., p. 7.
17. Augustine (A.D. 354–430) viewed some of the Apocrypha as inspired. He frequently quoted from Sirach and the Wisdom of Solomon. Yet, near the end of his life, he retracted some statements about Sirach stating that it was not right to ascribe the words of Sirach 10:9 to a prophet since "they are not found in a book by an author we are absolutely certain should be called a prophet." Augustine, *Revisions*, I.10.3.
18. The first explicit definition of the Catholic Canon is the Tridentine Canon of the Council of Trent, Session IV, 1546. After listing all of the books accepted into their canon, including the Apocrypha, the Council declared, "If anyone does not accept as sacred and canonical the aforesaid books in their entirety and with all their parts, as they have been accustomed to be read in the Catholic Church and as they are contained in the old Latin Vulgate Edition, and knowingly and deliberately rejects the aforesaid traditions, let him be anathema."

are not found anywhere in the biblical canon. Praying for the dead is endorsed in 2 Maccabees 12:39–45; the importance of the intercession of the dead (saints) is found in Baruch 3:4 and 2 Maccabees 12:44; and the value of charitable giving to earn forgiveness is encouraged in Tobit 4:10 and 12:9.

On the other hand, Protestant churches since the time of the Reformation have never accepted the Apocrypha as part of the revelation of God, and for many good reasons. As we have seen, not only are there obvious historical errors in some of the books of the Apocrypha, especially in Tobit and Judith, but Josephus, Philo, the Jewish Talmud, and the Council of Jamnia (c. A.D. 100) never used the Apocrypha as Scripture. In addition, the Jewish scribes who copied what are known to us as the Dead Sea Scrolls never referred to the apocryphal books as Scripture, and none of the apocryphal books ever claims divine inspiration for itself; there is nothing equivalent to the "this is what the LORD says" of the Old Testament prophets. In A.D. 170, Melito, the leader of the church in Sardis, traveled to Jerusalem to ascertain the exact limit of the Jewish Scriptures, and he returned with a list precisely as ours with the exception of the book of Esther that apparently some Jews questioned.[19]

While a few of the early church leaders did quote from the Apocrypha, though quite infrequently when compared to their use of the Old Testament, there is no evidence that they recognized these as equivalent to the Old Testament.[20] However, first among all the reasons for the Protestant unwillingness to accept the Apocrypha as part of the Bible is the fact that although there are literally hundreds of quotations from and allusions to the Old Testament books by Jesus and the Apostles, there is not a single quotation from the Apocrypha, even though most of it was available to them had they wanted to use it. On that authority alone, the Apocrypha ought never be added to the Bible. As Professor F.F. Bruce commented, "Our Lord and his apostles might differ from the religious leaders

---

19. Perhaps this was the view of the Essene community at Qumran, now famous for writing the Dead Sea Scrolls. Copies or fragments of every Old Testament book were found at Qumran with the exception of Esther. There are several possible reasons why Esther was not found there. Perhaps it was simply not preserved or it has not yet been discovered. A likely explanation is that the Essenes did not highly regard Esther because it describes the origin of the festival of Purim, a holiday the Essenes did not celebrate.

20. See Wenham, *Christ and the Bible*, p. 146–147.

of Israel about the meaning of the Scriptures [but] there is no suggestion that they differed about the limits of the Scriptures."[21]

Other Books?

The **Book(s) of Enoch** is not part of the Apocrypha, but many assume that it is, and some have suggested that it should be. Jude 14–15 consists of a quote from 1 Enoch 1:9. But just because Jude quoted from this work does not mean he attributed any divine authority to the book as a whole. It only means that he approved of using the verse that he quoted to make his point. Likely written sometime during the second century B.C., it claims to be authored by the Enoch referred to in Genesis 5:18–24. The book refers to the Flood in the time of Noah and the fall of the angels (much is made of Genesis 6:1–8). There are visions of hell and heaven, the "Son of Man" (chapters 46–49), the cosmology of earth and the heavens (chapters 42, 72–80), and apocalyptic prophecies of the history of the world from the beginning to the kingdom of the Messiah (chapters 85–90). Very little comports with the Bible. Instead there are portions that had an influence on the early heresy of Gnosticism or were influenced by it, depending upon which was developed first.[22] It was never a contestant for a place in the Bible.

The **Sibylline Oracles** are a collection of Jewish and Christian poems composed between 200 B.C. and A.D. 250.[23] But these are never referred to in the New Testament, and no early extant Christian writings ever considered them to be Scripture.

We must not forget that an occasional quotation or allusion to a book by a biblical writer does not mean that he considered the quote or the work from which it was taken as being authoritative in any way. Paul's quotation in 1 Corinthians 15:33, possibly from Menander,[24] his reference from Aratus while preaching in Athens (Acts 17:28),[25] and his summary

---

21. F.F. Bruce, *The Canon of Scripture* (Downers Grove, IL: IVP Academic, 1988), p. 28.
22. Enoch is typically viewed as being written before Gnosticism flourished, but the dating of Enoch is questionable and many of the Gnostic elements in Enoch could have been written after Gnosticism became popular.
23. See *The Old Testament Pseudepigrapha*, James H. Charlesworth, editor (New York: Doubleday and Co., 1985), p. 317–472.
24. "Evil communications corrupt good manners" is uncertainly attributed to the lost comedy *Thais* by the fourth century B.C. Greek dramatist Menander. Paul does not offer his source and only later writers suggest Menander as the author.
25. Aratus, a third century Greek poet, *Phaenomena* 5.

of the Cretans in Titus 1:12–13 taken from Epimenides[26] are no more or less significant than a preacher's illustrations and quotations used in sermon.

The Septuagint

The Septuagint is the Greek translation of the Hebrew Old Testament; the name means "70" because it was supposedly translated by 70 (probably 72) scholars. The work was begun around the middle of the third century B.C. in the Egyptian capital city of Alexandria. By the time of Jesus, Greek was still the common language across the Roman Empire and so the Septuagint became the Old Testament text used by the Apostles and the early church. This led them occasionally to quote from the Septuagint, which was in places slightly different in form, though not in meaning, from the Hebrew text. Occasionally, quotations of the Old Testament in the New Testament appear to be taken from another translation altogether. For example, Matthew 12:18–21 is neither precisely the same as the Hebrew or the Greek (Septuagint) text of Isaiah 42:1–4; however, the differences are small, make no change to the meaning, and are simply matters of which text was being used rather than another book altogether. The earliest complete texts of the Septuagint do contain the Apocrypha, but these are dated from the fourth and fifth centuries A.D., and therefore we cannot know exactly how early it was when the Apocrypha was included.

Conclusion

It is beyond reasonable dispute that the Jews, Jesus and His Apostles, and the majority of Christians during the first three or four centuries A.D. had no doubt that the 39 books that make up our Old Testament were the only divinely given texts for the canon of the Hebrew Scriptures. These, and these alone, were considered to be fixed in their number, divine in their origin, and authoritative in their claims.

---

26. Epimenides was a semi-legendary sixth century B.C. Greek poet who supposedly fell asleep in a cave on Crete and woke up with the gift of prophecy. The fact that Paul refers to him as "one of their own prophets" does not imply that he accepted the stories as true, though he clearly endorsed the widely held sentiment about the Cretans!

Chapter 22

The "Missing"
New Testament Books?

Brian H. Edwards

᛭᛭᛭᛭᛭᛭᛭᛭᛭᛭᛭᛭᛭᛭᛭᛭᛭᛭

Forgers existed even when the Apostle Paul corresponded with the churches. Writing to the Christians at Thessalonica, he was anxious that they would not become "soon shaken in mind or troubled, either by spirit or by word or by letter, as if from us" (2 Thessalonians 2:2). Paul often used a scribe to write his letters at his dictation, but he found it necessary to sign off his correspondence in his own handwriting to reassure the recipients that the letter came from him and was not a forgery. To the Thessalonians, he refers to his "distinguishing mark" or signature (2 Thessalonians 3:17).[1]

In addition to this, some pretended apostles (Revelation 2:2 and 2 Corinthians 11:5) were distorting the truth and claiming hidden "wisdom" understood only by the initiated. Paul reassured the churches: "We have renounced secret and shameful ways; we do not use deception, nor do we distort the word of God. On the contrary, by setting forth the truth plainly we commend ourselves to every man's conscience in the sight of God" (2 Corinthians 4:2; NIV).

---

1. See also 1 Corinthians 16:21; Galatians 6:11; Colossians 4:18; Philemon 19.

So who were these people? What were they writing? How did the first-century church distinguish between the forgeries, false writings, and the truth?[2]

The "Super Apostles" and Forgers

Early in the life of the Christian community, there were many who claimed special access to the truth, or invented "authentic" stories about Christ or forged letters from the Apostles. Space will allow us to refer only to some of the most significant.

The **Gnostics** were the most dangerous and widespread of the early heresies in the Church, and an early form of their heresy seems to have been the target of both Paul and John in the New Testament. Their name comes from a Greek word for knowledge (*gnosis*), and they believed that salvation was through personal enlightenment of the secret mysteries revealed in their own writings. There were several strands with different leaders and beliefs, but generally they all dismissed the Old Testament as the product of an evil inferior god, claiming that the natural, physical world was created by that god. Therefore, the physical world was evil and opposed to the spiritual world. The Gnostics considered that salvation was through self-enlightenment and freeing oneself from the body, which they thought of as the prison house of the soul. Jesus was the one to give this enlightenment, but their Jesus was very different from the God-man portrayed in the four New Testament Gospels. Most Gnostics believed that the Christ only *seemed* to be a real man (a view known as Docetism from the Greek verb *dokein*, "to seem"), and that just before the Cross, the Christ was substituted by another. Many Gnostics believed this substitute was Simon of Cyrene.

Marcion arrived in Rome in the summer of A.D. 144. Whether or not he was a Gnostic is debated, but certainly he accepted many of their views. Marcion rejected the Old Testament and used only part of Luke's Gospel and ten of Paul's letters, which he edited.[3] Marcion was put on trial by the church in Rome, found guilty of heresy, and expelled.

---

2. A more detailed account of the early pseudepigrapha can be found in Brian H. Edwards, *Why 27?* (Darlington, England: Evangelical Press, 2007).
3. For an analysis of Marcion's editing, see F.F. Bruce, *The Canon of Scripture* (Downers Grove, IL: IVP Academic, 1988), p. 134–144.

Valentinus was another influential Gnostic leader, a native of Alexandria and contemporary of Marcion, who made use of *The Gospel of Truth*, which came to light among the Nag Hammadi texts (see below).

Basilides was born in Alexandria and was the most able and literary of the Gnostics. He produced 24 books to expound his views. One of the early Christian leaders, Irenaeus, understandably called these books "an immense development to his doctrines."[4] Only fragments of these remain today, but Basilides presents a mixture of Greek mythology and twisted gospel narrative, including the "fact" that Simon of Cyrene was crucified in place of Jesus who, meanwhile, "received the form of Simon, and, standing by, laughed at them."[5]

Irenaeus also targeted **Carpocrates,** who headed up a sect of Gnostics that believed Jesus was little more than any other man.[6] Possibly, *The Secret Gospel of Mark* (see below) came from the Carpocratians, and Irenaeus referred to their sordid nighttime rites.[7]

Marcus was a disciple of Valentinus, and when Irenaeus condemned the Marcosians, he specifically condemned them for inventing "an unspeakable number of apocryphal and spurious writings, which they themselves have forged, to bewilder the minds of foolish men, and of such as are ignorant of the Scriptures of truth." Irenaeus referred to many of their false statements that are found in *The Gospel of Truth*.[8]

It is out of these Gnostic stables that most of the false writings of the first few centuries came, and it was the Gnostic writings that influenced the first misunderstandings of the Christian gospel by Islam in the seventh century. The Koran perpetuates the long discredited stories put around by the Gnostics.[9]

---

4. Irenaeus, *Against Heresies*, Book 1, ch. 24:3.
5. Ibid., Book 1, ch. 24:4.
6. Ibid., Book 1, ch. 25:1. "They also hold that Jesus was the son of Joseph, and was just like other men, with the exception that he differed from them in this respect, that . . . he perfectly remembered those things which he had witnessed."
7. Ibid., "They practise also magical arts and incantations; philtres [a drink to inflame the passions] and love-potions; and have recourse to familiar spirits, dream-sending demons, and other abominations."
8. Ibid., Book 1, ch. 20:1.
9. As an example, the story of Simon substituting for Jesus on the Cross, or a similar story, is alluded to in the *Koran*, Surah 4:158.

A Few of the False "Gospels"

During the first few centuries of the Christian church, forged letters pretending to come from the Apostles and others appeared. These are known as pseudepigrapha, which literally means "false writing," but refers to writings falsely attributed to an individual. There are perhaps 60 of these documents in total. The false gospels are often referred to as "apocryphal gospels," and there are no more than a dozen or so of these. Although some of these "gospels" are mere fragments, none were ever contenders for the New Testament canon.

There are bizarre forgeries, like the *Letter of Herod* (unfortunately, the forger forgot that the Herod of the time of our Lord's birth was not the same Herod at His trial and crucifixion!), and letters from Pilate, Joseph of Arimathea, the woman healed of an issue of blood (Matthew 9:20–22), correspondence between Paul and Seneca (the Roman Philosopher and Nero's tutor), and a letter by Jesus Himself. No one today seriously accepts these as authentic.

The Gospel of Judas

In April 2006, the *National Geographic Magazine* published a long-lost fragment of a false gospel that had been known about since Irenaeus (c. A.D. 180) called it "a fictitious history . . . which they style the Gospel of Judas."[10] Foolishly, *National Geographic* suggested that the publication "could create a crisis of faith." The papyrus discovered is dated to A.D. 220 at the earliest, though clearly it was a copy of an earlier manuscript since Irenaeus knew of it by A.D. 180.[11]

The Gospel of Judas tells the "secret account of the revelation that Jesus spoke in conversation with Judas Iscariot a few days before the Passover."[12] It recounts a story of Christ laughing at His disciples for praying to the God of the Old Testament, and reassuring Judas that he was the only disciple who understood Christ's mission. By his betrayal of Jesus, Judas would "exceed all of them [the disciples]. For [he] will sacrifice the man that clothes [Jesus]." This is the Gnostic view that the man Jesus went

---

10. Irenaeus, *Against Heresies*, Book 1, ch. 31:1.
11. The story of its discovery and publication is briefly told in Edwards, *Why 27?* p. 137–141.
12. Rodolphe Kasser, Marvin Meyer, and Gregor Wurst, editors, *The Gospel of Judas* (Washington, DC: National Geographic Society, 2006).

to the Cross, but not the Christ. As such, Jesus encouraged Judas to betray him, which made Judas the hero of the story. Unquestionably, it was a Gnostic writing.[13] It is not difficult to understand why *The Gospel of Judas* disappeared under the sand sometime in the third or fourth centuries. It did not merit a place in anyone's library — it still does not.

The Infancy Gospel of Thomas

Probably written in the middle of the second century, *The Infancy Gospel of Thomas* (not to be confused with *The Gospel of Thomas*, part of the Nag Hammadi Library) does nothing more than fill in the gap of the life of Christ up to the age of 12, where God has chosen to be silent. The book begins: "The stories of Thomas the Israelite, the philosopher, concerning the works of the childhood of the Lord."[14]

We are informed, for example, that at the age of five Jesus fashioned 12 sparrows out of clay which, when he clapped his hands, flew away. This is immediately followed by the account of a young boy who, having spoiled one of Jesus' miracles, was punished by Jesus and promptly "withered up wholly." One boy who "dashed against his shoulder" dropped dead on the spot after Jesus essentially cursed him. Others who admonished him, including his teachers, were struck with blindness or otherwise punished. More positively, the exceptional wisdom of Jesus amazed His teachers, and he was able to heal and even raise the dead. The account closes with the story of Jesus being left behind in Jerusalem, similar to that recorded in Luke 2:42–52, implying that the author had access to the Gospel.

The Arabic Gospel of the Infancy

This writing fills in details of what happened when Joseph, Mary, and Jesus fled to Egypt. It is doubtful whether it was written much earlier than the eighth century, but clearly its author's intent was to exalt Mary who is

---

13. Sophia, the goddess of wisdom, is referred to and that is typical of Gnostic writing. Irenaeus refers to her cult more than 30 times and mocks the stupidity of Gnostic beliefs concerning her.
14. B. H. Cowper, *The Apocryphal Gospels and Other Documents Relating to the History of Christ* (London and Edinburgh: Williams and Norgate, 1870), p.128–169. All of these apocryphal books can be read online by searching under their title, but I have sometimes chosen to quote from a 19th-century volume to emphasize that there is nothing new in our knowledge of them.

the worker of a number of miracles. The family even meets the two thieves whom the Christ child prophesies would later be crucified with Him! Having returned to Bethlehem, Jesus, at the age of seven, makes animals and birds of clay that then walk and fly. Some phrases are scattered throughout that show the author's acquaintance with the Gospels.

The *Gospel of Pseudo Matthew*

The Gospel of Pseudo Matthew begins: "The Book of the Birth of the Blessed Mary and of the Infancy of the Saviour. Written in Hebrew by the Blessed Evangelist Matthew, and translated into Latin by the Blessed Presbyter Jerome."[15] The earliest copies are from the fifth century, and it is intended to encourage the veneration of Mary.

Mary is presented to us as a perfect child who received her food from the angels who talked often with her. She determined to remain a virgin all her life and eventually was committed to the care of Joseph. Mary becomes pregnant by the Holy Spirit, and, with many embellishments, the story runs more or less parallel to the Gospels at this point. Significantly, Luke 2:1–2 is quoted verbatim, but then the nativity is filled out with many imaginary details. The story clearly reflects the widespread view in the fifth century of the perpetual virginity of Mary, and a few miracles are even added in an attempt to prove this idea. The story continues through the circumcision of the child, the visit of the Magi, the slaughter of the boys in Bethlehem by Herod, and the flight to Egypt. Various miracles follow, such as the idols of Egypt falling down. From here we are taken to the childhood of Jesus, and some of the stories reflect those in *The Infancy Gospel of Thomas*.

The *Gospel of Peter*

This short and incomplete account was discovered in the Egyptian desert by a French archaeologist around 1886. It was a copy of an original that may have been written in the middle of the second century. It begins with the trial of Jesus and assumes that Herod was responsible for the Crucifixion of Jesus. Since only the Roman governor had the authority to pronounce and carry out the death sentence, this immediately betrays the late date of writing and the author's poor knowledge of history. In light of

---

15. Cowper, *The Apocryphal Gospels*, p. 29–83

this opening historical gaffe, additional details need not be taken too seriously. The story switches to Mary Magdalene and the women who came to the tomb; this part follows fairly closely the Gospel records. Peter then takes up the story from his own perspective, admitting that the disciples were all afraid. The account ends abruptly, and the rest is lost.

The Gospel of Peter is irrelevant as a document to throw any new light on the trial and death of Christ, and once again, it is not difficult to appreciate why it was rejected by the early church as spurious. It certainly was not written by Peter.

The Secret Gospel of Mark is now lost and known only from a letter from Clement of Alexandria who is said to have denounced it as a "falsification."[16] *The Gospel of the Lord* is largely a synopsis of Luke's Gospel dated around A.D. 130. *The History of Joseph the Carpenter* was probably written in the fourth century A.D. to support the later view that Mary was a perpetual virgin. These add nothing to our understanding of the life of Christ.[17] *The Acts of Paul and Thecla* was invented by a presbyter in Asia who admitted "that he had done it from love of Paul."[18] Someone in the fourth century wrote *The Epistle to the Laodiceans* to make up for the letter referred to by Paul in Colossians 4:16. It is very brief and contains nothing to make it worth the while for the Colossians to send a messenger to Laodicea to collect a copy. It is hard to imagine how it would be possible to construct a less convincing forgery. *The Preaching of Peter, The Acts of Peter*, and *The Apocalypse of Peter* are no less easy to detect as forgeries and were never accepted by the churches during the first two centuries.

The Nag Hammadi Library

In 1945, a peasant discovered under the sand near the village of Nag Hammadi on the east bank of the Nile what proved to be a collection of 13 books containing 52 separate documents. They had been written some time in the fifth century, though they are considered to be copies of earlier works, possibly from the third century. The much-mutilated

---

16. There is great debate as to whether this book even existed or if it was simply the product of an elaborate hoax perpetrated by the man who allegedly discovered it in 1958.
17. Cowper, in *The Apocryphal Gospels*, claims that the story "is characterised by features by no means devoid of interest, although most improbable, unreasonable, and in the worst possible taste."
18. Tertullian, *On Baptism*, chapter 17.

documents were translated into English in 1977 and their importance is that from their own writings we can now read much more of the beliefs of the early Gnostics. Most of the Gnostic writing is "tedious and verbose,"[19] so we have space to survey only a representative sample of the books from Nag Hammadi.

The Gospel of Truth

The Gospel of Truth is the fullest expression of the Gnostic mind of all the books in the Nag Hammadi Library, and some believe that it is the work of the leading and influential Gnostic Valentinus, written around the middle of the second century. It reveals the Gnostic love of the obscure, and the expressions and thoughts are a world away from the records of the four canonical Gospels. The theme is that ignorance of the Father is darkness, and the darkness is dispelled only by attaining true knowledge of oneself and the world. This is classic Gnosticism.

The Gospel of Truth bears no resemblance to the New Testament record of salvation, and presents a philosophy that cannot be considered as Christian spirituality at all. By A.D. 180, Irenaeus was aware of this so-called "gospel," since it had only just begun circulating when it came to his attention: "Indeed, they have arrived at such a pitch of audacity, as to entitle their comparatively recent writing *The Gospel of Truth*, though it agrees in nothing with the Gospels of the Apostles, so that they have really no Gospel which is not full of blasphemy. For . . . what they have published . . . is totally unlike those which have been handed down to us from the apostles."[20]

The Gospel of Thomas

The Gospel of Thomas (not the same as *The Infancy Gospel of Thomas*) is perhaps the most important of the Nag Hammadi documents. It contains 114 sayings, supposedly of Jesus, revealed to the Apostle Thomas. Many of these bear similarities with the teaching of Jesus. Some are straightforward quotations which reveal a clear knowledge of the Gospels. However, much else is vague and obscure. Irenaeus made no direct reference to *The Gospel of Thomas*, and since he was familiar with most of

---

19. Bruce Metzger, *The Canon of the New Testament* (New York: Oxford University Press, 1997), p. 77.
20. Irenaeus, *Against Heresies*, Book III, ch.11:9.

the Gnostic writings, it is possible that this one had not been written before A.D. 180 — long after the death of the Apostles and the circulation of the four Gospels.

It is claimed by some today that one reason why the Gnostic gospels were destroyed was because they revealed the "true" story of the positive role of leadership of women in the first century church. If this is so, what should we make of the following statement from this "gospel": "Simon Peter said to them, 'Let Mary leave us, for women are not worthy of Life.' Jesus said, 'I myself shall lead her in order to make her male, so that she too may become a living spirit resembling you males. For every woman who will make herself male will enter the Kingdom of Heaven' "?[21]

The Gospel of Philip

The Gospel of Philip is essentially a handbook of Gnostic thinking. Much of it is obscure. Whatever one's view of The Gospel of Philip might be, it is impossible to read it without appreciating the simplicity and clarity of the four New Testament Gospels.[22] Clearly, this is the work of one who stood outside the mainstream of Christian teaching, because some of the expressions are heretical. For example, the book denies the virgin birth and claims that the world came into being through a mistake.

It is The Gospel of Philip that introduces the relationship of Mary Magdalene with Jesus, and wildly extravagant claims are made suggesting that it reveals that Jesus and Mary were married.[23] In fact, the book does not make this claim, but these ideas have been read into it.

The Gospel of Mary

It is hardly possible to assess what Mary really said because large sections are missing — barely a thousand words survive. As with The Gospel of Philip, it is misleading to refer to it as a Gospel since we learn nothing

21. The Gospel of Thomas Collection, The Gnostic Society Library, http://www.gnosis. org/naghamm/nhl_thomas.htm.

22. Wesley Isenberg, trans., "The Gospel of Philip," The Gnostic Society Library, http://www.gnosis.org/naghamm/nhl.html.

23. Many of these false claims were critiqued by Tim Chaffey, "What about the Factual Claims in The Da Vinci Code?" in Ken Ham and Bodie Hodge, editors, How Do We Know the Bible Is True? Vol. 1 (Green Forest, AR: Master Books, 2011), p. 139–148. See also Brian Edwards, The Jesus Gospel or the Da Vinci Code — Which? (Taylors, SC: Day One Publications, 2006).

about the life of Christ. What we have here is mystic teaching falsely attributed to Mary Magdalene. After the ascension of Christ, the disciples were in despair, and it is Mary who rouses them to action and courage.[24]

Mary now delivered the secret things she had learned from Jesus. The little we have does not advance our understanding much apart from confirming the mysteries of Gnosticism. The book reveals Mary Magdalene as a favorite of Jesus and one who possessed a knowledge and spirituality superior to that of the Apostles. Nothing is said about her relationship to Jesus to suggest a marriage.

The Gospel of the Egyptians

The most bizarre of all the documents in the Nag Hammadi Library is *The Gospel of the Egyptians*. Some of the early church leaders were aware of it, and Clement of Alexandria referred to it, but all rejected it as spurious. Large sections are missing, and it is not a Gospel in any sense. It has virtually nothing to do with the Christian story or the Christian religion, giving the impression more of the ramblings of a deranged mind than a serious attempt at religious writing.[25] Written by "Eugnostos the beloved" (whoever he was), it claims to be "The Holy Book of the Great Invisible Spirit" and is full of pretended symbol and unintelligible language.

It is not difficult to see why leaders of the early church were so strident in their rejection of this wacky philosophy. It is equally hardly surprising that such material was lost beneath the sands of Egypt for 1,800 years.

The Apocryphon of James

These are supposedly secret revelations to James, the brother of Jesus, and to Peter. It is in the form of a conversation between Jesus and His disciples, and apparently these are things that Jesus "did not wish to tell to all of us, his twelve disciples." Though why this would be the case is hard to imagine since, even if the sayings here are true, they are hardly such as should be kept secret. It adds nothing to our certain knowledge of Christ and His teaching, or to our knowledge of the Gnostics either. We may well question whether Jesus would have said, either openly or in secret: "The

24. *The Gospel According to Mary Magdalene*, The Gnostic Society Library, http://www.gnosis.org/library/marygosp.htm.

25. Alexander Bohlig and Frederik Wisse, trans., *The Gospel of the Egyptians*, The Gnostic Society Library, http://www.gnosis.org/naghamm/goseqypt.html.

Father has no need of me, for a father does not need a son, but it is the son who needs the father, though I go to him. For the Father of the Son has no need of you."[26]

"Some Mighty Fiction"

Thankfully, the Church was not without its strong defenders of the truth. Respected Church leaders during the first two centuries, like Polycarp, Justin Martyr, Irenaeus, and Tertullian, had no problem distinguishing the false writing from the true; the *Muratorian Canon* observed: "It is not suitable for gall to be mingled with honey."[27]

Two of the most able leaders, Tertullian of Carthage (155–220) and Irenaeus of Lyons (130–202) wrote strongly against Marcion and Valentinus.[28] Tertullian contrasted the methods of these two men:

> Maricon expressly and openly used the knife, not the pen, since he made such an excision of the Scriptures as suited his own subject-matter. Valentinus, however, abstained from such excision, because he took away more, and added more, by removing the proper meaning of every particular word, and adding fantastic arrangements of things which have no real existence.[29]

In his five-volume *Against Heresies*, Irenaeus showed he was well acquainted with the false writings circulating in his day, and he summarized them. "Every one of them generates something new day by day, according to his ability; for no one is deemed 'perfect,' who does not develop among them some mighty fiction."[30]

Early in the fourth century, the church historian Eusebius had little difficulty listing those books that were to be rejected. It is true that parts of the Church across the empire accepted some of the apocryphal works as canonical for a while. However, that does not tell us what the majority of churches believed, anymore than the views of modern cults would tell

---

26. Francis Williams, trans., *The Apocryphon of James*, The Gnostic Society Library, http://www.gnosis.org/naghamm/jam.html.
27. *The Muratorian Canon* (discovered by an Italian scholar in Milan in 1740 and dated around A.D. 150) Section 3.
28. Irenaeus, *Against Heresies*, Book 3, ch.17:4; Tertullian, The Prescription Against Heresies.
29. *The Prescription Against Heresies*, ch. 38.
30. Irenaeus, *Against Heresies*, Book 1, ch.18:1 and 21:5.

us what the Christian churches today believe. It is also true that occasionally some of the early Church leaders themselves made allusions to apocryphal writings, though never to any of the so-called Gospels referred to above, but they never referred to the apocryphal writings with the authority they gave to the New Testament books.[31] A few scattered weeds do not describe a field.

The Middle Ages saw a revival of interest in the apocryphal documents, and some were useful to bolster — perhaps were even written for — the creeping errors of the Roman Church. For example, the *History of Joseph the Carpenter* supports the Roman Catholic doctrine of the perpetual virginity of Mary. Many of the apocryphal stories found their way into the Morality and Miracle plays that were popular in the Middle Ages, and into art, the Breviary,[32] and later into our Christmas carols as well. For example, the ox and the ass adoring the infant Christ is taken directly from *The Gospel of Pseudo-Matthew*.[33] It is a tragic matter of history that Mohammed in the seventh century was more familiar with the apocryphal gospels than the four New Testament Gospels.[34] Sadly, "Old falsehoods have been preferred to older truths."[35]

Good Books for the Churches

Aside from the promotion of the strange and obscure Gnostic teaching and the desire to fill in the gaps left in the four Gospels, there were some good books that were read and even quoted by the early Christian leaders. *The Didache* provided teaching that was mostly in line with orthodox faith. *The Epistle of Barnabas* and *The Shepherd of Hermas*, while at times fanciful and visionary, were often popular among the churches.

---

31. In *The Apocryphal Gospels*, Cowper refers to his own work and that of others and concludes that at the most there are "some probable traces of the Apocryphal Gospels" (p. xx) in the writings of the church Fathers — but no more than this.

32. A Catholic website devoted to the Breviary defines the term as follows: "The word breviary . . . is applied to the liturgical work which contains the psalms and the hymns, the readings from Sacred Scripture and from the writings of the Fathers, the prayers and the responses, which are combined to form the canonical hours of the divine office of prayer recited daily throughout the world by priests and religious." From www.breviary.net/breviary/brevintro.htm, accessed May 22, 2012.

33. Cowper, *The Apocryphal Gospels*. p. 53.

34. A useful survey of this subject is in Cowper, *The Apocryphal Gospels*, p. xxviii–xlvii.

35. Cowper, *The Apocryphal Gospels*, p. xlv.

Authentic letters written by Clement, Ignatius, Polycarp, Justin Martyr, Clement of Alexandria, and others, valuable to varying degrees and popular in their time, were never admitted to the divinely inspired canon, and they never claimed to have been God-breathed.

The Ring of Truth Is Missing

Since we have only a tiny fraction of the work and teaching of Christ over approximately three years of public ministry, there is much more that could have been told, as the Apostle John himself declared (John 20:31–31, 21:25). But God has chosen what we need to know.

Those who are well read in the books of the New Testament will have little difficulty recognizing the wholly different genre of the apocryphal gospels. The literary scholar and critic C.S. Lewis made this point well when he commented that such a reader might find himself saying: "No, it's a fine saying, but not his. That wasn't how he talked."[36] As the New Testament scholar Bruce Metzger pointed out, some set out to supplement and others to supplant the four Gospels.[37] But their attempts are poor: the "ring of truth" is missing, the historical context (such as there is) is often inaccurate, the additional sayings of Jesus are mostly either unintelligible or irrelevant, and the miracles are frequently frivolous. Metzger, a usually cautious and restrained writer, commented: "One can appreciate the character of the canonical Gospels and the near banality of most of the gospels dating from the second and third centuries."[38]

It is a simple fact of the story of the Bible that there were only ever the four Gospels accepted by the churches. From the earliest records, there is not a shred of evidence that any other gospel was even a remote contender for a place in the canon of the New Testament. The false "gospels," mostly known to us by incomplete fragments, were rejected by the churches as unreliable and, falling into disuse, eventually disappeared. Their chief value today is to reveal, by contrast, the beauty, simplicity, and integrity of the New Testament Gospels.

---

36. C. S. Lewis, *Christian Reflections* (Grand Rapids, MI: Eerdmans, 1967), p. 150.
37. Bruce Metzger, *The Canon of the New Testament*, p. 166.
38. Metzger, *The Canon of the New Testament*, p. 173. Compare similarly Cowper, *The Apocryphal Gospels*, p. xxv, and Bruce, The Canon of Scripture, p. 251.

Chapter 23

Has the Bible's Text Been Changed Over the Years?

Dr. Ron Rhodes

❧❧❧❧❧❧❧❧❧❧❧❧❧❧❧❧❧❧❧

It was sad to see Matt become conflicted over his Christian faith. He had attended a private Christian school his entire life. He was excited about the Bible. In his later teen years, he was very active in his church's youth ministry.

Everything changed when Matt left for college. One of the required courses at this "Christian" university was an "Introduction to Christianity" course. The professor taught many ideas he was unfamiliar with, including that the Bible had been changed over the years.

After the first month of the course, Matt's spiritual life took a nosedive. He called his parents, who had helped him select this "Christian" university. They were stunned at what their son had been taught. To this day, they continue undoing the damage caused in their son's life by this course.

Today, there is a battle for the Bible. The Bible is under relentless attack by authors of bestselling books, mainstream news magazines, Internet blogs, television specials, and more. New Testament critic Bart Ehrman is a case in point. In one of his best-selling books, he claims that the New Testament manuscripts "all differ from one another, in many thousands of places."[1]

---

1. Bart Ehrman, *Misquoting Jesus* (San Francisco, CA: HarperOne, 2007), p. 10, 12.

This is obviously a critically important issue. If the Bible *has* been changed, then you and I cannot trust what it says about God, Jesus, the gospel, our beginnings in Genesis, the Resurrection, or anything else found within its pages.

So — let's look at the evidence. Let's examine the *hard facts* to discover the *real* truth about the trustworthiness of the Bible.

God's Word Endures Forever

We begin by noting the "forever" nature of God's Word. Isaiah 40:8 affirms, "The word of our God stands forever." First Peter 1:25 likewise affirms that "the word of the Lord endures forever" (see also Mark 13:31).

Jesus implicitly assumed the perpetual preservation of His Word when He informed the disciples that the gospel would eventually span the entire globe: "This gospel of the kingdom will be preached in all the world . . . and then the end will come" (Matthew 24:14). How could the gospel be preached in all the world up till "the end" if the Word of God were not preserved from age to age?

The perpetual preservation of Scripture is also assumed in Christ's Great Commission (Matthew 28:19–20). How could disciples be made in "all the nations" to the end of the age if the Word of God were not preserved from age to age? The reason Jesus could instruct His followers in this way is because He sovereignly knew Scripture would be preserved.

Preservation through the Written Word

God's will has always been for His revelations to be permanently recorded and preserved for coming generations. We read that "Moses wrote all the words of the Lord" (Exodus 24:4). Joshua "wrote these words in the Book of the Law of God" (Joshua 24:26). Samuel wrote "in a book and laid it up before the Lord" (1 Samuel 10:25). The Lord instructed Isaiah, "Take a large scroll, and write on it with a man's pen . . ." (Isaiah 8:1).

Paul affirmed that "the things which I write to you are the commandments of the Lord" (1 Corinthians 14:37). John was commanded by the Lord to "write the things which you have seen" (Revelation 1:19). All of these biblical books were written by the inspiration of the Holy Spirit (2 Timothy 3:16; 2 Peter 1:21).

Jesus' View of Scriptural Preservation

The biblical evidence further reveals that the God who sovereignly inspired Scripture, and caused it to be written down, also preserved it in the ongoing transmission of the written biblical manuscripts from one generation to the next (see Colossians 1:17; Hebrews 1:3). Consider Jesus' attitude toward the Old Testament Scriptures. Neither Jesus nor His Apostles had in their possession the original books penned by Moses, David, Isaiah, Jeremiah, or other Old Testament authors. They had access *only* to manuscript copies of these books.

Nevertheless, Jesus had full confidence that the Old Testament Scriptures He used during His three-year ministry had been faithfully preserved through the centuries. This is so, despite the fact that there were some minor differences or variants in the Old Testament manuscript copies.

The respect that Jesus and His Apostles held for the Old Testament manuscript copies of their day is an expression of their confidence that God providentially preserved the Word of God in these written copies. They expressed no doubts whatsoever. Likewise, we today can trust that both the Old *and* New Testaments have been accurately preserved in our manuscript copies.

The Amazing Manuscript Evidence for the Bible

There is overwhelming manuscript evidence that points to the accuracy and reliability of the Bible. Because the primary target of critics today is the New Testament, let's focus our primary attention on New Testament manuscripts.

Today there are 5,686 known partial and complete manuscript copies of the New Testament. Following are some representative samples.

One early New Testament manuscript is the Chester Beatty papyrus, P45. The manuscript was named after the person who acquired it, Chester Beatty. The letter P refers to *papyrus*, a durable writing material manufactured from a river plant in ancient Egypt. The number 45 is an identifying number.

P45 dates to the third century A.D., within 150 years of the original New Testament documents. That's very early! It contains the four gospels and the Book of Acts (chapters 4–17).

Another Chester Beatty papyrus is P46. It dates to about A.D. 200. It contains ten Pauline epistles (all but the pastoral epistles) and the Book of Hebrews. Yet another Chester Beatty papyrus is P47. It dates to the third century A.D., and contains Revelation 9:10–17:2.

One extremely early fragment is P52, also called the John Rylands Fragment. Scholars date this fragment to about A.D. 117–138. It contains portions of John's gospel, and is within a generation of John's original text.

An important manuscript that contains the entire New Testament is the Sinaiticus uncial manuscript, which dates to the fourth century. "Uncial" manuscripts were written entirely in capital letters, and were commonly used from the third through the eighth centuries A.D.

The Vaticanus uncial manuscript dates to the fourth century. It contains most of the New Testament except for part of Hebrews, the pastoral epistles, Philemon, and Revelation.

There are many, many other such manuscripts. If one adds into the mix over 10,000 Latin Vulgate manuscripts and at least 9,300 other early versions — including Ethiopic, Slavic, and Armenian versions — the total approximates 25,000 manuscripts that cite portions of the New Testament. The manuscript support for the New Testament is truly staggering![2]

Quotations of the New Testament in the Church Fathers

In addition to the many New Testament manuscripts, there are over 36,000 quotations of the New Testament from the early church fathers and several thousand lectionaries (church service books from the early centuries of Christianity). There are enough quotations from the early church fathers alone that even if we did not have a single manuscript copy of the New Testament, scholars could still reconstruct over 99 percent of it from material written within 150 to 200 years of the time of Christ.

A Comparison with Other Ancient Literature

Most ancient classical literary works have an extremely long gap between the writing of the original document and the earliest extant manuscript copy. To illustrate, we have only ten copies of Caesar's *Gallic Wars*, the earliest of which is dated a thousand years after the time of Caesar. We

2. See Josh McDowell, *The New Evidence that Demands a Verdict* (Nashville, TN: Thomas Nelson, 1999), p. 34.

have only seven copies of Plato's writings, the earliest of which dates to about 1,300 years after the time of Plato. We have 643 copies of Homer's *Illiad*, the earliest of which dates to about 400 years after the time of Homer.

The New Testament has far better manuscript support. As Bible scholar Norman Geisler put it, "There are more [New Testament] manuscripts copied with greater accuracy and earlier dating than for any secular classic from antiquity."[3] Geisler rightly concludes that if you can't trust the New Testament, you can't trust any ancient book.

But What About the Variants?

In the many thousands of manuscript copies we possess of the New Testament, scholars have discovered between 200,000 and 400,000 variants (minor alterations), depending on who you ask. This may seem like a staggering figure to the uninformed mind. To those who study the issue, however, the numbers are not so disturbing as it may initially appear.

Foundationally, the reason we have so many variants in the New Testament manuscripts is that *we have so many New Testament manuscripts*. Moreover, keep in mind that the sheer volume of manuscripts we possess greatly narrows the margin of doubt regarding what the original biblical document said.

New Testament scholar F.F. Bruce puts it this way: "If the number of [manuscripts] increases the number of scribal errors, it increases proportionately the means of correcting such errors, so that the margin of doubt left in the process of recovering the exact original wording is not so large as might be feared; it is in truth remarkably small."[4]

Moreover, the claim that there are hundreds of thousands of variants can be misleading. The truth is, if a single word is misspelled in 3,000 manuscripts, that counts as 3,000 variants. That fact alone substantially reduces the severity of the variant problem.

Unintentional and Intentional Alterations

Most of the variants in the Bible manuscripts resulted from unintentional errors on the part of the scribe. There were some cases in which the

---

3. Norman Geisler, *Christian Apologetics* (Grand Rapids, MI: Baker, 1975), p. 306, insert added.
4. F.F. Bruce, *The New Testament Documents: Are They Reliable?* (Downers Grove,IL: InterVarsity, 1984), p. 19, insert added.

copyist experienced what some have called a "slip of the eye." This occurs when a copyist reads the second instance of two similar (or identical) words that are near each other, and he inadvertently omits the words in between. To illustrate, "I am *very* hungry and *very* tired" might inadvertently get copied as "I am very tired."

There were other cases in which a copyist experienced what some have called a "slip of the ear." Sometimes there were groups of copyists listening to a person dictating the manuscript. In such a case, the copyist might misspell a word or two, or perhaps insert a similar sounding word (like "there" instead of "their").

Faulty word divisions were another problem. In modern English, all our words are separated by a space. However, in early biblical manuscripts, letters were not separated into words with spaces. So, for example, "HEISNOWHERE could either mean HE IS NOW HERE or HE IS NOWHERE."[5]

Still other variants might be caused by the faulty memory of the scribe. He might occasionally forget the exact word and substitute a synonym. He might also inadvertently insert a wrong word as a result of remembering a parallel Bible passage.

There were other cases in which *intentional* changes were made to a manuscript (made by scribes *with good intentions*). For example, there were different schools of scribes, each of which had unique stylistic and linguistic idiosyncrasies. They would often make minor alterations to conform with the "house style" of their group — including the spelling of proper names and tweaking the grammar here and there.

In other cases, scribes might make slight alterations in order to harmonize accounts. For example, they might seek to harmonize the Lord's Prayer in the different gospel accounts.

Today, Bible scholars use well-defined principles to help them ascertain the original text when there are minor variations in the manuscript copies:

1. The more difficult reading is to be preferred, for scribes tended to improve the readings.
2. The shorter reading is to be preferred, for scribes tended to add clarifying words.

---

5. Norman Geisler and William Nix, *A General Introduction to the Bible* (Chicago, IL: Moody, 1986), Logos Bible Software.

3. Different readings among parallel passages are preferred, for scribes tended to harmonize accounts.
4. The less-refined grammatical reading is preferred, for scribes tended to improve the grammar.
5. The reading that best explains the variants is to be preferred.
6. The reading with the widest geographical support is to be preferred.
7. The reading that most conforms to the style and diction of the author is to be preferred.

Such principles are part of the science of textual criticism. Textual criticism seeks to examine all the manuscripts with a view to producing a text that is as close as possible to the original text.

Of course, the word "criticism" for many people carries negative connotations. Actually, though, the word carries the idea, "to exercise judgment about." When modern Bible scholars engage in textual criticism of the Bible, they are seeking to exercise judgment about the biblical manuscript copies so they can determine what the original text said.

I often do conferences across the United States with my friend and colleague Norman Geisler, who has done detailed study on textual criticism. He gives a great illustration on ascertaining the original text from faulty manuscript copies.

Suppose you received the following notification in the mail:

Y#U HAVE WON TEN MILLION DOLLARS.

Would you go claim your money? Of course you would.
But what if it said:

YO# HAVE WON TEN MILLION DOLLARS.

or perhaps:

YOU #AVE WON TEN MILLION DOLLARS.

Would you go claim your money? Of course you would.

Geisler's point is that even with mistakes (variants), we are able to reconstruct 100 percent of the message in the above statements. This illustration is admittedly quite simplistic. The truth is, however, that even with variants in the biblical manuscripts, we can reconstruct the original text with an incredibly high degree of certainty.

Four Families of Manuscripts

The differing readings among New Testament manuscripts tend to group themselves into families of manuscripts. This grouping is based on the similarity of slight variations in wording in particular verses. In other words, in Bible verses where manuscripts have different readings, manuscripts in a particular text family agree with each other in supporting one reading. A different text family supports a different reading on that verse.

Comparisons of thousands of New Testament manuscripts have yielded four families of text types: the Alexandrian, the Western, the Caesarean, and the Byzantine. It would appear that early Christian scribes copied the New Testament manuscripts according to varying guidelines in different parts of the Mediterranean world, hence giving rise to these families.

While it is beyond the scope of this chapter to present a detailed study of these families, we can note that the Alexandrian text family arose in Egypt, just as the Byzantine text family became common in the Byzantine world. The Western text family originated in early centers of Christianity in the Western Roman Empire, while the Caesarean text family was widely used in Caesarea.

Bible scholars debate over which family (or families) of text types are the best. While the debate will no doubt continue, the good news is that we have *thousands* of these various manuscripts. By comparing them, we can analyze the minor variations and reconstruct the original text.

Most Variants: Little or No Significance

Out of all the variants in the New Testament manuscripts, we can definitively state that 99.9 percent of them hold virtually no significance whatsoever. When all the facts are put on the table, only about 40 of the variants in the New Testament manuscripts have any real significance.

Even then, these 40 variants do not affect Christian doctrine. J. Harold Greenlee, in his book *Introduction to New Testament Textual Criticism*, asserts that "no Christian doctrine hangs upon a debatable text."[6]

Even liberal critic Bart Ehrman admits that the variants in the manuscript copies do not affect the theology of the Bible: "Most of the changes

---

6. J. Harold Greenlee, *Introduction to New Testament Textual Criticism* (Grand Rapids, MI: Baker, 1993), p. 68.

found in early Christian manuscripts have nothing to do with theology or ideology."[7]

Confirmation in the Dead Sea Scrolls

In 1947, an Arab shepherd-boy made the initial discovery of the Dead Sea Scrolls at Khirbet Qumran. Since then, thousands of fragments belonging to over 800 manuscripts have been discovered in 11 different caves in Qumran.

Previous to the discovery of the Dead Sea Scrolls, our earliest Old Testament manuscript was the Cairo Codex, which dates to about A.D. 895. The word "codex" is a Latin term meaning *book*. A codex was a manuscript bound in book form rather than as a scroll. The Cairo Codex contains the latter and former prophets.

The Dead Sea scrolls, by contrast, provide manuscripts that date a thousand years earlier — from the third century B.C. to the first century B.C. The significant thing is that when one compares the two sets of manuscripts, it is clear that they are essentially the same, with very few changes.

The copies of the Book of Isaiah discovered at Qumran illustrate this accuracy. Previous to the discovery of the Dead Sea scrolls, our earliest manuscript copy of the Book of Isaiah dated to A.D. 895. The Dead Sea Scroll copies date to about 125 B.C.

Old Testament scholar Gleason Archer examined the Dead Sea Scroll copies and found that "they proved to be *word for word identical* with our standard Hebrew Bible in more than 95 percent of the text. The 5 percent of variation consisted chiefly of obvious slips of the pen and variations in spelling."[8]

F.F. Bruce concludes, "It may now be more confidently asserted than ever before that the Dead Sea discoveries have enabled us to answer this question [of the reliability of Bible manuscripts] in the affirmative with much greater assurance than was possible before 1948."[9]

---

7. Ehrman, *Misquoting Jesus*, p. 55.
8. Gleason Archer, *A Survey of Old Testament Introduction* (Chicago, IL: Moody, 1964), p. 19.
9. F.F. Bruce, *Second Thoughts on the Dead Sea Scrolls* (Grand Rapids, MI: Eerdmans, 1956), p. 61–62.

A Confident Assurance in the Bible

In view of all this evidence, we conclude that — contrary to the claims of modern critics — the Bible *has not* been changed through the centuries. To summarize:

- God's Word endures forever (Isaiah 40:8; 1 Peter 1:25).

- One way God insured His Word would endure and be preserved was to have it written down (Exodus 24:4; Joshua 24:26; Isaiah 8:1).

- Though Jesus possessed only manuscript copies of the original Old Testament documents, He expressed full confidence in them as the "Word of God."

- There are close to 25,000 manuscript copies that contain portions of the New Testament. These are copied with great accuracy and many are dated early.

- There are enough quotations from the early church fathers alone to reconstruct over 99 percent of the New Testament.

- While there are variants in the biblical manuscripts, most are minor, and none affect doctrine.

- The sheer volume of manuscripts we possess greatly narrows the margin of doubt regarding what the original biblical document said.

- The Dead Sea scrolls prove the accurate transmission of these biblical manuscripts.

My friend, you can trust your Bible! And Matt, my hope is that you learn to understand this debate and learn how various manuscripts are a great confirmation of the Bible's accuracy.

Chapter 24

Nazca Lines — Defying Evolutionary Ideas?

David Wright

ʀ❀❀❀❀❀❀❀❀❀❀❀❀❀❀❀❀❀❀❀

It's a bird! It's a monkey! It's a whale? Wait, no. It's all of the above! It's the Nazca Lines! The what? If you've heard of these geoglyphs, you know they're quite the mystery to archaeologists and most other experts.

Discovered by accident from an airplane in 1927, their purpose remains a conundrum. Plenty of fantastical and plain ideas abound — from UFO landing zones to religious rituals. Who knows? Maybe it was some rebellious Nazca teen's version of graffiti. One thing is sure. The complexity of these lines defies the evolutionary assumption of "primitive" ancestors.

What Are the Nazca Lines?

The name "Nazca Lines" pretty much says it all. But what's so special about a bunch of lines? The Nazca Lines are geoglyphs — huge pictures or hieroglyphs that are formed by digging trenches or building up earth. Geoglyphs are so long that what they depict can usually only be seen from an elevated point.

From the ground they can just look as though someone was a little tired and dragged his plow all the way home from the field. As a matter of fact, many of these can even be seen using Google Earth. Just type in "Nazca, Peru," fly in a little closer, and you'll see some incredible things.

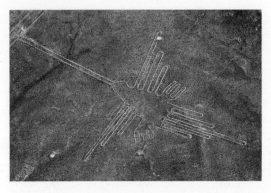

The most popular parts are the many animal drawings, like a monkey, a few birds, whales, and an unmistakable spider. From the ground it would be nearly impossible to tell what the figures are, but from the air their form becomes quite clear. Also, there are many trapezoids, spirals, "runways," and straight lines.

The trapezoids are usually larger than a football field, and they appear to be placed randomly. "Runways" are not literally runways; they just look as such. And some of the lines are spirals or zigzag patterns. Though a straight line seems like an unimpressive feat, how about a nearly perfect straight line that goes on for miles without curving or being thrown off by obstacles such as hills? And these are seen all over the desert. Many of the straight lines have a tendency to trace back to a radiant point — a point from where groups of lines emanate.

Who and When?

The Nazcas thrived, it is believed, from the first century to the early eighth century A.D. They lived near and around the desert areas of southern Peru. The lines and figures weren't the only things they constructed. Because they lived in a very dry climate — maybe an inch of rain per year (*if* things were the same then as now), they also constructed many wells and aqueducts to help channel the water for irrigating their crops. Many of these wells and aqueducts still exist and function today — talk about quality workmanship!

It is believed that the Nazca Lines were created by the ancient Nazca people sometime between A.D. 1 and 650, though they were not all created at the same time. Most dating for the lines is based on wooden stakes or broken pottery pieces nearby. While this method can give us an idea of when they were possibly constructed, it is not absolute.

The lines could be much older. This would be like dating a piece of trash found next to a trail and then using that to date the trail. The only problem is that the trash could be a year old and the trail hundreds of years old. Though this method is not perfect, it does help to give a minimum relative age for the lines.

How?

Unfortunately, the prevailing thought is that the ancient Nazcas were primitive and so had no advanced technology. Thus, a few people believe that aliens were responsible. However, this explanation is rejected by most experts since there is no evidence, and the idea is completely unnecessary.

Many people have studied the Nazca Lines and have even recreated some of them. While the lines and designs are not so advanced that they would have needed help from a higher intelligence (i.e., aliens), neither are they so simple that any primitive man could chalk one up.

Some have even ranked the lines in an order of complexity. The idea is that they started with straight lines, and then, as their knowledge of geometry grew, so did the complexity of the shapes — trapezoids, zigzags, spirals, and then finally animal and plant shapes. But this idea is based on the assumption that the Nazcas had no prior knowledge of geometry and/ or land surveying. However, this is an unfounded assumption based mostly on evolutionary presuppositions.

The lines were simply formed by scraping the darker pebbles and rocks that lay atop the desert floor away from the lighter clay soil underneath. These geoglyphs have remained nearly untouched for centuries due to the fact that there is very little wind and rain. As for the straightness of many of the lines and geometry of the spirals and animals, some simple land surveying equipment could have been used. For example, ropes and stakes, triangles and

plumb lines can be used to help construct straight lines over long distances.

Also, many ancient cultures have been credited with having impressive mathematical prowess, and the Nazcas, no doubt, were one of them. Even though we know they are responsible for the lines and shapes, we don't know exactly how they formed them. From the precision of the lines and figures, we can ascertain that they had the necessary tools for surveying and construction and also had in-depth knowledge of mathematics and geometry.

Further evidence that the Nazcas knew what they were doing is supported by what is seen in an area outside of the town of Nazca. Upon viewing, one can see this was used as a practice area where they looked from the surrounding mountaintops to view the lines below. Some have even speculated the Nazcas could have used hot air balloons. In the 1970s, Jim Woodman theorized that the Nazcas had the knowledge and materials to build one. So he and ballooning expert Julian Nott set out to construct the world's "first" hot air balloon, using only materials the Nazcas would have had access to, such as totora reeds, cloth, and rope. In 1975 in the desert pampa[1] of Nazca, Peru, Woodman and Nott took flight and achieved an average altitude of 300 feet. Though they did not prove the Nazca used hot air balloons, it at least became plausible that the Nazcas *could have*. Such a tool would have been very helpful in the construction of the lines and figures.

Why?

When Paul Kosok came across the lines in 1941, he came up with the idea that the lines pointed to star constellations so that farmers could predict the underground flow of water from the Andes Mountains. Since their initial (re)discovery, many theories have come about as to their purpose: a

---

1. A pampa (from Spanish *bolson*, "large purse") is a semi-arid, flat-floored desert valley or depression, usually centered on a playa or salt pan and entirely surrounded by hills or mountains. It is a type of basin characteristic of basin-and-range terrain. *Pampa*, Dictionary.com. © Encyclopedia Britannica, Inc. http://dictionary.reference.com/browse/pampa, accessed April 24, 2012.

celestial calendar, a form of artistic expression, roads for trade and travel, indicators of ground water, and religious rites pertaining to the worship of mountain-gods and the provision of water.

As for an astronomical calendar, only a few lines have been shown to track the rising and setting of the sun to keep track of the rainy season. But other than these, few scientists and researchers have been able to make any certain connections between the lines and the positions of the stars. It is possible, though, that the plant, animal, and other pictures represent constellations.

The pampa was (and still is) fairly dry due to the lack of rainfall. This is because of the Andes Mountains. As water vapor travels up over the mountains, the majority of it tends to fall on the mountains. Because of the height of the mountains, the air becomes very thin and cold, thus causing most of the remaining water in the air to precipitate and fall on the mountains. All that's left for the valley is dry air. Some of this water, however, ends up in underground channels that flow from the Andes to the desert. So some have speculated that certain formations, like the trapezoids, were used as indicators as to where the underground water sources were located. Although interesting, this model is not widely accepted.

Probably the most plausible and accepted idea is that the lines were used for religious ceremonial purposes, especially the trapezoids and figures. Since this was a dry climate, it is believed the Nazca constructed these lines and figures as tools for ceremony and worship.

For example, it was noted by Anthony Aveni that "the large trapezoids attached to the lines seemed to be situated in the spits of elevated land in between the ancient streambeds. Often the axes of the lines are parallel to the direction of the flow of water."[2] He goes on to explain that since these were usually situated next to waterbeds they were probably places of worship and prayer. It can also be observed that many of the straight lines emanate from elevated radial points. It's possible these "center points" were focal points of worship and sacrifices.

Religious rites and ceremonies for the geometric and animal shapes seem to make the most sense. One possible connection may be between the spiral geoglyphs and the wells that were dug by the Nazcas. A quick look at the wells shows how they spiral downward into the earth to the

---

2. Anthony F. Aveni, *Archaeology*, vol. 53, issue 3 (May/Jun2000): p. 26–35.

water. The spiral geoglyphs could possibly be an artistic and ritualistic representation of their wells.

Archaeology

Archaeology serves as a useful teaching tool. Those in the field understand the difference between facts and interpretations. Archaeologists and other scientists look at the lines (evidence/facts) and then interpret their purpose: "religious ceremonies," "they were roads," "they marked underground water," and so on. But they usually keep their minds open since not all the facts are known because no one was there to witness the lines being formed and ask the Nazcas why they were doing it.

As new information arises, certain theories are disproven, and certain theories are given further credence. But most archaeologists, if not all, will admit that there is no way to know *absolutely* and *exactly* what the purposes of the Nazca Lines were since we don't have all the information. This honest and candid approach to archaeology is what science should be about. Unfortunately, this open-minded approach is rare in evolutionary camps when it comes to their dogmatic (religious) stance on the history of the earth.

Conclusion

When taking a closer look at the Nazca Lines and putting aside evolutionary bias, it becomes clear the Nazcas were not "primitive" at all, but rather intelligent civil engineers.

Once we take a step back from our preconceived notions about earlier mankind, we see they were ingenious.[3] The next time you hear about how ancient man was "primitive," just remember that our minds have undergone more than 6,000 years of the debilitating effects of the Curse, so those who came before us likely had a much greater capacity for intelligence than ourselves.

---

3. For more examples of our intelligent ancestors, I recommend reading Donald Chittick's book *The Puzzle of Ancient Man* (Newberg, OR: Creation Compass, 1998).

Chapter 25

Did Atlantis Exist? What We Can Learn from Bible History

Bodie Hodge

Atlantis is the theme of modern science fiction, hotels, cartoons, and much, much more. Questions about Atlantis come into Answers in Genesis more than you might think. Let's take a fresh look at it from a biblical perspective.

A Little Background

The island of Atlantis was primarily discussed and recorded by Plato in his dialogues *Timaeus* and *Critias*.[1] Plato mentions that this rather large island was later destroyed by a great earthquake. The time frame for this written account by Plato is said to be about 350–400 years before Christ.[2]

According to Plato, Atlantis was named for Atlas, who was supposedly the oldest twin of Poseidon, the son of Cronus in Greek mythology. Often mythology grew out of a remnant of truth. Chronos has often been

---

1. Though much has been written about Atlantis from various sources since Plato, I will focus most of this paper on the original sources; this is to keep from going into the many "bunny trails" that one could follow.
2. A side note of history is that Socrates taught Plato, Plato taught Aristotle, Aristotle taught Alexander the Great, who later conquered most of the known world at the time. This is why Greek was the popular language of the time of the New Testament, which was written in Greek. This may give you an idea of the time frame that Plato wrote.

identified as the biblical Kittim/Cethimus (other variants are Cyprus, Ce-thim, Cethima, or Citius).

Kittim is the son of Javan (translated "Greece" in the Old Testament), the son of Japheth, the son of Noah. This leads to the possibility of these people being real, but the embellished mythology relating to them was likely the handiwork of subsequent descendants. This was quite common. For example Mercury was the "god" name of Ashkenaz (Kittim's first cousin and grandson of Japheth),[3] and Hercules was the Greek embellish-ment of Samson.[4]

Furthermore in the story, Poseidon was the owner of the island and named it for his son. Other place names also reflect Atlas, such as the At-lantic Ocean and the Atlas Mountains extending from Morocco to Algeria.

According to Plato's account (of Socrates' account of Solon's account that he received from the Egyptians), the Athenians (people of the city of Athens and perhaps others in Greece) went to war with those inhabiting the island of Atlantis. The Atlantians had conquered parts of modern-day Italy and North Africa and were threatening Greece and Egypt. Accord-ing to the account, many of the Athenians may have died while fighting the Atlantians not long before the island's destruction.

Pre-Flood or Post-Flood Possibilities

When it comes down to it, either Atlantis was a real place or it wasn't. If it wasn't, then the discussion is more or less finished. And considering that this story was passed down several times before Plato recorded it, we can assume that it has some inaccuracies.

Regardless, let's assume for a moment that it was a real place and use a biblical framework to place it. Big-picture biblical explanations could be:

1. Atlantis was destroyed by the Flood, and we should not expect to find remnants of it.
2. Atlantis was destroyed after the Flood, and its remnants may still exist.

---

3. Dr. James Anderson, *Royal Genealogies* (London, England: James Bettenham Publisher, 1732), Part 1, Table CCXIII, p. 442.
4. *Adam Clarke Commentary* (New York: J. Emory and B. Waugh, for the Methodist Episcopal Church, J. Collord, printer, 1831), notes, Judges 16:31.

So could Atlantis have been a pre-Flood continent? If so, there would be little evidence left due to such a worldwide cataclysm. However, the *Critias* account by Plato reads:

> . . . which had elapsed since the war which was said to have taken place between those who dwelt outside the Pillars of Heracles and all who dwelt within them; this war I am going to describe. Of the combatants on the one side, the city of Athens was reported to have been the leader and to have fought out the war; the combatants on the other side were commanded by the kings of Atlantis, which, as was saying, was an island greater in extent than Libya and Asia, and when afterwards sunk by an earthquake, became an impassable barrier of mud to voyagers sailing from hence to any part of the ocean.

Also in Plato's account of Atlantis, he refers to the Atlantic Ocean as well as these "pillars of Hercules," which is likely the Strait of Gibraltar between modern-day Spain and Morocco. Plato said that Atlantis was as large as "Libya" and "Asia." (Asia was originally seen as a portion of modern-day Turkey). Keep in mind that this is not what we think of today as Libya and Asia, but the way the Greeks viewed them about 350–500 B.C. Take note that these are post-Flood features and names. Plato's *Timaeus* says:

> Many great and wonderful deeds are recorded of your state in our histories. But one of them exceeds all the rest in greatness and valour. For these histories tell of a mighty power which unprovoked made an expedition against the whole of Europe and Asia, and to which your city put an end. This power came forth out of the Atlantic Ocean, for in those days the Atlantic was navigable; and there was an island situated in front of the straits which are by you called the Pillars of Heracles; the island was larger than Libya and Asia put together, and was the way to other islands, and from these you might pass to the whole of the opposite continent which surrounded the true ocean; for this sea which is within the Straits of Heracles is only a harbour, having a narrow entrance, but that other is a real sea, and the surrounding land may be most truly called a boundless continent. Now in this island of Atlantis there was a great and wonderful empire which had rule over the whole island and several

others, and over parts of the continent, and, furthermore, the men of Atlantis had subjected the parts of Libya within the columns of Heracles as far as Egypt, and of Europe as far as Tyrrhenia. This vast power, gathered into one, endeavoured to subdue at a blow our country and yours and the whole of the region within the straits; and then, Solon, your country shone forth, in the excellence of her virtue and strength, among all mankind. She was pre-eminent in courage and military skill, and was the leader of the Hellenes. And when the rest fell off from her, being compelled to stand alone, after having undergone the very extremity of danger, she defeated and triumphed over the invaders, and preserved from slavery those who were not yet subjugated, and generously liberated all the rest of us who dwell within the pillars. But afterwards there occurred violent earthquakes and floods; and in a single day and night of misfortune all your warlike men in a body sank into the earth, and the island of Atlantis in like manner disappeared in the depths of the sea. For which reason the sea in those parts is impassable and impenetrable, because there is a shoal of mud in the way; and this was caused by the subsidence of the island.

Much of *Critias* is a description of the island and its inner politics, but Timmeaus helps us establish a post-Flood understanding of Atlantis. Tiras's descendants (Noah's grandson) inhabited the area of Tyrrhenia between Italy and Greece. Libya was inhabited by descendants of Lybyos (as given by Josephus) who was the son of Mizraim (Egypt); they are known as the Lehabites in Genesis 10. So this is definitely referring to post-Flood places.

In *Critias*, Plato also gives the dimensions of the main island of Atlantis in a measurement called "stadia," which are about 600 feet each. The dimensions were 2,000 by 3,000 stadia. It was an oblong-shaped island. Translating this into modern measurement, it would have been about 227 miles by 340 miles, giving an estimated 77,000 square-mile area. This is about the size of the state of Nebraska. Plato's measurement makes Atlantis much smaller than a continent.

Since the modern continent scheme was changed significantly from the Flood, and Plato was referring to post-Flood places, it is very unlikely that this Atlantis was pre-Flood. Plato's book *Critias* gives details of the island and much more (such as the ancient Egyptians originating the account), implying that if it existed, it was likely post-Flood. Egypt was formed by Mizraim, Noah's grandson, and is still known as *Mizraim* in the Hebrew language. So for Egypt to be aware of it requires Noah's grandson Mizraim to have existed to begin Egypt. If so, descriptions given by Plato appear to place it outside of the Mediterranean in the Atlantic Ocean.

In the past, people have proposed likely places for Atlantis, such as the Americas or parts of it, remnants of the island of Thera (in the Mediterranean — which should be ruled out by Plato's statements), or the Azores in the Atlantic, but there has never been a consensus by researchers that any of these were indeed Atlantis.

Before or after the Tower of Babel?

Plato also informs us that Atlantis was inhabited by Poseidon and his family (including Atlas). Before people begin thinking "Are you taking Greek mythology seriously?" take note that Poseidon was son of Cronus, which is a variant of Cethimas/Kittim (Cronus/Kronos, Κρόνος).[5] Biblically, Kittim is the son of Javan, the son of Japheth, the son of Noah. With this in mind, Atlas was likely Noah's great, great, great grandson.

So when Plato speaks of Poseidon inheriting land from the dispersion of people around the earth, this makes sense. Kittim, Poseidon's father, was mentioned in the Tower of Babel account. With the Tower of Babel dispersion happening just over a hundred years after the Flood according to Ussher, then the earliest Atlantis could have been inhabited was soon after that time.[6]

When Might Have Atlantis Been Destroyed?

According to Plato, Poseidon's control of Atlantis had already been given to Atlas, after whose death several kings had ruled by the time the disaster struck the island. If Poseidon was the great, great grandson of Noah (the same as Eber, who is the father of the Hebrews, and in a different lineage), then it is reasonable to assume that his life expectancy would

---

5. It makes sense that many early ancestors on the earth after the Flood were raised up to "god-like" status because they outlived great, great grandsons. For example, Noah outlived great, great, great grandson Peleg. Of course, this doesn't make them "gods" at all.

6. James Ussher, *The Annals of the World*, trans. Larry and Marion Pierce (Green Forest, Arkansas: Master Books, 2003), p. 22.

be near the same as Eber and Atlas may have been near the same as Eber's son Peleg. The ages of the post-Flood patriarchs dropped off after Noah.[7]

Eber, who was born 66 years after the Flood, would have died 530 years after the Flood. Had Poseidon lived about this long as well, then this would have been about 1818 B.C. (according to Ussher who put the Flood at 2348 B.C.).[8] This would have been about the time Abraham died as well.

Patriarch	Age
Noah	950
Shem	600
Arphaxad	438
Shelah	433
Eber	464
Peleg	239

Peleg died sooner, and assuming that Atlas was his contemporary, he too should have died much sooner than Poseidon, as should the next few in line. Using these assumptions, about 1818 B.C. would have been the *earliest* that Atlantis could have been destroyed. To give you some context, Moses and the Exodus from Egypt would have occurred in 1491 B.C. or about 850 years after the Flood (using Ussher's numbers). So it makes sense that there would be some time before the destruction of Atlantis. Plato records:

> Now Atlas had a numerous and honorable family, and they retained the kingdom, the eldest son handing it on to his eldest for many generations. . . .

Remembering the limitations of Plato's account, this suggests several generations of rule well after Poseidon's son Atlas. Plato even records that their law had been passed down by Poseidon. It appears Poseidon had probably died by the time of the destruction of the island. So let's use the earliest estimated date for Poseidon's death at 1818 B.C.

The latest Atlantis could have been destroyed would have to be prior to Socrates, who died around 400 B.C. But the account came through an aged Solon, who got it from the Egyptians and their accounts of the past. So the latest date would surely be a few hundred years prior to Socrates' death. To be generous, let's set 600 B.C. as the latest date. So we have a range of 1818 B.C. to about 600 B.C.

7. Ancient Patriarchs in Genesis, Answers in Genesis website, Bodie Hodge, January 20, 2009, http://www.answersingenesis.org/articles/2009/01/20/ancient-patriarchs-in-genesis.
8. James Ussher, *The Annals of the World*, trans. Larry and Marion Pierce (Green Forest, Arkansas: Master Books, 2003), p. 21.

What Happened to Atlantis — If It Did Exist?

First, it could have been completely destroyed by earthquake, volcano, or other disaster.[9] Or perhaps the remnants of Atlantis that Plato wrote of have been destroyed since the time of his writing. Plato records that it was associated with a great earthquake — perhaps it was even felt in Greece.

According to Plato's account in *Timaeus*, the ocean where Atlantis used to be was nearly impassable by boat due to the mud and debris from the island. However, in 2,000 to 3,000 years such sediment could have easily traveled and settled out in other areas due to ocean currents, tides, storms, and so on.[10] So that may not be a good sign to look for today. Perhaps groups of islands may be the place to look in the Atlantic Ocean extending from the mouth of the Mediterranean Sea. But this is just speculation; we may never know where it was, if it did exist.

Could the destruction of Atlantis have been caused by a sudden rise in sea level? Creationists have often pointed out there was a post-Flood Ice Age that was triggered by the Flood. In brief, conditions following the Flood would have yielded warm oceans and cool summers due to massive volcanic activity associated with the Flood, plate movements during the Flood, and mountain building at the end stages (and soon after the Flood). With fine ash hovering in the upper atmosphere and being replenished with each volcano, this reflects sunlight back to space, hence cooling the

---

9. If an island the size of Nebraska did burst with volcanic explosions that were able to destroy it and cause it to sink, one would think it surely left some marks. One can't help but notice that one of the plagues on Egypt was a thick darkness for three days during the time of Moses. This is the sort of thing that ash would do downwind if an island that size blew up. Interestingly, down wind runs over Egypt today — perhaps God utilized a miracle of timing and directed the ash to cover the Egyptians with darkness and not the Israelites (Exodus 10:22–23). If Atlantis were just in the Atlantic Ocean from the Mediterranean Sea, was this the time when it was destroyed? We simply do not know, but it is within the time frame of when it could have blown up. Though again this would merely be speculation.

10. The recent tsunami in Japan (Great East Japan Earthquake) washed much debris out to the ocean on March 11, 2011. Immense debris from that tsunami has made its way to North America over the course of only one year, including heavy items like the famous motorcycle that washed up in Canada. "Tsunami Motorcycle: Japan Tsunami-Swept Harley Found in Canada," Malcolm Foster, 5/12/2012, Associated Press, http://www.huffingtonpost.com/2012/05/02/tsunami-motorcycle-japan-harley-canada_n_1470541.html.

globe. Warmer oceans due to plate movements and heated rock under the oceans increased evaporation, which caused more rainfall or, in winter months, more snowfall. With cooler summers not melting the snow, it accumulates into ice — many layers of ice quickly form. Therefore, the world would have rapid growth of glaciers and ice caps.[11]

From a big picture, an Ice Age takes water out of the ocean and deposits it on land. This means the ocean levels would have been reduced. Both Christians and non-Christians agree that an Ice Age would reduce ocean levels significantly — to a point where land bridges open up — which is likely how many people and animals could have migrated to most continents.

But at the end of the peak of the Ice Age, water levels in the ocean began to rise as glaciers and ice caps melted. Creationists have pointed out that the peak of the Ice Age would have been in the neighborhood of about 500 years after the Flood. For example, creationist researcher Mike Oard has estimated that there was extensive melting for the next 200 years. If Atlantis' destruction was 700 or 800 years after the Flood, it may have had something to do with the rising ocean levels. Keep in mind that an island being overtaken by rising sea levels appears identical to an island sinking!

Where Might Atlantis Have Been?

The Americas can easily be ruled out due to size, but also because *Timaeus* refers to a continent set beyond it. This continent is likely the Americas. Most obviously, the Americas still exist and have not sunk into the sea. In addition, the island of Thera is within the Mediterranean Sea, so this would be ruled out.

Perhaps the most famous report of Atlantis came from Athanasius Kircher from *Subterraneus* in 1669. He drew a map and placed Atlantis between Africa/Europe and the Americas. Take note that north is facing the bottom in his map.

The size of Kircher's Atlantis is much larger than Plato's description, but it is in the Atlantic Ocean. In fact, Kircher's version of Atlantis appears as large, if not larger, than Greenland. So this may not have been as accurate

---

11. Ken Ham, general editor, *New Answers Book 1*, "Where Does the Ice Age Fit?" by Mike Oard (Green Forest, AR: Master Books, 2006), p. 207–219, http://www. answersingenesis.org/articles/nab/where-does-ice-age-fit.

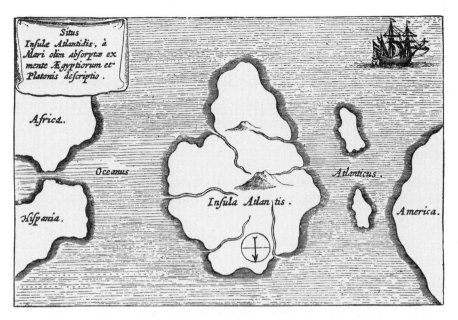

Athanasius Kircher's map of Atlantis from *Subterraneus* in 1669.

as it could have been. However, the island is where the Azores now sit. And of the logical places Atlantis could have been, the remnants spoken of by Plato could be the Azores or perhaps the Canary Islands or the Madeira Islands. Plato states:

> The consequence is, that in comparison of what then was, there are remaining only the bones of the wasted body, as they may be called, as in the case of small islands, all the richer and softer parts of the soil having fallen away, and the mere skeleton of the land being left.

This is, of course, assuming the mountaintops still remain to this day as islands. The Azores sit above the Mid-Atlantic Ridge, where many creationists believe some of springs of the great deep burst forth (Genesis 7:11). This area was likely wrought with earthquake and volcanic activity. But would this area be an obvious impasse of mud and debris for several years for those sailing out of the Mediterranean Sea? Since it seemed rather well known that mud and debris caused a near impasse for ships, this may not be where Atlantis was. It doesn't seem as logical, since fewer ships were traveling that far into the Atlantic as opposed to the other two locations.

Madeira Island and the Canary Islands are aloft volcanoes as well, and these areas may be more apt to cause a problem with ships trying to pass if demolished so near the Straight of Gibraltar. A few potential areas are shown on the map below for the island of Atlantis.

Conclusions

We may never know where Atlantis existed. If it did exist, it was most likely a post-Flood island somewhere in the Atlantic Ocean, not far from the Strait of Gibraltar.

Atlantis, if the accounts were reasonably accurate, would have been destroyed, leaving only much smaller islands still sitting above the Atlantic Ocean's surface. The most logical remnants would seem to be the Canary or Madeira Islands as well as other underwater islands in their vicinity that may have further been destroyed 3,000 years ago or so.

Several of these island chains, such as the Azores (A.), Madeira (B.), or Canary (C.) islands, could be the remnants Plato wrote about. But without further research, it would not be wise to comment further.
Map credit: 2009 Google - Imagery NASA, Data SIO, NOAA, U.S. Navy, NGA, GEBCO

Chapter 26

The Authority Test:
Christianity or Humanism?

Bodie Hodge

✿✿✿✿✿✿✿✿✿✿✿✿✿✿✿✿✿✿✿✿

Part 1: Testing Christians' Ultimate Authority

Why the Need for This Test?

There are many Christians who say they believe in biblical authority. They may even claim to adhere to biblical inerrancy and say they take the Bible "literally," or as it is written. However, in *practice,* many of these Christians often ignore the Bible.

The primary reason many Christians do not adhere to biblical authority in practice is that they are influenced by the religion of humanism — and may not even realize it. Humanism is the common religion of the times. As Christians, we need to be able to effectively recognize and refute it. In this article I will present the "authority test" to help Christians recognize when humanism is trying to overstep the authority of God. But before I explain what I mean by "the authority test," let's look at the influence of humanism.

Influence of Humanism

In today's culture, the religion of humanism has infiltrated the thinking of Christians, whether laity, pastors, elders, or professors. Humanism is a religion that essentially places humans on top and everything else below. So in this religion, God would be lower than man — or there is really no God at all.

Humanism really began taking hold in the Western world with the widespread rejection of God as the authority beginning about 200 or so years ago. Humanism has become the staple religion in universities and state schools around the world and is directly opposed to biblical authority.

Some famous humanists are Dr. Eugenie Scott, who heads up the National Center for Science Education, and Dr. Richard Dawkins, who openly professes atheism and writes books that attack Christianity. Both were signers of the Humanist Manifesto III. However, many people think humanisticly (having man as the authority), whether they realize there is a Humanist Manifesto or not. With humanism being the prime religion taught in today's schools, it is no surprise that younger generations think as though mankind is the authority.

God Is the Authority

Contrary to what the world believes, we know that God, being the Creator and Sustainer of all things, is the ultimate authority in all things. Consider God's Word:

> All Scripture is given by inspiration of God, and is profitable for doctrine, for reproof, for correction, for instruction in righteousness, that the man of God may be complete, thoroughly equipped for every good work. I charge you therefore before God and the Lord Jesus Christ, who will judge the living and the dead at His appearing and His kingdom: Preach the word! Be ready in season and out of season. Convince, rebuke, exhort, with all long-

suffering and teaching. For the time will come when they will not endure sound doctrine, but according to their own desires, because they have itching ears, they will heap up for themselves teachers; and they will turn their ears away from the truth, and be turned aside to fables. But you be watchful in all things, endure afflictions, do the work of an evangelist, fulfill your ministry (2 Timothy 3:16–4:5).

God determines what is right or wrong. Therefore, His Word, i.e., Scripture, is useful for rebuking and correcting. Even people, families, and governing authorities for various cultures can get laws and rules for civil life correct from time to time, but this is because they are borrowing from what God has determined as right and wrong.

The context surrounding 2 Timothy 3:16 reveals that there is a time when people no longer adhere to sound doctrine from God but leave the concepts of right and wrong up to their own desires. When one raises up his own desires to be the authority, this is humanism, where humans think they can sit in authority over God. Paul writing to Timothy here says that this philosophy will influence teachers and turn people away from the truth to fables. In today's culture, this is exactly what is happening with universities and schools and why Christians need to be exceptionally discerning lest they be led astray to fables by humanism (e.g., molecules-to-man evolution) instead of resting on Scripture.

The Authority Test

First Thessalonians 5:21 says that we must "Test all things; hold fast what is good." God helps us think through the issues, using the standards of Scripture, to determine what is good and right. Then we should hold fast to that.

Using the following authority test can play a big part in the process of thinking through the issues. The authority test is this: "Does the idea/

statement/presupposition that I am confronted with have man as the ultimate authority or the God of the Bible as the ultimate authority? Are man's thoughts exalted above God's Word, or is the Word of God honored?" This authority test can be used two ways:

1. To better yourself by realizing where humanism has infiltrated your life and accordingly changing to align with God's Word (2 Corinthians 13:5)
2. To recognize when others are thinking "humanisticly" and being able to reveal that fallacy to prepare to refute it (2 Corinthians 10:3–6)

Brief Examples in Scripture

There are quite a number of examples in Scripture where God's authority was reduced and man's ideas were raised up to be greater than what God said. Here are a few of the many biblical examples that illustrate this:

1. Adam and Eve, Genesis 3: When the woman (later named Eve in verse 20) was presented with two different options (what God said and what the serpent said), she raised her thoughts up to be the authority on the subject. The woman saw the fruit and desired it. She raised her own thoughts of the fruit above what God said about the fruit in Genesis 2:17, which she was more or less aware of (Genesis 3:2–3). She, thus, was first to exhibit this humanist trait. Then Adam followed suit.
2. Cain, Genesis 4:1–12: Cain's sacrifice didn't mimic sacrifices of animals as God did in Genesis 3:21 for Adam and Eve (coats of skins). His sacrifice for this or other reasons was not acceptable compared to Abel's, who did have animal sacrifices. God advised Cain, yet Cain did not listen to God, and, in his anger over God's

authority to determine what is and what is not acceptable, went out and killed his brother Abel. This violates God's transcendent law against murder. So Cain raised up his own thoughts to be greater than God's by rejecting them. Once again, humanist thinking.

3. Saul, 1 Samuel 15: Instead of listening to God, Saul decided to keep back what he considered the best animal plunder to supposedly sacrifice to God, as opposed to destroying them as the Lord had commanded. Saul opted to have his own thoughts on the matter to be greater than God.

4. Pharisees, Matthew 12:38: The Pharisees wanted to see a sign from Jesus. They placed themselves in authority by trying to force Jesus, the Almighty God, to submit to their wishes to prove Himself to them, thus putting themselves in authority over God.

Putting Ideas and Comments to the Test in Today's Culture

Christians should learn from these types of examples, because once one reduces God as the authority, then man's ideas, by default, become the authority. Sadly, many Christians fail to realize that when this happens, the authority is transferred over to man's erroneous ideas and philosophies and no longer comes from Christ. Consider:

> Beware lest anyone cheat you through philosophy and empty deceit, according to the tradition of men, according to the basic principles of the world, and not according to Christ (Colossians 2:8).

As Christians, we need to be able to discern if the ideas of men (even our own) are sitting in a position of authority over God's Word. Here are three examples:

1. Cults: Many cults claim to add to the Word of God. In reality, they are raising up man's words to be equal to or greater than God's Word. This is a form of humanism. As soon as one refers to a book, magazine, organization, etc., as having equal or greater authority than the Bible, then that should be a red flag to anyone that humanism has infiltrated.

2. The deity of Christ: John 1, Colossians 1, and Hebrews 1 are clear that Jesus Christ is the Creator God. Some people demean this and reduce the deity of Christ. This is man sitting in authority over God's Word — again. For more on this see the article "Is Jesus the Creator God?"[1]

3. Millions of years: In no place in Scripture is the idea that the earth is millions of years old. Adding up genealogies will not get anyone even close to millions of years. The idea of millions and billions of years comes from fallible man's ideas about the past. These fallible men interpret the geological rock layers as accumulating over millions of years, and hence, these men reject God's Word in Genesis 6–8 about a global Flood. If one accepts these ideas, knowing that these ideas contradict God's Word, then one is putting man's ideas over God's ideas. Isn't it clear how humanistic this really is? Unfortunately, even sincere Christians can begin to adjust their methods of interpretation so that their interpretation of the Bible becomes consistent with the secular "findings" of science. These Christians may not be willfully setting up their ideas over God's Word, but they are being heavily influenced by the results of humanistic thinking. There is no legitimate reason to reject a plain reading of the Genesis record of creation and the Flood. It is when Christians examine the "evidence" of secular geology in light of God's Word, rather than the other way around, that they will be able to understand that the evolutionary time-line is in error. The antidote for the influence of humanistic thinking is to view Scripture as authoritative.

Consider these comments and try to spot the humanism in these:

1. My pastor said that our particular church agrees that evolution and the Bible are compatible.

2. The Bible doesn't mean a normal day in Genesis 1 because science says it is much longer.

With #1, the writer of this statement appeals to the pastor, who appeals to the specific local church, which appeals to man's ideas about millions of

---

1. Bodie Hodge, "Is Jesus the Creator God?" Answers in Depth, December 12, 2007, http://www.answersingenesis.org/articles/aid/v2/n1/jesus-the-creator.

years and evolution. There can be multiple levels to search through before you spot the humanism at the root.

With #2, again the person appeals to "science," but really they mean a secular interpretation of scientific facts.

We must use our God-given mind to reach logical conclusions, but if our minds interpret facts in such a way that our conclusion contradicts God's Word, then we must reject that conclusion and give God the benefit of the doubt. Otherwise, we are guilty of humanistic thinking. We must allow God's Word to be the ultimate authority.

My prayer is that each one of us will use the authority test on a daily basis to correct our thinking. This is one of the first steps to get back to biblical authority.

It is important to realize that when man tries to sit in authority over the Word of God, then man is trying to judge God. But God makes it clear that it is He and His Word that will judge us.

Part 2: Testing Humanism and Witnessing

Once Christians begin to get themselves back to biblical authority, then the next challenge is humanism in the culture. Consider these comments that are common in today's society and try to spot the humanism:

1. The paper from the latest scientific journal says dinosaurs and man didn't live at the same time.
2. Most scientists believe in evolution, so it must be true.
3. The Bible can't be true because it is full of contradictions.

In #1, the paper from the journal is given authority over the Bible's statement that on day 6, God created both man and land animals (dinosaurs). Where did the paper come from? Fallible man.

In #2, it appeals to multiple humans (scientists) as an authority over God and implies consensus is the method by which we determine truth — but how often has that consensus changed? The consensus in Noah's day was that there would be no Flood!

In #3, the person is sitting in authority over God's Word claiming there are contradictions (which there aren't), and, in effect, that God is lying or can't get His facts straight in what He claims is His Word, true, perfect, and complete (Revelation 22:18–19; 2 Timothy 3:15–16, 2:15; Romans 2:16, 3:2; Hebrews 4:12, etc.).

Following up the Test in Practice

The authority test simply allows you to recognize the root of a belief system — either going back to God or going back to humanity. But what is the next step? The goals are threefold:

1. To reveal to that person the real religion that they believe or have been influenced by is humanism
2. To show the foundational problems with that view
3. To present what the Bible says and culminate with the gospel

Many people who think humanisticly simply don't realize it. So, the first goal is to reveal this to them — perhaps challenge a humanistic worldview (in kindness) by asking questions about how they view the world and how their beliefs relate to things in reality. This is usually a non-threatening way to get people to think about their beliefs (Christian or not) more deeply because they probably haven't — especially the foundation for their belief system.

This also reveals problems with the foundation of humanism. For example, ask that person why people wear clothes in general. The person may be a bit taken aback, but what this shows is that a humanistic view of the past really doesn't explain the world. Ultimately, of course, clothing is a Christian aspect that goes back to sin, shame, and sacrifice in Genesis 3.

Or ask about marriage — where does the idea of marriage come from? (Ultimately, it comes from the Bible, too.) Ask why death exists and if "right and wrong" exist and what is the ultimate standard by which we judge what is right or wrong. Ask if truth exists; if so, what exactly is it? And then ask if truth is the same for everyone. Ask where the world and universe came from; and where the stars came from; and where life came from; and so on.

A few questions like these should get the person thinking — without being "preachy." What will likely happen, though, is that a person will reveal what he or she really believes about origins . . . which is probably a mixture of some big bang, long ages, and evolution with some spirituality — or even some Christianity — mixed in.

When some of that comes out, point out the areas in which they are thinking as a humanist (evolution, naturalism, long ages, big bang, etc., are subsets of humanism). You may even have to explain it. Once they realize how humanism has influenced them, then proceed to point out that humans (or even that person individually) are really raising themselves up to be "a god" by placing themselves as the ultimate authority. Point out that humanism is really a polytheistic religion where each human is his own "god."

This should get through any humanist thinking, but then suggest to them that the Bible does explain things like the origin of matter, space, time, stars, marriage, clothing, truth, and so on. Then go into the doctrine of sin and that a perfect God originally created everything perfect. It was due to man's sin that the world is like this — full of death and suffering. Then this can lead into the gospel, and how Christ came to save us from sin and death.

While witnessing, remember to be kind and patient (1 Peter 3:15; 2 Timothy 2:24). After all, we were each enemies of the gospel ourselves at one point (Colossians 1:21) — but Jesus Christ was patient with us and performed the ultimate act of kindness on the Cross.

Chapter 27

Was Jesus Wrong?
Peter Enns Says Yes

Tim Chaffey and Roger Patterson

❀❀❀❀❀❀❀❀❀❀❀❀❀❀❀❀❀❀

Introduction

At Answers in Genesis, we have frequently warned about the dangers of forcing man's fallible ideas into the text of Scripture, because it unlocks a door of compromise that will inevitably be pushed open further by the next generation. This can be traced throughout Church history in many areas. When it comes to the age-of-the-earth controversy, the various harmonistic views developed from a quasi-literal interpretation of much of Genesis 1 (the gap theory)[1] to modern views which have completely reclassified the text (the framework hypothesis)[2] so that people can believe whatever they want about origins while claiming they are being "faithful" to the Bible.

While liberal theologians have long bought into theistic evolution, many conservative Christians have flirted with the idea of long ages (and some have bought into it), but they have almost universally rejected any

---

1. For a refutation of the gap theory, see Ken Ham, "What about the Gap & Ruin-Reconstruction Theories," in *The New Answers Book 1*, Ken Ham, editor (Green Forest, AR: Master Books, 2006).
2. For a refutation of the framework hypothesis, see Tim Chaffey and Bob McCabe, "Framework Hypothesis," in Ken Ham and Bodie Hodge, editors, *How Do We Know the Bible Is True?* Vol. 1 (Green Forest, AR: Master Books, 2011).

notion that the first man was not a special creation of God. In the past few years, however, a handful of books from ostensibly conservative Christians have challenged the traditional interpretation that God created man from the dust of the ground. Instead, these authors have argued for some eclectic blend of creation and evolution when it comes to mankind's origin.

An Old Error Given New Life

We have consistently challenged the Church to reject any attempt to reinterpret Genesis because of the dangerous hermeneutical precedent this sets. That is, if we desire to reinterpret (i.e., reject) certain parts of God's Word because of man's fallible opinions about the past that are based on anti-supernatural presuppositions, then at what point do we stop reinterpreting the Bible? If Genesis should be reinterpreted to accommodate billions of years and the other evolutionary ideas proposed by the majority of scientists, should we not also reinterpret other sections of Scripture that are at odds with the majority of scientists, such as the virgin birth, Resurrection, and ascension of Christ?

"Oh, come on, that will never happen," some Christians might protest. We have been told this time and time again by Christians who think AiG has made a proverbial mountain out of a molehill or committed the slippery slope fallacy. Well, that door of compromise has now been opened to such an extent that the gospel itself is under attack. In his recent book, intended to provide a rationale for rethinking Christianity in light of the claims of current evolutionary theories,[3] Dr. Peter Enns promotes the idea that Adam and Eve were not real, historical people. To bolster this claim, Enns relies on the discredited documentary hypothesis to say that the Pentateuch (first five books of the Bible) was not written

---

3. It is important to note that the evolutionary ideas endorsed by Dr. Enns and others extend beyond the common notion of biological evolution. Biological evolution is dependent on the time and processes involved in the geological evolution of the earth. The formation of the earth is based in the nebular hypothesis as an extension of the big-bang cosmology that demands the universe is approximately 14 billion years old. These three areas, cosmological, geological, and biological, are impossible to divorce if one embraces the mainstream scientific consensus. The result is that the current scientific understanding becomes the authority when considering the origin of the universe, the earth, and the life on it — including humans made in the image of God.

until after the Babylonian exile.[4] Moses did not write them, but instead it was some scribe or group of scribes that compiled oral and written traditions and stuck them together. Despite a wealth of biblical and historical evidence to the contrary, Enns portrays this idea as a given, accepted by any scholar worth his or her salt. In a footnote in his new book, Dr. Enns addressed one of the objections to this view — namely, that Jesus said that Moses wrote about Him:

> Although treating this issue fully would take us far afield, I should mention at least a common line of defense for Mosaic authorship: Jesus seems to attribute authorship of the Pentateuch to Moses (e.g., John 5:46–47). I do not think, however, that this presents a clear counterpoint, mainly because even the most ardent defenders of Mosaic authorship today acknowledge that some of the Pentateuch reflects updating, but taken at face value this is not a position that Jesus seems to leave room for. But more important, I do not think that Jesus' status as the incarnate Son of God requires that statements such as John 5:46–47 be understood as binding historical judgments of authorship. Rather, Jesus here reflects the tradition that he himself inherited as a first-century Jew and that his hearers assumed to be the case.[5]

Before looking at the disastrous conclusions that follow from such a belief, let's read the passage in question.

> "Do not think that I shall accuse you to the Father; there is one who accuses you — Moses, in whom you trust. For if you believed Moses, you would believe Me; for he wrote about Me. But if you do not believe his writings, how will you believe My words?" (John 5:45–47).

Jesus did not just *seem* to attribute authorship of the Pentateuch to Moses, He clearly affirmed in this passage that Moses wrote at least some of it. Earlier in the confrontation, Jesus told the Jews that they searched

---

4. For problems with the documentary hypothesis, see Terry Mortenson and Bodie Hodge, "Did Moses Write Genesis?" in Ham and Hodge, *How Do We Know the Bible Is True?* vol. 1.

5. Peter Enns, *The Evolution of Adam: What the Bible Does and Doesn't Say about Human Origins* (Grand Rapids, MI: Brazos Press, 2012), p. 153.

the Scriptures because in them they thought they had eternal life, but Jesus said that the Scriptures testify of Him and that the people needed to come to Him for eternal life. Then He narrowed it down to a particular section of the Old Testament. The Jews divided their Scriptures into two (sometimes three) sections: the Law and the Prophets (see Luke 24:27; sometimes the Prophets were divided into the Prophets and the Writings). So by referring to Moses, it appears that Jesus was attributing Mosaic authorship to the first five books of the Bible.

Since Jesus said Moses wrote about Him, that settles the issue. "Not so fast," says Enns, who offered two arguments in response to this claim. First, Enns stated that "even the most ardent defenders of Mosaic authorship today acknowledge that some of the Pentateuch reflects updating, but taken at face value this is not a position that Jesus seems to leave room for." It is true that some portions of the Pentateuch reflect updating. For example, Deuteronomy 34 was almost certainly not written by Moses, since it is the account of his death. It may very well have been recorded by Joshua.[6] Enns apparently appeals to a straw man argument here in claiming that all who disagree with his view are hyper-literalists, when he states that Jesus did not leave room for any updating. Enns implies that when Jesus called Moses the author, it must be understood that every letter was penned by Moses himself or else Moses could not truly be called the author. Candidly, this is simply an absurd contention. Authors today have

---

6. Of course, it is possible that God enabled Moses to prophetically write about his own death, but the easiest and most likely solution to this alleged dilemma is to propose that Joshua or another person wrote the chapter after Moses died. Another example of this "updating" is found in the phrase "to this day." Several times these words appear with a place name or a custom (Genesis 22:14, 26:13, 32:32, 35:20, 47:26), indicating that the place name or custom was still in effect in the time the book was written or compiled. This does not in any way provide a strong argument against Mosaic authorship of the Pentateuch. First, one of the popular explanations for the authorship of Genesis is that it originally consisted of several eyewitness records from some of the key figures in the book (Adam, Noah, Abraham, Isaac, etc.) but was eventually compiled and edited by Moses. If this is accurate, then the words "to this day" simply reflect the words of Moses who told his readers that a place name or custom established in Genesis was still in use in his day. The fact that the words "to this day" are not used in the same manner in the other books of the Pentateuch supports this idea. Second, if God revealed the content of Genesis to Moses, it does not negate the possibility of Moses inserting these updates. Third, even if these updates were added long after Moses, it would not negate Mosaic authorship of the Pentateuch as a whole.

editors who contribute to and revise their work, but this does not cause anyone to deny authorship to the person who wrote the majority of the text. The Apostle Paul had others write for him, but this does not mean Paul was not the author.

The Accommodation Theory

Enns acknowledges that this is not his strongest argument. His more important claim is that Jesus was not really making an authoritative historical statement about Mosaic authorship.[7] "Rather, Jesus here reflects the tradition that he himself inherited as a first-century Jew and that his hearers assumed to be the case." Please read that statement again and try to understand the seriousness of this charge. According to Dr. Peter Enns, Jesus wrongly attributed the writing of the Pentateuch to Moses because He accepted an erroneous tradition of His day.

The idea advanced by Dr. Enns here is known as the accommodation theory and was first advanced in the 18th century by Johann Semler, the father of German rationalism. The accommodation theory is very popular among liberal theologians and basically asserts that Jesus accommodated (accepted and taught) the various ideas of His day, even if they were wrong.[8] Allegedly, since Jesus was primarily concerned with spiritual matters, He did not bother to correct some of their false historical or scientific beliefs because doing so might have distracted from His real message.

There are many problems with this type of thinking. First, Jesus routinely rebuked people who held beliefs contrary to Scripture and corrected those who were in error. He specifically told the Sadducees, "You are mistaken, not knowing the Scriptures nor the power of God" (Matthew 22:29). This is hardly accommodating someone's errors. Furthermore, Jesus often

---

7. This is not a new claim for Enns. He raised similar notions in a 2002 article: Peter Enns, "William Henry Green and the Authorship of the Pentateuch: Some Historical Considerations," *Journal of the Evangelical Theological Society* 45 (September 2002): p. 386–405.

8. A related heresy is known as the limitation theory. This view focuses on apparent limitations Jesus had because of His humanity. Since He became hungry, thirsty, and tired, then why could He not be limited in His understanding and be wrong about many things as long as they were not directly related to His work of redemption? This view neglects the truth that Jesus was (and is) also God, and God cannot make a mistake. It also fails to account for the many instances where Jesus was able to know the thoughts of those He was addressing (e.g., Matthew 9:4, 12:25; John 2:24–25), which is a strong argument for His divinity.

reacted strongly to accepted practices that were contrary to the Word of God. He drove the moneychangers out of the temple (John 2:15–16) and excoriated the scribes and Pharisees (Matthew 23:16–33). If Jesus simply accommodated the errors of His time, He never would have done these things.

Those who promote the accommodation theory emphasize that Jesus said not even He knew the timing of His return: "But of that day and hour no one knows, not even the angels of heaven, but My Father only" (Matthew 24:36). However, one scholar correctly pointed out, "Limits on understanding are different from misunderstanding. The fact that He did not know some things does not mean He was wrong in what He did know."[9] We can be certain that when Jesus affirmed something to be true, He knew it was true, and He spoke with absolute authority. Jesus never accommodated the erroneous thinking of His day. He always spoke the truth, the full truth, and nothing but the truth.

So why does it matter whether Jesus accommodated the errors of His day? Well, if Jesus taught error, then He would have lied to His listeners, in which case He would have been a sinner. If He unwittingly taught error, then He would have misled His followers, making Him a false teacher. Either option leaves us with a Jesus who is sinful and less than God. If Jesus had sinned, then He could not have been the spotless Lamb who appeased God's wrath by His sacrificial death on the Cross, because He would have needed to die for His own sins. If Jesus did not die for our sins, then we are still in our sins and are headed for an eternity in the lake of fire.

Did Jesus really say Moses wrote about Him? Consider His words in the following verses:

> He said to them, "Moses, because of the hardness of your hearts, permitted you to divorce your wives, but from the beginning it was not so" (Matthew 19:8; cf. Deuteronomy 24:1–4)

> "But go and show yourself to the priest, and make an offering for your cleansing, as a testimony to them, just as Moses commanded" (Luke 5:14; cf. Leviticus 14:2–32).

---

9. Norman L. Geisler, *Systematic Theology*, Vol. 1 (Minneapolis, MN: Bethany House, 2002), p. 276.

Abraham said to him, "They have Moses and the prophets; let them hear them" (Luke 16:29).

But even Moses showed in the burning bush passage that the dead are raised, when he called the Lord "the God of Abraham, the God of Isaac, and the God of Jacob" (Luke 20:37; cf. Exodus 3:1–6).

Then He said to them, "These are the words which I spoke to you while I was still with you, that all things must be fulfilled which were written in the Law of Moses and the Prophets and the Psalms concerning Me" (Luke 24:44).

"Did not Moses give you the law, yet none of you keeps the law? Why do you seek to kill Me? . . . I did one work, and you all marvel. Moses therefore gave you circumcision (not that it is from Moses, but from the fathers), and you circumcise a man on the Sabbath. If a man receives circumcision on the Sabbath, so that the law of Moses should not be broken, are you angry with Me because I made a man completely well on the Sabbath?" (John 7:19, 21–23; cf. Exodus 24:3; Genesis 17:9–14).

And just in case you are not convinced yet that the absolute truthfulness of Jesus is essential, think carefully about these words Jesus spoke to the Jews:

"When you lift up the Son of Man, then you will know that I am He, and that I do nothing of Myself; but as My Father taught Me, I speak these things. And He who sent Me is with Me. The Father has not left Me alone, for I always do those things that please Him" (John 8:28–29).

Since Jesus only spoke the words the Father taught Him, to say that Jesus accommodated the errors of His day is to also claim that God the Father made these same mistakes. It may sound unkind to say it, but the accommodation view promoted by Dr. Enns is heresy. It charges our precious Savior with error and accuses the Father of instructing the Son to teach error.

Conclusion

In this book, Enns demonstrates a low view of Scripture, and that low view of Scripture logically leads to a low view of the Savior. In both Hebrews

6:18 and Titus 1:2 we are given a clear statement — God cannot lie! To assert that Jesus knowingly told His hearers falsehoods or affirmed something that He knew was false can only be called a lie. To rightly understand the nature of the Scriptures and their inerrancy and infallibility, we must clearly connect these ideas with the character of God. Since God cannot lie, neither can His Scriptures. As the incarnate Son of God, Jesus would not mislead anyone, even though He was a first-century Jew. To suggest that Jesus would lie, even if it is called an "accommodation," is to deny the deity of Christ.

This is not a side issue. This is not a "can't we all just get along" dispute. This is a false teaching that strikes right at the heart of the gospel, and it should never be accepted by those who claim to love Jesus Christ. This problem has been addressed by many writers since its introduction in the 18th century. The basic problems with the accommodation view have been described in detail and we will summarize them here.[10] To accept accommodationism is to accept that God is not able to use language in a way that perfectly communicates His meaning without embracing falsehoods. Wayne Grudem states succinctly that to embrace accommodation "essentially denies God's effective lordship over human language."[11] Secondly, as noted above, to say that God has communicated using a falsehood denies His moral character as described in Numbers 23:19, Titus 1:2, and Hebrews 6:18. Further, since we are to be imitators of God and His moral character (cf. Leviticus 11:44; Ephesians 5:1; 1 Corinthians

---

10. The following is a brief list of articles and books that address the accommodation theory: Norman L. Geisler, *Systematic Theology*, Vol. 1, (Minneapolis, MN: Bethany House, 2002), p. 274–280; Wayne Grudem, *Systematic Theology* (Leicester, England: InterVarsity Press, 1994), p. 97–100; "Chicago Statement of Biblical Inerrancy," Article XV, see Grudem, p. 1206; Charles Hodge, *Systematic Theology*, Vol. 1 (Grand Rapids, MI: Eerdmans, 1997), p. 153–188; John W. Wenham, "Christ's View of Scripture" in Norman L. Geisler, editor, *Inerrancy* (Grand Rapids, MI: Zondervan, 1979), p. 14; G.K. Beale critiqued Enns's particular understanding of the accommodation view in a review of an earlier work by Peter Enns entitled *Inspiration and Incarnation: Evangelicals and the Problem of the Old Testament* (Grand Rapids, MI: Baker, 2005). Beale's review appeared in the *Journal of the Evangelical Theological Society* (June 2006) and was followed by a response from Enns. Beale included his review, a summary of the response by Enns, and a critique of that response in his book, *The Erosion of Inerrancy in Evangelicalism: Responding to New Challenges to Biblical Authority* (Wheaton, IL: Crossway, 2008).
11. Grudem, *Systematic Theology*, p. 97.

11:1; and others), then if God misled people, should we not also use intentionally misleading or false ideas to communicate? All of these ideas are contrary to the clear teaching of Scripture and deny the holiness of God.

We pray that Dr. Enns and others who hold this view will recognize the seriousness of this error and repent, and we ask you to pray to that end as well. This single footnote has exposed how the church desperately needs to stop thinking they can innocuously incorporate secular philosophies with God's Word (and even, wittingly or unwittingly, undermine the deity of Christ along the way). Christians need to take an absolute and uncompromising stand on the Word of God as the ultimate source for doctrine.

Chapter 28

Were There Really Giants as Described in the Old Testament?

Tim Chaffey

❧❧❧❧❧❧❧❧❧❧❧❧❧❧❧❧❧❧❧

Introduction

Critics and skeptics often scoff at the Bible because it describes many individuals as giants, and it also mentions several giant people groups.[1] Interpreters have speculated about the size of these people with guesses ranging anywhere from 6 feet to more than 30 feet in height. A great deal of misinformation about biblical giants has been proliferated on the Internet along with some fake pictures of supposed giants.

This chapter surveys all of the individuals and people groups described as giants in Scripture. Since the Bible tells us about these giants, we can be certain of their existence. It is also helpful to know that some ancient records and archaeological data corroborate some of the biblical data in this area, so these will be examined as well.

Old Testament Giants

One of the earliest mentions of giants in Scripture is found in Genesis 14.

---

1. This chapter is an abridged version of Tim Chaffey's article "Giants in the Old Testament" available at http://www.answersingenesis.org/articles/aid/v7/n1/ot-giants, accessed June 7, 2012. The web article includes some extra details exploring the possible height of these giants as well as discussion about modern "giants."

> In the fourteenth year Chedorlaomer and the kings that were with him came and attacked the *Rephaim* in Ashteroth Karnaim, the *Zuzim* in Ham, the *Emim* in Shaveh Kiriathaim, and the Horites in their mountain of Seir. . . . Then they turned back and came to En Mishpat (that is, Kadesh), and attacked all the country of the Amalekites, and also the *Amorites* who dwelt in Hazezon Tamar (Genesis 14:5–7, emphasis added).

Genesis 14 does not reveal that the Rephaim, Zuzim, Emim, or Amorites were giants, but this information can be found in other places.

The Amorites

The Amorites are mentioned more than 80 times in Scripture and, early on, some were allied with Abraham (Genesis 14:13). They were descendants of Noah's grandson Canaan (Genesis 10:15–16). Although the Bible does not provide this information, the Jewish general-turned-historian Josephus gives the name of their ancestor as Amorreus.[2] While the Amorites are mentioned in the same contexts as other giants a few times, they are specifically described as giants in the Minor Prophets.

> Yet it was I who destroyed the Amorite before them, whose height was like the height of the cedars, and he was as strong as the oaks; yet I destroyed his fruit above and his roots beneath. Also it was I who brought you up from the land of Egypt, and led you forty years through the wilderness, to possess the land of the Amorite (Amos 2:9–10).

Through Amos, God clearly stated that the Amorites were generally very tall and strong. Some may downplay the description of the Amorites in this passage, since these verses employ figurative language, but there are some good reasons to take this passage in a straightforward manner.

John C.P. Smith has worked with Centre for Biblical and Hebraic Studies in the UK, and he is the founder of Jot & Tittle, a ministry focused

---

2. Flavius Josephus, *The Antiquities of the Jews*, I.6.139, in William Whiston, translator, *The Works of Josephus: Complete and Unabridged* (Peabody, MA: Hendrickson Publ., 1996). For a good comparison of the Table of Nations in Genesis 10 and the writings of Josephus on this subject, see Bodie Hodge, "Josephus and Genesis 10: A Wonderful Stepping Stone," www.answersingenesis.org/articles/aid/v4/n1/josephus-and-genesis-chapter-ten.

on teaching Christians the Hebrew language. Regarding the claim that Amos 2:9 is poetic so one can downplay the comparison of the Amorites' height to cedars and strength to oaks, Smith wrote the following:

> Is it any more poetical than Job 40–41? And even if the language is poetic, it does not necessarily follow that it is exaggerated, especially given that it is God who is describing the size of the Amorite here (and the giant creatures of Job 40–41).

> An important word here is כְּ (ke), meaning "as" or "like." In English, a significant range of meaning exists between describing two things being vaguely *like* each other in some general sense and being precisely the same *as* each other. Dictionary.com defines "as" in the following way: "to the same degree, amount, or extent; similarly; equally." So the wording in the NKJV and NASB, "like the height of cedars," might give the impression of vague similarity (i.e., they were both tall.), whereas the wording in the NIV and NJB, "tall as the cedars," implies a greater sense of equality. The context gives a clue to the correct interpretation here. The verse does not simply say, "like/as cedars and oaks"; it explicitly qualifies the comparison with the words "height" (*govah*) and "strong" (*chason*). The relevant clause translates literally: ". . . which as [or like] height of cedars is his height and strong is he as [or like] oaks . . ." (Amos 2:9). The evidence appears to support a close, as opposed to a loose, correlation between the height of the Amorite(s) and the height of cedars.[3]

Since they dropped out of history so abruptly, it is not surprising that we find little or no records of giants outside of the Bible. In the absence of any contrary evidence, it is surely best to take God at His word, however extraordinary it may appear to us. If He did not mean it literally, then why did He use such specific wording?

The idea that the Amorites were giants is supported by the report of the spies whom Moses sent through the land of Canaan. The Amorites were one of the people groups they saw (Numbers 13:29), and they claimed that "all the people whom we saw in it are men of great stature"

---

3. From personal correspondence, Johann Carl Friedrich Keil and Franz Delitzsch, *Commentary on the Old Testament*, Vol. 10, "The Minor Prophets" (Peabody, MA: Hendrickson Publishers, 2006), p. 172.

(Numbers 13:32). It is telling that in their response, Joshua and Caleb did not challenge the size of the land's inhabitants (Numbers 14:6–9).[4]

The Emim

Deuteronomy 2 reveals that the Emim, which likely means "terrors," were giants:

> The Emim had dwelt there in times past, a people as great and numerous and tall as the Anakim. They were also regarded as giants [Hebrew *rephaim*], like the Anakim, but the Moabites call them Emim (Deuteronomy 2:10–11).

Moses told the people that the Emim used to live in the territory that God had given to the descendants of Lot's son Moab (Genesis 19:37).

The Zuzim (Zamzummim)

The Zamzummim (almost certainly the same as Zuzim in Genesis 14:5) were also called giants and listed in the same chapter as the Emim:

> [The land of Ammon] was also regarded as a land of giants [Hebrew *rephaim*]; giants [*rephaim*] formerly dwelt there. But the Ammonites call them Zamzummim, a people as great and numerous and tall as the Anakim. But the LORD destroyed them before them, and they dispossessed them and dwelt in their place (Deuteronomy 2:20–21).

These verses explain that a group of giants known as Zamzummim had lived in the land of Ammon, "a land of giants." God destroyed the Zamzummim so that the descendants of Lot's son Ben-Ammi (the Ammonites) could live in the land (Genesis 19:38).[5]

---

4. The non-canonical (Apocrypha) books of Baruch 3:22–28 and Sirach 16:6–9 indicate that giants (Greek; *gigantes, gigantōn*, respectively) previously lived in the land of Canaan before Israel conquered them. The passage in Baruch states that they "perished because they had no wisdom, they perished through their folly" (Baruch 3:28, NRSV).
5. The next verse in this passage (v. 22) mentions the Horites, who may also have been giants, although they are not specifically called *giants* in Scripture. However, in two of the three chapters in which they are mentioned, they appear in the same contexts with other giants (Genesis 14:6; Deuteronomy 2:12–22), so they may also have been giants.

According to Genesis 14:5, the Zuzim were in the land of Ham. This may be in reference to Noah's son, Ham, since they descended from him. But it is more likely a reference to the Hamathites, who were descendants of Canaan, Ham's son. While the Zuzim and Zamzummim may have been different people groups, there are enough similarities in name, description, and geographical location to infer that they were variant names for the same group.

Rephaim

The most common term used to describe giants in the Bible is "rephaim" (e.g., Deuteronomy 3:11, 13). It may refer to a certain people group,[6] or it may be a term that simply means "giants." The singular form, *raphah*, also appears several times (e.g., 2 Samuel 21:16, 18, 20).[7]

The third chapter of Deuteronomy contains an interesting account of the victory of the Israelites over Sihon, the king of the Amorites, and Og, the king of Bashan.[8] It is here that we learn an intriguing detail about Og:

> For only Og king of Bashan remained of the remnant of the giants [*rephaim*]. Indeed his bedstead was an iron bedstead. (Is it not in Rabbah of the people of Ammon?) Nine cubits is its length and four cubits its width, according to the standard cubit (Deuteronomy 3:11)

Some translations use the word "sarcophagus" (NEB) or "coffin" (TEV, CEV) in place of "bedstead," for the Hebrew word עֶרֶשׂ (*eres*). The majority of English Bibles render this term as "bed" or "bedstead," which

---

6. This was the view of C.F. Keil, who, in commentating on 2 Samuel 21:16–22, asserted that "Raphah was the tribe-father of the Rephaim, an ancient tribe of gigantic stature, of whom only a few families were left even in Moses' time." (Johann Carl Friedrich Keil and Franz Delitzsch, *Commentary on the Old Testament*, Volume 2, Joshua, Judges, Ruth, 1 and 2 Samuel [Peabody, MA: Hendrickson Publishers, 2006], p. 680).

7. Strictly speaking, there are two singular Hebrew forms with slightly different spellings (and originally pronounced slightly differently): רָפָא (*rapha*) and רָפָה (*raphah*). But these appear to be simply two spellings for the same word, since 2 Samuel 21:20 and 1 Chronicles 20:6 are nearly identical in their wording, with the former employing רָפָה (*raphah*) and the latter רָפָא (*rapha*).

8. Sihon, the Amorite king of Heshbon, may also have been a giant. He was an Amorite and is listed in the same contexts as other giants (e.g., Numbers 21:21–35; Deuteronomy 2:24).

makes sense since *eres* means couch, divan, bed, or bedstead. Also, it would be indeed strange to translate it as "sarcophagus" since these were made of stone or marble, and Og's "bedstead" was made of iron.[9]

Whether Moses referred to Og's bed or coffin is not particularly relevant to the discussion at hand. However, the size of this object is noteworthy. We are told that it was nine cubits long and four cubits in width "according to the standard cubit." Since the standard cubit is approximately 18 inches long, then Og's bed or coffin was about 13.5 feet long and 6 feet wide. To put this in perspective, if stood up on end, the height of this bed would have been exactly twice as tall as a person who is 6 foot 9 inches tall. Of course, he may not have been as large as his bed. Some authors have attempted to downplay the significance of these dimensions, but the Bible clearly identifies Og as a giant.

The Nephilim

The earliest mention in Scripture of giants is just prior to the Flood account.

> There were giants [nephilim] on the earth in those days, and also afterward, when the sons of God came in to the daughters of men and they bore children to them. Those were the mighty men who were of old, men of renown (Genesis 6:4).[10]

The word translated as "giants" in this verse is the Hebrew word nephilim, and many Bible versions simply transliterate it as such. There has been much debate over the meaning of this word. Some believe it comes from the Hebrew verb *naphal*, while others claim that it is from

---

9. For example, William White wrote, "As to Og's famous bed, it may have been a sarcophagus which was large not because Og was a giant but because other objects would have been buried with him." Robert Laird Harris, Gleason Archer, Bruce Waltke, *Theological Wordbook of the Old Testament*, electronic ed., (Chicago, IL: Moody Press, 1999), s.v. 2198d. Other items may have certainly been buried with Og, but he was called a giant. Why bother to mention the massive size of this item if Og were not a giant? Perhaps the bed was made of iron instead of wood to support such a large man.

10. It is beyond the scope of this article to discuss the identity of the "sons of God," other than to clear up a point that confuses many: the sons of God in this passage are not the same group as the giants (nephilim). For more information on this fascinating subject, please see my article, "Battle Over the Nephilim," http://www.answersingenesis.org/articles/am/v7/n1/battle-nephilim.

the Aramaic noun *naphil*.[11] These individuals are described in Hebrew as *gibborim* ("mighty men").[12] The *nephilim* were mentioned again when the

---

11. The Hebrew verb *naphal* can theoretically take the form of an active or passive participle, נֹפְלִים (*nophelim*) or נְפוּלִים (*nephulim*) respectively. The former occurs 18 times in the Hebrew Scriptures, mostly meaning "those who fall" (as in battle, see Ezekiel 32:22–24 for three examples), but the latter is unattested. Neither of these terms matches the morphology (shape, including vowel pattern) of nephilim (נְפִלִם in Genesis 6:4 and Numbers 13:33b or נְפוּלִים in Numbers 13:33a). The Hebrew language does not require that the morphology of every single word follow a predetermined pattern. This is particularly true of proper nouns, which sometimes sound like other words sharing the same root letters. If a different vowel pattern was used for this term, then it could possibly be connected to the Hebrew verb *naphal* ("to fall"). One example of this type of vowel pointing is found with the Hebrew verb מָשַׁח (*mashach*), which means "to anoint." The active participle form is מֹשְׁחִים (*moshchim*, "anointing [ones]"), equivalent in form to *nophelim*. The passive participle form is מְשֻׁחִים (*meshuchim*, "anointed [ones]"), equivalent in form to *nephulim*. An adjectival noun form of the word is מְשִׁיחִים (*meshichim*, also "anointed [ones]") is equivalent in form to nephilim. Strictly speaking, the Old Testament does not include the precise form of this final word, but it does exist in combination with a suffix in 1 Chronicles 16:22 and Psalm 105:15.

    On the other hand, by comparing the variant spellings of nephilim it is easy to see the extra י (*yod*) in the word from Numbers 13:33a. This may not seem like a big deal, but according to Dr. Michael Heiser (PhD, Hebrew Bible and Ancient Semitic Languages), this extra letter provides a strong clue as to the word's origin. Aramaic is closely associated with Hebrew, and some small sections of the Old Testament were written in Aramaic. In Aramaic, the word *naphil* (נְפִיל) has the extra י (*yod*) and means "giant." The plural form of this noun is *nephilin*, which is equivalent to the Hebrew word nephilim (Aramaic masculine plurals have an "-in" ending, whereas Hebrew masculine plurals have an "-im" ending.). Interestingly, this is also the Aramaic word used for the constellation Orion, named for the giant hunter of mythology. Michael S. Heiser, "The Meaning of the Word Nephilim: Fact vs. Fantasy," available at www.michaelheiser.com/nephilim. pdf, accessed December 6, 2011. Some of the lexicons and dictionaries that support the rendering of nephilim as "giants" include *The Hebrew-Aramaic Lexicon of the Old Testament* (HALOT, Koehler, Baumgardner), *The New International Dictionary of Old Testament Theology and Exegesis)NIDOTTE*, VanGemeren(, *The Analytical Hebrew and Chaldee Lexicon* (Davidson), and *Dictionary of the Targumim, the Talmud Babli and Yerushalmi, and the Midrashic Literature* (Jastrow). *Brown-Driver-Briggs Hebrew and English Lexicon* (Brown, Driver, Briggs) also defines the word as "giants" but lists its etymology as dubious.

12. Many other individuals in Scripture are classified as "mighty men" (*gibborim*), but this does not necessarily mean they were giants (e.g., Nimrod in Genesis 10:8 and David's "mighty men" in 2 Samuel 23:8–39). So although not all *gibborim* were giants, it seems as though all giants were *gibborim*.

    It is intriguing that in the Septuagint, the Greek translation of the Hebrew Old Testament, Nimrod is called a "giant" and a "giant hunter" (Genesis 10:8–9) — not a hunter of giants, but a giant who was a hunter. Indeed, the Greek word

spies returned from their exploratory mission of the land of Canaan. These men reported that Ahiman, Sheshai, and Talmai (descendants of Anak, progenitor of the Anakim) dwelt in Hebron. They also stated, "The people who dwell in the land are strong; the cities are fortified and very large; moreover we saw the descendants of Anak there" (Numbers 13:28). The chapter concludes with ten of the spies giving "a bad report" trying to convince the Israelites that they could not conquer the land:

> The land through which we have gone, in spying it out, is a land that devours its inhabitants; and all the people whom we saw in it are men of great size. There also we saw the Nephilim (the sons of Anak are part of the Nephilim); and we became like grasshoppers in our own sight, and so we were in their sight (Numbers 13:32–33; NASB).[13]

γίγας (*gigas*) — the plural form is γίγαντες (*gigantes*) — used in the Septuagint's rendering of Genesis 10:8–9 is also used to translate both *nephilim* and *gibborim* in Genesis 6:4. There are some difficulties with this view of Nimrod. Genesis 10:8 states that Nimrod "began to be a mighty one [*gibbor*] on the earth." How does one *begin* to be a giant? Either you are one or you're not. The solution may be found in the ESV's rendering of this verse, which states that Nimrod "was the first on earth to be a mighty man." Yet there were certainly "mighty men" on the earth prior to the Flood, so how could he be the first one? Perhaps the meaning of this phrase is that he was the first giant after the Flood, or it could be that the Septuagint is inaccurate here.

13. There is some debate over the truthfulness of these claims since they are included in the "bad report" made by the spies. Some interpreters have argued that the reports of giants were simply exaggerations made by the spies in their efforts to discourage the people. However, the term "bad report" (Hebrew *dibbah*) does not focus on falsehood, but grave intentions. Brown-Driver-Briggs place the use of this word in Numbers 13:32 under its third definition: "*evil report*, specif. a (true) report of evil doing" (Francis Brown, Samuel Rolles Driver, and Charles Augustus Briggs, *Enhanced Brown-Driver-Briggs Hebrew and English Lexicon*, electronic ed. [Oak Harbor, WA: Logos Research Systems, 2000], p. 179.) This same word is used of Joseph's report of his brothers' activities in Genesis 37:2, and there is no reason to think he was lying. Also, the narrative reporting found in Numbers 13:21–24 shows that the spies did find out that Ahiman, Sheshai, and Talmai were in Hebron. Furthermore, neither Joshua nor Caleb disagreed with these facts, but they did encourage the people that they could win the battle because God was on their side. Finally, it appears that the words in parentheses — "the sons of Anak are part of the Nephilim" (Numbers 13:33; NASB) — were not spoken by the spies but were an editorial comment from the author (i.e., Moses or a later editor added these words for clarification). Nevertheless, and despite the omission of the parenthetical text in some ancient manuscripts including the Septuagint, the fact remains that the spies claimed to have seen the

The Anakim

The Anakim were mentioned in several of these passages. They were perhaps the best known of the giants dwelling in the land of Canaan at the time of the Exodus. As stated in the verse above, they were part of the nephilim. If nephilim simply refers to giants in general, then the Anakim are just said to be giants in Numbers 13:33, which is consistent with their description in this passage. So the Amorites and other giant people would also be nephilim. If nephilim refers to a particular giant tribe, then the Anakim were part of this line.

Numbers 13:22 states that Ahiman, Sheshai, and Talmai were descendants of Anak, who was obviously the namesake of the Anakim. Both the Emim and Zamzummim were compared to the Anakim, as they were both "a people as great, numerous, and tall as the Anakim" (Deuteronomy 2:10, 21; see also 9:2).

Anak was the son of Arba (Joshua 15:13). Little is known about Arba, and his ancestry is not provided. However, he was apparently somewhat legendary as indicated by the parenthetical statements in the text when his name appears. The city of Hebron, where Abraham, Isaac, and Jacob settled and were buried was also called Kiriath Arba.[14] We are told that "Arba was the greatest man among the Anakim" (Joshua 14:15), and "the father of Anak" (Joshua 15:13; 21:11).[15] Kirjath Arba was also called "Mamre" in Genesis 35:27. Mamre was an Amorite, who was an ally of Abram (Genesis 14:13). This man owned some trees by which Abram settled, and at some point, part of Hebron became synonymous with his name.

Joshua fought several battles with the Anakim and the Amorites. Eventually, he "cut off the Anakim from the mountains: from Hebron,

---

nephilim.

14. Genesis 23:2, 35:27; Joshua 15:13, 54, 20:7; Judges 1:10. Genesis 23:19 states, "Abraham buried Sarah his wife in the cave of the field of Machpelah, before Mamre (that is, Hebron) in the land of Canaan."

15. Some have proposed that Arba was not a personal name but was merely the name of the main city of the Anakim. This is how Arba is viewed in the Septuagint. For example, this particular version of Joshua 15:13 states, "καὶ ἔδωκεν αὐτῷ Ἰησοῦς τὴν πόλιν Αρβοκ μητρόπολιν Ενακ (αὕτη ἐστὶν Χεβρων)." Literally translated, this would be, "and gave him Joshua the city of Arbok [Arba], capital of Anak (this is Hebron)." Similar wording is found in the Septuagint's rendering of Joshua 21:11.

from Debir, from Anab, from all the mountains of Judah, and from all the mountains of Israel; Joshua utterly destroyed them with their cities. None of the Anakim were left in the land of the children of Israel; they remained only in Gaza, in Gath, and in Ashdod" (Joshua 11:21–22). These actions set the stage for the famous account of Goliath in 1 Samuel.

Goliath

Of course, the most renowned giant was the mighty Philistine slain by David. Here is how he is described in Scripture.

> And a champion went out from the camp of the Philistines, named Goliath, from Gath, whose height was six cubits and a span. He had a bronze helmet on his head, and he was armed with a coat of mail, and the weight of the coat was five thousand shekels of bronze. And he had bronze armor on his legs and a bronze javelin between his shoulders. Now the staff of his spear was like a weaver's beam, and his iron spearhead weighed six hundred shekels; and a shield-bearer went before him (1 Samuel 17:4–7).

Notice that Goliath was from Gath, which happened to be one of the three places where Anakim remained, according to Joshua 11:21–22. So although he is not called one in 1 Samuel 17, it is possible that Goliath was a descendant of the Anakim who mixed with the Philistine population in that area.[16]

There is some debate about Goliath's height due to the textual variants in ancient manuscripts. Most English translations follow the Masoretic text in listing his height at "six cubits and a span" (approximately 9'9"). However, the NET Bible puts Goliath at "close to seven feet tall." The reason for the discrepancy is that the Masoretic Text differs from some ancient texts, including the Septuagint and an ancient manuscript found among the Dead Sea Scrolls, labeled 4QSam[a], which list Goliath's height as four cubits and a span (approximately 6'9").

Many modern scholars believe there is stronger textual support for the shorter Goliath.[17] But while he is not specifically called a giant in this

---

16. The word "Philistine" may mean "immigrant" or "stranger," and the Bible informs us that the Philistines came from Ham's son Mizraim, who was the father of the Casluhim, "from whom came the Philistines" (Genesis 10:14).

17. J. Daniel Hays, "Reconsidering the Height of Goliath," *Journal of the Evangelical*

passage, 2 Samuel 21:15–22 seems to identify Goliath as the "giant" (*raphah*) from Gath. There are other details provided that make the "six cubits and a span" the more likely figure. For example, the sheer weight of his armaments required that he must have been of enormous size and strength. His coat of mail weighed about 125 pounds and just the tip of his spear was 15 pounds. This does not even take into account his helmet, armor on his legs, javelin, or sword.[18] Also, I personally find it hard to believe that every member of Israel's army would have been terrified of someone who was my height (6'9").[19]

There are many other details about the account of David and Goliath that are often overlooked. Most people assume David was a short young man when he fought against the giant, but the Bible is very clear that David was considered "a mighty man of valor, a man of war" (1 Samuel 16:18) prior to fighting Goliath.[20]

Other Giants

The Bible mentions four more Philistine giants who were relatives of

Theological Society 48:4, electronic ed. (December 2005): p. 702–715.

18. Ibid, p. 709. Hays appealed to the size and strength of an offensive lineman in the National Football League, claiming that one "could carry [the amount of weight] easily." The question is not whether a person could carry this weight but whether he could be an effective warrior while carrying the extra 125 pounds of scale armor, plus the helmet and bronze armor on his legs, and wield such a massive weapon. In a footnote, Hays also cited modern soldiers who sometimes need to carry guns and mortars which are similar in weight to Goliath's gear. Again, this misses the point. The type of gun (MK 19) mentioned by Hays is not carried into hand-to-hand combat but is a grenade launcher often set up on the ground or mounted on a vehicle. A mortar is also fired from a distance. Hays also claimed that only Saul would have had the armor or weapons to match Goliath. He based this on 1 Samuel 13:19–23, which speaks of a time in which the Philistines had subjugated the Israelites and did not allow them to have blacksmiths in the land. He admitted that things may have been slightly different by the time of David's battle with Goliath, but he missed the fact that 1 Samuel 15:8 reveals the Israelite army destroyed the Amalekites and "utterly destroyed all the people with the edge of the sword." The Israelite army was well-equipped to battle the Philistines in 1 Samuel 17, and they routed their enemies after David defeated Goliath.

19. King Saul was said to be a head taller than any of the people (1 Samuel 9:2), yet he was not considered a giant. If Goliath was a mere 6'9", it seems strange that Saul would not also have been considered a giant.

20. I have elsewhere written at length about the misconceptions people have about David's stature. See "David: Little Guy or Mighty Man of War?" at www.answers-ingenesis.org/articles/2011/02/01/little-guys-big-things, accessed June 7, 2012.

Goliath from the region of Gath. Second Samuel 21:15–22 provides a more detailed account of these giants than the record of 1 Chronicles 20:4–8, but the latter passage does give some extra information that helps us make sense of the passage. The additional details from 1 Chronicles are in brackets.

> When the Philistines were at war again with Israel, David and his servants with him went down and fought against the Philistines; and David grew faint. Then Ishbi-Benob, who was one of the sons of the giant, the weight of whose bronze spear was three hundred shekels, who was bearing a new sword, thought he could kill David. But Abishai the son of Zeruiah came to his aid, and struck the Philistine and killed him. Then the men of David swore to him, saying, "You shall go out no more with us to battle, lest you quench the lamp of Israel."
>
> Now it happened afterward that there was again a battle with the Philistines at Gob [or "Gezer"].[21] Then Sibbechai the Hushathite killed Saph [or "Sippai"], who was one of the sons of the giant. Again there was war at Gob with the Philistines, where Elhanan the son of Jaare-Oregim [or "Jair"] the Bethlehemite killed ["Lahmi"] the brother of Goliath the Gittite, the shaft of whose spear was like a weaver's beam.
>
> Yet again there was war at Gath, where there was a man of great stature, who had six fingers on each hand and six toes on each foot, twenty-four in number; and he also was born to the giant. So when he defied Israel, Jonathan the son of Shimea, David's brother, killed him.
>
> These four were born to the giant in Gath, and fell by the hand

---

21. It is quite simple to resolve this difference in detail. Gob may have simply been a smaller town near the larger city of Gezer or within the area of Gezer (or vice versa). We do the same type of thing today. For example, if someone from another area of the country asked me where the Creation Museum was located, I could say that it's near Cincinnati. They might think that the museum is in Ohio because Cincinnati is in Ohio, but the Creation Museum is actually near Petersburg, a small town located in northern Kentucky. My direction gave them clear enough details for them to know the approximate location of the museum. If someone from the Cincinnati area asked me where the museum was, then I would tell them that it is located in Petersburg because they will likely know where that is.

of David and by the hand of his servants. (2 Samuel 21:15–22)

David's mighty men killed giants named Ishbi-Benob, Saph (Sippai), and Lahmi, as well as an unnamed giant with six fingers on each hand and six toes on each foot.[22] Each of these men could have descended from the remnant of Anakim that survived in the region of Gath, Gaza, and Ashdod (Joshua 11:22).

An Egyptian Giant?

One of David's mighty men, Benaiah the son of Jehoiada, defeated a large Egyptian man:

> And he killed an Egyptian, a man of great height, five cubits tall. In the Egyptian's hand there was a spear like a weaver's beam; and he went down to him with a staff, wrested the spear out of the Egyptian's hand, and killed him with his own spear (1 Chronicles 11:23).

Although he is often considered a giant, the Bible does not specifically identify this man as one, nor does it place this account with the exploits of David's other men who slayed giants, but it does provide his height as being "five cubits" (approximately 7'6"). The KJV, NKJV, NASB, ESV, and others insert the word "great" before "height" or "stature," but "great" does not appear in the Hebrew. This may have been done for stylistic and readability purposes or because his height is provided later in the verse. Young's Literal Translation renders this verse in an almost perfect word-for-word match of the Hebrew: "And he hath smitten the man, the Egyptian — a man of measure, five by the cubit — and in the hand of the Egyptian *is* a spear like a beam of weavers" (1 Chronicles 11:23).

In the parallel account given in 2 Samuel 23:21 the Egyptian is called "a spectacular man" in the NKJV and "an impressive man" in the NASB. While modern man may think of a 7'6" man as a giant, it is intriguing that the Bible does not identify him as such. Perhaps this is a clue that those who are identified as giants were larger than the Egyptian slain by Benaiah. Another explanation for this omission is that many of the giants were called by their particular tribes (Anakim, Emim, etc.), but the tall Egyptian is not said to belong to any of these giant groups. If that is the case, it

---

22. This somewhat common condition is known as polydactyly. Many popular-level works have ascribed this trait to all of the biblical giants, but the Bible only describes this particular giant in this way.

is curious why the biblical writers would not simply use a generic term for "giant," such as *rapha*.

Following these accounts in 2 Samuel and 1 Chronicles, the giants fade from the pages of Scripture (other than the retrospective mention of the Amorites as giants in Amos 2:9).

Extra-biblical References to Giants

Scores of giant skeletons have been allegedly unearthed in the past couple of centuries. These claims were especially popular in the 19th century. So far, no concrete evidence of these claims has been brought forth. Although some claim the evidence was ignored, destroyed, or hidden by places like the Smithsonian, it seems more likely that the vast majority of these reports were hoaxes created for various reasons.

Several websites display pictures of people standing next to or holding a giant human femur, but these bones are sculptures, allegedly replicas of a real bone found in Turkey or Greece. Once again, there are fantastic claims, but little or no hard evidence to support them.

As far as I know, no one has discovered definitive fossil evidence of giant humans. But then again, human fossils are quite rare altogether, since humans are often capable of avoiding conditions that lead to fossilization (e.g., like being rapidly buried in sediment). What is indeed significant is that many giant versions of other creatures existed in the past or still exist today. To name just a few, these include the following:

- spiders (e.g., the bird-eating spider, up to 12-inch leg span)
- moths (e.g., the Atlas moth, with a wing span of 11 inches)
- centipedes (up to 13 inches long)
- snails (e.g., the African giant snail, up to 15½ inches long)
- frogs (e.g., Beelzebufo, 16 inches high)
- dragonflies (e.g, Meganeura, with a wing span of more than 2½ feet)
- rats (e.g., Josephoartigasia, with a conservatively estimated body mass of 772 pounds or 350 kg)
- beavers (e.g., Trogontherium, about 7½ feet long)
- scorpions (e.g., the sea scorpion Jaekelopterus, estimated at more

than 8 feet long)

- crabs (e.g., the giant spider crab, with a claw span more than 12 feet)
- armadillos (e.g., Glyptodon, up to 13 feet long)
- turtles (e.g., Archelon, up to 16 feet long)
- fish (e.g., Xiphactinus, 19 feet long)
- sloths (e.g., Megatherium, which stood about 20 feet)
- worms (e.g., the giant earthworm, up to 22 feet long)
- sea cows (e.g., Hydrodamalis, 25 feet or more in length)
- crocodiles (e.g., Sarcosuchus, up to 40 feet long)
- snakes (e.g., Titanoboa, over 42 feet long)
- crustaceans (e.g., supergiant amphipods 10 times larger than those previously discovered)
- squid (e.g., Mesonychoteuthis, 50 feet or more in length)
- sharks (e.g., Rhincodon, up to 65 feet long)
- octopuses with 100 foot long tentacles[23]

The fact that scientists have discovered animals with body sizes far greater than those observed today suggests, at least in theory, the possibility of there having also been giant humans in the past, as recorded in the Bible.

Many modern scholars scoff at the idea that there could have been giant warriors in excess of seven and a half feet tall. Consequently, the biblical dimensions of these people have often been downplayed or ignored. However, the biblical data about these people can be trusted because it is in the Word of God. Furthermore, other ancient sources describe giants, and the Anakim are even mentioned as dwelling in the land of Canaan.

Egypt

---

23. Sources include: *The Book of Comparisons* (London: Sidgwick & Jackson, 1980); Carl Wieland and Darrell Wiskur, *Dragons of the Deep* (Green Forest, AR: Master Books, 2006); http://newswatch.nationalgeographic.com/2009/02/04/biggest_ animals_of_all_time; http://news.bbc.co.uk/1/hi/sci/tech/7408743.stm; Online Encyclopedia, http://www.encyclo.co.uk; http://prehistoricearth.wikia.com/wiki/ Glyptodon; http://en.wikipedia.org/wiki/Meganeura; http://www.bbc.co.uk/ news/science-environment-16834913.

During the 12th dynasty of ancient Egypt, traditionally dated from the 20th to 19th centuries B.C.,[24] the Egyptians practiced something akin to the modern use of voodoo dolls. A potter would make a clay figurine of an enemy they feared. The figurine had its arms behind its back and the name of the group or its leaders would be written upon it. Sometimes a bowl or block of clay was used for listing the enemies. The figurine or bowl was then smashed in a symbolic way of cursing the enemies so that they could be defeated.

Archaeologists have reconstructed many of these Execration texts (also called Proscription Lists), and some very interesting details have been found concerning the Anakim. This is an example of a text which mentions them:

> The Ruler of Iy'anaq, Erum, and all the retainers who are with him; the Ruler of Iy'anaq, Abi-yamimu and all the retainers who are with him; the Ruler of Iy'anaq 'Akirum and the retainers who are with him (emphasis added).[25]

It should be noted that *anaq* (i.e., with a *q* in place of the *k*) is a common transliteration of the Hebrew word for "Anak," עֲנָק (Numbers 13:33).

Another Execration text places the Anakim in the land of Canaan and even mentions the city of Jerusalem.[26] The ancient Egyptians also called the inhabitants of the land of Canaan "Shasu." A later text entitled *The Craft of the Scribe* (c. 1250 B.C.), which was used to train Egyptian scribes, discusses a Canaanite mountain pass during a past battle.

> The face of the pass is dangerous with Shasu, hidden under the bushes. Some of them are 4 or 5 cubits, nose to foot, with wild faces.[27]

Egyptian cubits were longer than the Hebrew common cubit. At

24. Many biblical creationists would place the 12th dynasty in the 16th to 17th centuries B.C. See John Ashton and David Down, *Unwrapping the Pharaohs* (Green Forest, AR: Master Books, 2006), p. 78.

25. James B. Pritchard, editor, *The Ancient Near East*, Volume I, "An Anthology of Texts and Pictures" (Princeton, NJ: Princeton University Press, 1958), p. 225.

26. Ibid.

27. W.W. Hallo, editor, *The Context of Scripture*, 3 vols. (Leiden: Brill, 2003) 3.9, cited in Clyde E. Billington, "Goliath and the Exodus Giants: How Tall Were They?" *Journal of the Evangelical Theological Society*, volume 50:3 (September 2007): p. 487–508.

20.65 inches per Egyptian cubit, the Shasu mentioned in this letter would have measured between 6'10" and 8'7". This description shows that the traditional measurement of Goliath is not as outlandish as many critics believe.

Other Ancient Reports

Nearly every place around the world has legends of giants dwelling in the land. Certainly, one must exercise caution when reading these stories on the Internet since so much of the information online is contrary to the Word of God. For example, a few years ago, pictures of giant skeletons started to appear on websites, but they were clearly doctored (apparently part of a graphic design contest). However, a recent discovery of a Peruvian mummy *could* be that of a giant toddler. At 20 inches in height, the skull is much larger than adult skulls today, yet exhibits features characteristic of children under two years of age, such as an open fontanelle.[28] Popular news reports have introduced speculation that this discovery is evidence of the existence of aliens, but the Bible provides solid reasons why this is wishful thinking, and even secular sources are crying "hoax" about such alien speculation. DNA tests are underway to verify the humanity of the specimen (presumably to preclude it being "another" human-like earth creature) — so far there seems to be little doubt that the specimen itself is at least genuine. It has been postulated that some of its abnormality was perhaps caused by disease or by ritual skull manipulation for cultural reasons, but no one explanation seems to explain all the unusual features (note the large eye sockets and unusual chin, for example).

Greek and Roman mythology mentions the Titans, Kyklopes (Cyclops), and several other giants.[29] Norse mythology contains stories of the

---

28. Brian Thomas, "Is Peruvian Mummy a Giant Toddler?" available at www.icr.org/article/6624, accessed February 17, 2012.

29. The apocryphal book of Judith mentions Titans and giants. According to this tradition, the Jewish people were about to be attacked by the invading Assyrians led by General Holofernes. (These names may have been cryptic for the Greeks and General Nicanor, respectively.) A beautiful Jewish widow was brought before the mighty general who attempted to seduce her. Four days later, Judith consented to eat and drink with him, but she only drank what her maid had prepared, while Holofernes drank so much that he passed out. She proceeded to cut off his head, which eventually led to a Jewish victory. In Judith's song, the people expressed how the Lord defeated Holofernes: "For their mighty one did not fall by the

Frost giants of Jötunheim. But these records are not limited to European mythologies or only to the ancient past. African and Asian peoples also have legends of giants, as do Native Americans.

For example, in his autobiography, "Buffalo" Bill Cody wrote the following words about a legend recounted to him by members of the Sioux tribe.

Mummy recently discovered in Peru.

> It was taught by the wise men of this tribe that the earth was originally peopled by giants, who were fully three times the size of modern men. They were so swift and powerful that they could run alongside a buffalo, take the animal under one arm, and tear off a leg, and eat it as they ran. So vainglorious were they because of their own size and strength that they denied the existence of a Creator. When it lighted, they proclaimed their superiority to the lightning; when it thundered, they laughed.
>
> This displeased the Great Spirit, and to rebuke their arrogance he sent a great rain upon the earth. The valleys filled with water, and the giants retreated to the hills. The water crept up the hills, and the giants sought safety on the highest mountains. Still the rain continued, the waters rose, and the giants, having no other refuge, were drowned.[30]

Undoubtedly, many of these stories contain exaggerations of the giants' prodigious height and strength. But is it reasonable to automatically reject every one of these traditions, or, like tales of dragons, is there possibly some truth behind the legends, as is often the case? It is interesting

---

hands of the young men, nor did the sons of the Titans strike him down, nor did tall giants [*gigantes*] set upon him; but Judith daughter of Merari with the beauty of her countenance undid him" (Judith 16:6, NRSV).

30. http://www.usgennet.org/usa/topic/preservation/bios/chpt19.htm, accessed November 2, 2011. Cody went on to write, "This tradition has been handed down from Sioux father to Sioux son since earliest ages. It shows, at least, as the legends of all races do, that the story of the Deluge is history common to all the world."

that much of giant lore includes descriptions of a flood sent by God (or the gods) to destroy these wicked people. Could it be that while the Bible contains the true history of our past, these groups are simply repeating their own distorted versions of world history prior to and perhaps after the dispersion at Babel?[31]

Conclusion

The Bible clearly teaches that giants existed in the past. Many of them lived in and around the land of Canaan, and Joshua was involved in several battles with them. David and his mighty men killed some Philistine giants. The Egyptians knew about the Anakim and feared them. Finally, cultures from around the world have legends that are often remarkably similar to biblical accounts, including the existence of giants.

The biblical accounts of giants are more than just "tall" tales. These enormous people truly existed, and no amount of scoffing or rationalizing by skeptics will change that fact.

---

31. During Solomon's day, "men of all nations, from all the kings of the earth who had heard of his wisdom, came to hear the wisdom of Solomon" (1 Kings 4:34). First Kings 10:22 explains the vast trade network enjoyed by Israel at the time. Details of Israel's history could have spread far and wide during Solomon's rule, which may explain why some of the ancient legends from other nations sound similar to biblical accounts.

Chapter 29

Did the Ten Plagues of Egypt Really Happen?

Steve Fazekas

❦❦❦❦❦❦❦❦❦❦❦❦❦❦❦❦❦❦

Egypt is a land of mystery and amazement. The wonder of the pyramids, the opulence of ancient dynasties, the abundance of temples, tombs, and obelisks collectively creates a tapestry of magnificence unequaled by our modern technological society.

In addition, there is the Nile River, for many centuries deemed the giver of life as the very bloodstream of the country, transforming a dry and thirsty desert into a verdant panorama of lushness by its yearly offering of rich black silt. Truly, Egypt is a remarkable place to the modern mind.

Yet to those of ancient Israel, the word "Egypt," evoked an emotion somewhat different to that of today.[1] The Bible records the words of Stephen as he speaks, full of faith and the Holy Spirit, recounting the incident of Moses receiving the promise of deliverance from God.

> "I have surely seen the oppression of My people who are in Egypt; I have heard their groaning and have come down to deliver them" (Acts 7:34).

---

1. Egypt in Old Testament Hebrew is literally Mizraim, Noah's grandson through Cush. It is translated as Egypt.

332 • How Do We Know the Bible Is True? Volume 2

There Are Detractors

There is much discussion today with regard to various theories surrounding ancient Egyptian slavery and the exact degree, if any, of forced bondage. Further, the veracity of the biblical text regarding the occupation of Goshen by Jacob's descendants and the appearance of Moses as deliverer from bondage along with the credibility of the ten plagues that gave rise to the "Exodus" is under continual historic revisionism and challenge.

The naysayers and detractors are legion in number. The subject is large and academic, much broader than can be dealt with in a chapter of this size. Nonetheless, there are aspects of the discussion, which, by being addressed, may help us to see in some respects that Charlton Heston and Cecil B. DeMille were more adept at Hollywood filmmaking than they were at biblical theology in the famous movie *The Ten Commandments* (1956).

Preaching in Antioch, the Apostle Paul reminds his hearers, "The God of this people Israel chose our fathers, and exalted the people when they dwelt as strangers in the land of Egypt, and with an uplifted arm He brought them out of it" (Acts 13:17).

Frankly, the whole drama found in the biblical narrative presupposes the supernatural, and this is precisely the issue. An enlightened age such as ours has no room for a supernatural God, who acts sovereignly in His creation, doing what He wants and when He wants, and especially establishing Himself in and through a people of His choice. This in itself to the modern mind is pseudo-historical, illogical, discriminatory, and just plain unscientific. Therefore, another explanation must be sought.

Ancient Egyptian society

The chronology that deals with the 10 Plagues of Egypt — where it fits in the time-line of the pharaohs and leading up to the actual exodus of the Hebrew nation from Egyptian bondage — is a broad discussion and outside the scope of this paper.[2] The biblical data gives us little specific

---

2. For more on this see *Unwrapping the Pharaohs* by David Down and John Ashton (Green Forest, AR: Master Books, 2006), and *The Annals of the World*, James Ussher, translated by Larry and Marion Pierce (Green Forest, AR: Master Books, 2003).

detail by way of chronology. *That* it happened is beyond question to the biblical record. Exactly *when* it happened may be a discussion for another time.

Amazing in itself is the silence of the ancient Egyptian historical record where neither tomb nor temple nor stele offers even a hint of the successive afflictions that ravaged the whole land in a manner which could only make the headlines.

However, before we raise the white flag, there could be a very plausible explanation for the silence. Egypt was a sacral society. In modern parlance, there was no separation of church and state. A complex pantheon of gods and goddesses were interwoven into the fabric of everyday life. The whole of society, whether in agriculture, business, family life, politics, or war, embraced a deity of some kind. For example, Hapi was the god of the Nile, the bringer of food and provision. Osiris was the god of the underworld, supervising the journey of the deceased to his final home.

William Ward points out the huge contrast between the gods of Egypt and the gods of surrounding nations. The deities of the Canaanite nations, for example, were bloodthirsty and capricious, given over to immorality and violence. The gods of Egypt were quite the opposite, peacefully pantheistic, being embodied in dogs, cats, wolves, hippopotami, crocodiles, frogs, trees, locusts, and other life forms.[3]

The Pharaoh himself was the sun in the sky of this sacral society. He was Horus, son of Hathor, literally one of the deities who ruled by divine fiat. To Egyptian life, the Pharaoh was absolutely sovereign, beyond fault, and without doubt. He was the divine agent of prosperity and national security and the source of all that was good and necessary for life itself. The media of the day was no different from ours centuries later. Things embarrassing to those who control the news need not be reported.

Certainly, someone with a huge ego such as Pharaoh would not record his own humiliating failures. This fact is well illustrated in the Battle of Kadesh, which was fought against the Hittites. Ramses II barely escaped with his life let alone a decisive victory. Yet the massive propaganda program by the young king embodied such a revision of historic fact that he was made out to have single-handedly guided his chariot into enemy ranks, bravely cutting them down on the right and the left.

---

3. William W. Ward, *The Spirit Of Ancient Egypt* (Beruit: Khayats, 1965).

How it is then remotely possible that a deity such as Pharaoh suffers embarrassment and defeat at the hands of two dusty shepherds named Moses and Aaron and their desert god, Jehovah? Unthinkable!

The Ten Plagues

On the other hand, deliverance from Egyptian bondage becomes the song of Israel (see Psalm 105:23ff). It becomes recorded, told, retold, celebrated, and commemorated from generation to generation. Why? Because their covenant-keeping God is faithful to His promises, bringing them out of captivity, forgiving their iniquities, leading them through the wilderness, into the land of Canaan as their promised possession.

Specifically then, the ten plagues involved blood, frogs, lice, flies, murrain (cattle disease), boils, hail, locusts, darkness, and death.

Generally speaking, there are at least three different ways people will view the plagues as they are recorded for us in the Pentateuch. The first is a simple, total denial that anything like this could ever happen in time and space. In this view, the purported ten plagues can be nothing more than tradition made of legend and myth mixed with fable. In other words, the biblical account is totally outside the bounds of the reasonable free thinker — but when is such a mere opinion from a fallible person who wasn't there the ultimate authority on the subject over God?

The second view shows a reluctance to jettison the biblical data completely, but searches for ways by which each of the plagues can be explained as "natural phenomena" that are part of a series of occurrences made explainable to the scientific mind by way of careful research. Sadly, this is quite common today in a world full of naturalism.

The third position accepts the historic accuracy of the Bible as a true account of God's dealings with the stubborn heart of the king of Egypt by way of ten plagues. Each of the plagues are supernaturally driven by God through His servant Moses, and supernaturally orchestrated toward a divine end by the One who says, "Then you shall know that I am the LORD God" (Exodus 6:7).

Judgment on the False Egyptians Gods Supernaturally

To ask if the ten plagues of Egypt really happened carries with it some interesting things. Secular researchers say, "No." The Bible says, "Yes."

The Scripture seems to suggest that the ten plagues were directed against the gods of Egypt including the Pharaoh.

"For I will pass through the land of Egypt on that night, and will strike all the firstborn in the land of Egypt, both man and beast; and against all the gods of Egypt I will execute judgment: I am the LORD" (Exodus 12:12).

For the Egyptians were burying all their firstborn, whom the LORD had killed among them. Also on their gods the LORD had executed judgments (Numbers 33:4).

Joseph P. Free, author of *Archaeology and Bible History*, makes five critical observations, and gives to us five key words descriptive of the ten plagues that underscore the uniqueness of the biblical record as it showcases a distinctly supernatural event.[4]

1. *Intensification.* The Egyptians certainly knew and understood plagues. However, a heightened escalation of locusts and frogs went beyond anything heretofore experienced by the general population. The extensive pollution of the waters turning to blood was an indictment of the river gods. The magnitude of the murrain or the intensity of the darkness went beyond anything that the court magician's limited repertoire could mimic, and so forth.
2. *Prediction.* Moses forecasts the time of the plagues with precision as well as the abatement of each. There was accuracy of prediction by Moses and Aaron that reached far beyond human guesswork.
3. *Discrimination.* The land of Goshen, where Israel was situated, became exempt from certain of the plagues. It would be difficult to keep hail, flies, and murrain within distinct geographical boundaries unless it were by a supernatural act.
4. *Orderliness.* Some see an increase in severity of the plagues culminating in the death of the firstborn male in each family. The plagues arrived in an order that progressed beyond those that could be imitated by the court magicians through their secret arts (Exodus 7:11). From the third plague onward, their imitations

---

4. Joseph P. Free, *Archaeology and Bible History*, revised edition (Wheaton, IL: Scripture Press Publications, Inc., 1969), p. 95.

stopped. The death of the firstborn was the ultimate stroke whereby Pharaoh relented.

5. *Moral purpose*. This could be the most important of these points.
The ten plagues were not flukes, but rather, each plague was a di-
vine assertion, "You shall know that I am the LORD your God"
(Exodus 6:7).

The Ten Plagues speak to at least three moral issues. First, there was
the complex of polytheism that saturated the Egyptian worldview. An
abundance of gods littered the moral landscape, yet not one of their gods
could lift a finger to ward off national calamity. Second, as a sacral society,
Egypt was led by soothsayers, sorcerers, magicians, and temple priests.
All the priestcraft and necromancy that Egypt could muster proved totally ineffective. The Pharaoh, himself considered as deity, could only
stand powerless before the God of Israel. Third, the nation of Israel
learned that they lived in a moral universe, created and ruled by one God,
and Jehovah is His name. It was His prerogative to define what was good
and what was evil, and punish or reward accordingly. At times, Israel was
no better than the heathen nations surrounding them, and it is no surprise that centuries later they found themselves in bondage again, under
Babylonian exile.

Modern-Day Thinking toward the Supernatural in Exodus

It is quite obvious that even a cursory reading of the biblical account
showcases the supernatural as the dominant element in the Exodus record. Many critics have tried to give a "scientific" explanation for each of
the ten plagues. However nothing satisfactory rises to the fore from the
annal's naturalistic explanation. For example, in the 19th century, scientist Dr. Greta Hort attempted to attribute the redness of the Nile River to
a species of red algae combined with the peculiar color of the dirt that
washes downriver during flooding. The work of Brad Sparks[5] is highly
commended as a well-researched counter to this kind of naturalistic approach, and the careful reader is left with no reasonable choice other than
the supernatural act of God as it is recorded in the Exodus account.

---

5. Brad Sparks, "Red Algae Theories of The Ten Plagues: Contradicted by Science,"
Bible and Spade 16 no.3 (2003) p. 66–77 and 17 no.1 (2004): p. 17–27.

Conclusion

In closing, the Scripture seizes the "Egyptian experience," not as some relic of the past, but with direct application to the Church of our day. The exhortation comes from the same sovereign Lord who sets the rules, not capriciously as the pagan gods of Canaan or Egypt might want to do, but framed within the integrity of all that He is in His gracious person and His work on our behalf, as the One who delivers His people from the bondage of sin and destruction.

"Now these things happened to them as an example, and they were written for our instruction, upon whom the ends of the ages have come. Therefore let him who thinks he stands take heed that he does not fall" (1 Corinthians 10:12–13; NASB).

Chapter 30

Spreading the Good News

Roger Patterson

✿✿✿✿✿✿✿✿✿✿✿✿✿✿✿✿✿✿✿

Every Christian is an ambassador for the Son of God who saved them from their sins and reconciled them to God. When writing to the Corinthian Christians, Paul reminded them of their job as ambassadors:

> Now all things are of God, who has reconciled us to Himself through Jesus Christ, and has given us the ministry of reconciliation, that is, that God was in Christ reconciling the world to Himself, not imputing their trespasses to them, and has committed to us the word of reconciliation. Now then, we are ambassadors for Christ, as though God were pleading through us: we implore you on Christ's behalf, be reconciled to God. For He made Him who knew no sin to be sin for us, that we might become the righteousness of God in Him (2 Corinthians 5:18–21).

Paul understood his role as an ambassador on behalf of God. His job was to communicate the gospel message — Christ's death on the Cross for the forgiveness of sins and His perfect obedience being credited to their account — to the entire world, begging them to be reconciled to God. In his previous letter to the Corinthians, Paul said, "Imitate me, just as I also imitate Christ" (1 Corinthians 11:1). The call for Christians today is no different.

While every Christian is called to proclaim the good news of the gospel of Jesus Christ, not all are called to do it in the same way. Jesus gives different roles to different individuals so that the entire Body of Christ can be equipped to do the work of ministry (Ephesians 4:11–12). Some people are called to be out on the streets proclaiming Christ, others within an office, others within a classroom, and others with their own children. Everywhere there is a sinner there is a need for the proclamation of the gospel. As there are different people in different situations, so the message of the gospel must reach those individuals through God's ambassadors.

At the Core

The core of the gospel message comes from the understanding of the universe we live in. What we experience today is not what the initial inhabitants of our planet experienced. Adam and Eve were placed into an environment that was free from corruption, disease, death, and rebellion. But they wrecked it — they disobeyed God's command and brought the curses of sin into the world. The world we live in now is broken and decaying, and the effects of that sin are present in each heart. Our hearts lead us to rebel against the God who created us and to hate and hurt those who are made in His image. Because God is a just judge (Psalm 7:11), He must punish all of those who disobey Him. As the Creator, He has that right. That is the bad news.

But God, who is rich in mercy, also demonstrates His love in providing a way for those who rebel against Him to be reconciled. That is the good news. Christ chose to step into our sinful mess as one of us, setting aside the glories of heaven. Unlike us, He lived a life of perfect obedience to God's laws and offered Himself as the perfect Lamb who could take away the sins of the world and then rose from the dead.

As the sinless Jesus received the punishment for sin upon the Cross, God's wrath against sinners was satisfied. Not only has God's wrath been turned from those sinners, Christ's perfect righteousness is credited to the account of all who repent and put their trust in Christ. The just Judge has justified us through Christ's perfect life and sacrificial death (Romans 3:20–28). What a glorious truth to proclaim!

As we survey the New Testament writings, we see the gospel message proclaimed in various ways. However, communicating in different ways does not mean that the heart of the message changes. Any proclamation of the gospel of Jesus Christ should include the following elements:

- All of humanity, back to Adam, has sinned against the Creator God by breaking His commands (Romans 3:23).

- Each individual is accountable for his or her own sins (Ezekiel 18:20).

- The penalty for sin is death and eternal punishment (Genesis 2:17, 3:19; Psalm 7:11; Matthew 8:12, 25:46; John 3:18; Romans 6:23; Hebrews 9:27).

- God, in His mercy, became flesh in Jesus Christ who died on the Cross as a substitute (to pay the penalty) for our sins and then rose from the dead (John 1:14, 3:16–21; Romans 5:8; 1 Corinthians 15:3–4; 2 Corinthians 5:21; 1 Timothy 2:5; Hebrews 9:22).

- By faith, we can each receive forgiveness of sins through repentance toward God (turning from our sin to go God's way) and placing our trust in Jesus Christ as our personal Savior and Lord (Mark 1:15; John 1:12–13, 3:3, 16–21, 36, 14:6; Acts 4:12, 16:30–34, 20:21; Romans 10:9–17; Ephesians 2:8–10).

- By faith, Christ's righteousness is credited to those who believe (Romans 1:17; Philippians 3:8–9).

Christ must be central to our proclamation of the good news — He is the one who has made salvation possible. When Paul preached the gospel, he emphasized a Savior who was crucified for sins and who rose from the dead as proof of His defeat of death and sin (1 Corinthians 15:1–5). He also made sin personal so that each individual would come under the conviction of the Holy Spirit (Acts 24:25). Proclaiming the gospel is a privilege, but also a responsibility.

A Bold Proclamation

Some believe that the gospel can be proclaimed by actions and (mis) quote the late Francis of Assisi: Preach the gospel every day, and, when necessary, use words. There are two problems with this idea. First, there is no evidence that he ever taught this. In fact, he was known to openly proclaim the gospel on the streets. Second, it is not a biblical idea. Think about it . . . if the gospel message includes the six points outlined above, how can your actions, without words, communicate those truths? Unless you are a really good mime, I don't know how you could explain those truths and expect someone to understand.

Evangelist Ray Comfort (and co-author in this book) has quipped that this sentiment is the spiritual equivalent of, "Feed starving children. Where necessary, use food."[1] As Paul tells us clearly in Romans 10, the gospel must be preached if it is to be understood and received by the lost.

That does not mean that the actions of a Christian are not important in preaching the gospel. Having a sound testimony before the world is of utmost importance. Peter exhorted the Christians being persecuted in the first century to live a blameless life so that those who were fighting against the gospel would have no reason to charge them (1 Peter 2:11–24, 3:13–17).

Likewise leaders within the Church are to be blameless (Titus 1:5–9; 1 Timothy 2:3–7). Living a life in accord with the truths of the gospel will only help as you seek to proclaim the gospel and the hope it offers. Let your light shine so that the words you speak will be illuminated by those actions — that God may be glorified in both.

Building a Toolbox

As a fix-it-yourself kind of guy, I appreciate a toolbox stocked with a variety of tools. A hammer doesn't do much when you need to tighten a screw on a light fixture. Likewise, different opportunities arise where one form of presenting the gospel might not be as appropriate as another. Any method that is faithful to the Scriptures and that presents the full gospel message is legitimate. Personally, I have studied many different methods and formats and have found all of them helpful in various situations.

When I hit the streets to share the gospel, I take tracts and props to help me communicate with large crowds. Sitting on a plane, I don't need those tools because the person is right there. Having the right tools, all grounded in the gospel truths, is a great encouragement as I seek to be an effective ambassador for the One who set me free from my sin.

---

1. Ray Comfort, "Saint Francis . . . A Sissy?" *Worldview Times*, http://www.worldviewweekend.com/worldview-times/article.php?articleid=2401.

I would encourage you to do the same. It can be very scary to communicate the gospel with others — whether friends, family members, or the stranger next to you on the bus. Being equipped with tools to help you communicate clearly can give you greater confidence in working alongside the Holy Spirit to spread the gospel message.

As you do this work, you are not alone. Jesus has sent the Spirit to empower us to obey His commands and proclaim the gospel. Ultimately, it is not our eloquence or ability to communicate with just the right words that is going to bring someone to conviction and repentance — that is the work of the Holy Spirit (John 16:7–11; 1 Corinthians 12:3). As we are faithful to proclaim the good news of the gospel, God will be faithful to call His children to Himself.

The following are various forms of evangelism. Some are promoted by specific ministries and others are more generic. All are aimed at proclaiming the gospel in its fullness to all who are lost and in need of the Savior. This is not an exhaustive list, but one that may help you as you think about stocking your own toolbox. Whether it is your first tool or another added to your collection, I trust these will give you added confidence in what the Lord can accomplish through you.

Creation Evangelism

Creation evangelism is using Genesis as a springboard to the gospel. The problem of sin has its foundation in the corruption of God's "very good" creation. Man exists in his sinful condition because of what happened when Adam rebelled against the Creator's authority. Understanding the true history of the universe provides a foundation for understanding our need for a Redeemer. Using the Bible as a starting point, the anti-biblical ideas of evolution and humanism (or other religions) can be shown false and the true nature of humanity can be presented. Using the Bible's history, the gospel can be clearly communicated.

The Answers in Genesis website offers many resources to communicate the gospel message starting with the very first verse of Scripture. The evangelistic booklets, videos, and the Seven C's Creation Evangelism Cube are great places to start learning and the *Pocket Guide for Effective Evangelism* will offer some great insights into sharing the gospel in our "evolutionized" culture. One great evangelistic book starting with creation is a book called *Begin*, which starts at the beginning of the Bible and takes people to Revelation to get a "big picture" of the Bible and the gospel.[2] Visit www.AnswersinGenesis.org for more information.

Evangelism Explosion

Developed by the late D. James Kennedy, *Evangelism Explosion* provides several unique ways to present the gospel. Using various memory aids and probing questions, you will develop confidence in your ability to clearly communicate the gospel. Visit www.EvangelismExplosion.org for more information.

Way of the Master/Living Waters

A ministry founded by Ray Comfort, *Living Waters* seeks to bring the use of God's Law back to evangelism — the way Jesus, Paul, and the Puritans used it. Studying the *Way of the Master* through their books, DVDs, and online resources will equip you to boldly proclaim the gospel. The ministry also produces many creative gospel tracts and other resources helpful for open-air preaching and personal evangelism. Visit www.LivingWaters.com for more information.

Open Air Campaigners

Just as Whitefield, Wesley, Knox, the Apostle Paul, and Jesus did, *Open Air Campaigners* train individuals to present the gospel message to large crowds. Using creative illustrations to draw the attention, the gospel message appears before the eyes of the onlookers as the words of life are brought to their ears. Visit www.oacusa.org for more information.

Wretched Radio and TV

"I'm the wretch the song refers to," is the tag line of Todd Friel and the ministry of *Wretched*. Through a daily television and radio show, they seek to inform Christians of current events, encourage them to share the gospel, and equip them to think biblically about the world we live in. The

---

2. *Begin* is a great witnessing book that has Genesis 1–11, the Ten Commandments, the Gospel of John, the Book of Romans, and last two chapters of Revelation. It has connecting material, some basics and the gospel presentation. It is a great place to start for seekers and new believers (Green Forest, AR: Master Books, 2011).

DVD-tract "The Biggest Question" is a great tool for sharing the gospel message with anyone and helping them to understand the amazing grace the God offers to wretched sinners. Visit www.WretchedRadio.com for more details.

Personal Testimony

If God has saved you from your sins, you have a story to tell! You were once an enemy of God, but now He has invited you to be a guest at His table as an adopted child. Use your personal experience to explain to others how God saved you and how He can do the same for them.

Gospel Tracts

Gospel tracts have been around for a long time. Today, there are many different styles available and in different formats. Take your pick from paper, optical illusions, fake money, DVDs, emails, and booklets. But as you do, consider the message carefully. Many tracts have a very limited amount of space, so make sure they point clearly to sin and the need to repent and trust in Christ alone for salvation. Include them in the bills you mail, pass them out at a local event, offer them to a waitress (with a handsome tip!), or toss them with a candy bar into the buckets of trick-or-treaters. Tracts can be a very effective way of spreading the gospel message and helping people understand their need for Christ.

Go!

Whatever you do, do it, and do it regularly. You know what Christ has done for you; now share that with everyone you can. Point them to the magnificence of Jesus and help them to see the love He displayed in laying down His life as the penalty for sin.

Then, help them continue to grow in their knowledge of Jesus as you disciple them. Help them find a local body of believers to be a part of. Encourage them to read their Bible every day, obeying what they read. Have them seek baptism in obedience to Christ, and help them learn how to share their new hope with others. What a joy to be a part of Christ's commission to make disciples of all the nations — wherever you are.

You can expect to face many different challenges as you spread the gospel, but don't let that prevent you from joyfully obeying Christ's call.

Jesus promised us that we would face persecution for His name's sake, but He also promised us He would be with us through those trials (John 15). Some people will ask questions, others will mock, some will be intrigued, and others will flatly reject their need for a Savior.

You don't have to know how to answer every possible question that arises or eloquently defend every point of doctrine to be an effective witness for Christ. Prepare your heart with prayer and prepare your mind with study to be able to answer the basic questions, but know you have many resources to look to for help. If you don't know the answer to a specific question, offer to research it and get an answer. This will show sincerity and give you an opportunity to follow up on your conversation. Using articles from www.AnswersinGenesis.org and other reputable websites, you can offer biblically based and reasonable answers to those who are interested in knowing the truth.

Go! Proclaim the truth of the One who set you free and bring Him the glory and praise that is due only to Him.

I leave you with this thought from the Apostle Paul:

> Continue earnestly in prayer, being vigilant in it with thanksgiving; meanwhile praying also for us, that God would open to us a door for the word, to speak the mystery of Christ, for which I am also in chains, that I may make it manifest, as I ought to speak. Walk in wisdom toward those who are outside, redeeming the time. Let your speech always be with grace, seasoned with salt, that you may know how you ought to answer each one (Colossians 4:2–6).

Chapter 31

Afterword:
Where Do We Draw the Line?

Bodie Hodge

✿✿✿✿✿✿✿✿✿✿✿✿✿✿✿✿✿✿✿

Answers in Genesis (AiG) is a unique ministry for this age! We are a biblical authority ministry. Many people see us as a creation and evolution ministry diving into scientific aspects of the creation. But many also view us as a worldview ministry, and many others see us as an evangelical ministry stressing the gospel (which should be an extremely important aspect of any ministry), and so on. And although these things seem to make the AiG ministry unusual, I am talking about *something else* that makes us unique.

AiG is a "parachurch" ministry. It could also be called a "non-denominational" ministry. It means that AiG is not a church in and of itself but is made of church members from various denominations (e.g. from Baptist to Christian to Lutheran to Reform, etc.) to focus on specific issues and challenges of today's culture.

Biblical Authority

AiG is made up of Christians who *unite* to defend the authority of the Bible in today's secular culture. And that is what we are "on about" — the authority of the Bible, specifically in Genesis but also other places (like the gospel message of the New Testament).

For example, the secular world has been teaching that the earth is billions of years old. The Bible, based on genealogies recorded throughout the Scriptures and the context of the Hebrew word *yom* (day) in Genesis 1, reveal that the earth is thousands of years old. So this question becomes a biblical authority issue. Is one going to trust a perfect God who created all things (Genesis 1:1), has always been there (Revelation 22:13), knows all things (Colossians 2:1-3), and cannot lie (Hebrews 6:18), or trust imperfect and fallible mankind who was not there and speculates on the past? See how this is an authority issue?

Also, take note that many of these issues ultimately overlap with worldview issues (biblical Christianity vs. secular humanism in this instance). Of course, this subject also gets into the character of Jesus Christ and His deity and, hence, the gospel. For a few other examples of biblical authority issues that AiG gets into, see table 1.

This is, of course, a small list of topics, but it should give the reader an idea. Basically, AiG will try to become involved in issues where the Bible clearly teaches and is the authority on something, and due to a source *other than the Bible*, someone takes a position against what the Bible clearly teaches.

Are Some Controversial Topics Battles over Biblical Authority?

Being a subset of the Church as a whole, this is why this ministry is unique. Christians from various denominations can *and should* be able to come together to defend the authority of the Bible against sources that are claiming the Bible, and ultimately God, is false or wrong.

But there are many who do not fully understand (or may have simply missed) what we mean by biblical authority — even within the various denominations from which we all come. Some want us to dive into issues that are not biblical authority issues. And although these issues are very important, they are not arguments that AiG will join.

For example, there are many denominational stances that AiG simply does not get into. One of these is Calvinism vs. Arminianism. Though this debate is important and we want to encourage people to know what they believe and why biblically, this is not a biblical authority debate.

Table 1: A few biblical authority topics that AiG dives into

Topic	A biblical authority issue?	Does AiG involve itself?
Millions of years	Yes; the Bible does not teach millions of years, but come from a source outside the Bible — e.g., God vs. autonomous man	Yes
Evolution	Yes; the Bible teaches man was created specially from dust, and the woman specially created from the man (Genesis 3) but in an evolutionary worldview, mankind came from an ape-like ancestor — e.g., God vs. autonomous man	Yes
Noah's Flood was local	Yes; Genesis 6–8 makes it clear that it was a global with the water over the highest mountain by over 15 cubits (Genesis 7:20). Those appealing to a local Flood trust secular authorities who say that the rock layers were evidence of millions of years, instead of Flood sediment — e.g., God vs. autonomous man	Yes
God is not triune	Yes; the Bible clearly teaches God is triune, so sources outside the Bible are going against the Bible (e.g., Watchtower organization, Koran, etc.), e.g., God vs. Watchtower or God vs. Koran, etc.	Yes
Racism	Yes; the Bible teaches there is one race that began with Adam and Eve, whereas the world had been teaching that there are perhaps four races (Caucasoid, Mongoloid, Negroid, and Australoid) — e.g., God vs. autonomous man	Yes

Both sides of this particular debate see the Bible as the authoritative Word of God and draw from its passages to make cases for their positions. Neither position is appealing to the Koran, autonomous human reason, or others for their interpretations of these verses.

Another example would be eschatology. For the most part, each position in this debate readily views the Bible, including the Book of Revelation, as authoritative. So the debate is about Scripture interpreting Scripture regarding various passages. This is not a debate into which AiG prefers to delve. A few other examples of debates that are important but not biblical authority issues that AiG refrains from taking a stance can be seen in table 2.

Table 2: Non-biblical authority topics that AiG tries to avoid

Topic	A biblical authority issue?	Does AiG get into it?
Calvinism vs. Arminianism	No; both positions view the Bible as the authority	No
Eschatology	No; each position views the Bible as the authority[1]	No
Modes of baptism	No; each position views the Bible as the authority	No
Speaking in tongues today	No; both positions view the Bible as the authority	No
Church government	No; each position views the Bible as the authority	No
Saturday vs. Sunday worship	No; both positions view the Bible as the authority	No
Covenant vs. dispensational theology	No; both positions view the Bible as the authority	No

Again, this is a fairly short list, but it should give you an idea of the debates in which AiG engages. These debates are important, though simply not the thrust of this ministry.

Naturally, there will surely be minor instances where, even with these subjects, some may try to insert an authority other than Scripture and so it may become a biblical authority issue. For example, if someone said that "no one ever spoke in tongues," then this becomes a biblical authority topic and *that particular point* could be dealt with because Scripture reveals that speaking in tongues has indeed taken place (Acts 2:4). So this would become an instance where it was God vs. autonomous thinking

---

1. Though "full" or "hyper" pretereism (which teaches Christ has returned and we are living in a restored perfect world where the Curse has been removed and there is no more death and suffering) is rejected by AiG due to the denial that Christ will return in the future and that the Curse has been removed, hence death, thorns, suffering, pain, etc., before sin and other theological problems. This is not to be confused with "orthodox" or "partial" pretereism where Christ has not yet returned and the Curse has not yet been removed.

man. But the issue of speaking in tongues today is a different debate than the issue of speaking in tongues ever — and we will let those involved in that debate "battle" that one out.

A Fine Line

The main reason we avoid some arguments is due to our focus of biblical authority issues and to keep us from getting distracted from what we have been called to do. We let others, including our various denominations, fight these battles (eschatology, tongues, etc.) with kindness and love among our brethren.

Naturally, though, it is a very difficult task to draw a fine "imaginary" line about the items we get into and the ones we avoid. In fact, it is very difficult simply because all doctrines of Christianity ultimately interconnect.

And so there are times where we tread a fine line in an effort to word things in a way that each position would agree with, without leaning toward one position or the other — and sometimes that line gets crossed. There are those times where a fine line may get crossed, when we work with outside authors who may not be well-versed in what we avoid (in fact, we worked with some great outside authors in this particular book series, and in their respective ministries they would get into more issues than we would here). Regardless, we ask for a little forgiveness and grace when it comes to these instances. As I said, this is an imaginary line that we try to remain within (like a self-imposed *speed limit*).

This is part of the reason why we have a Statement of Faith that reflects the issues where we do take stands and try to remain within that limit. There are those rare cases where some of these non-biblical authority topics that AiG tries to avoid may conflict with our Statement of Faith where doctrines interconnect. If this is the case, then AiG may get into it. For example in one form of eschatology ("hyper" or "full preterism"[2]), it is denied that Christ will have a future return and that the Curse has been removed, hence *death before sin* is believed and other theological problems that violate the Statement of Faith.

---

2. Again, this is not to be confused with "orthodox" or "partial preterism," where Christ will physically return in the future and the curse will then be removed and there will be no more death and suffering.

Conclusion

Again though, in reality all doctrines are interconnected and this makes it difficult to remain silent in some areas and vocal in others. Some well-meaning Christians prefer us to dive into one area more and others prefer that we not be involved in some areas at all. So we have to draw the line someplace and this is done so that we do not lose our focus on biblical authority surrounding origins, which is among the biggest debate in today's culture. In fact, by doing this, most denominations are readily open to working with and supporting AiG because we have common goals of promoting biblical authority, which is the foundation for many of the denominational debates from which we refrain.

We do want to encourage you to know what you and your denomination believe and do respect its importance — after all, those doing ministry at AiG are made up of Christians from various denominations. We also ask that you pray for us to stay focused and when we do walk this line that we do it with kindness and respect.